The Greater Key of Solomon
or
Clavicula Salomonis

A MODERN RENDERING of the 15TH CENTURY GRIMOIRE

With an Introduction, Commentary and
Appendix by DENNIS LOGAN

S.L. MacGregor Mathers
L.W. de Laurence

Introduction to *The Greater Key of Solomon*

From the 1914 Edition of L. W. de Laurence, Based on the Translation by S.L. MacGregor Mathers

The Greater Key of Solomon—also known by its Latin title *Clavicula Salomonis*—is a foundational text in the Western magical tradition, purporting to contain the teachings and rituals of King Solomon, the legendary Israelite monarch associated with divine wisdom and spiritual authority. The version herein presented, dated 1918, is derived from the English translation by S.L. MacGregor Mathers, a prominent member of the Hermetic Order of the Golden Dawn. This particular edition was later issued by L.W. de Laurence, a controversial publisher and occult entrepreneur whose name appears frequently in early twentieth-century esoteric literature.

It is important to note that all promotional material referencing *De Laurence, Scott and Co.*—a firm infamous for self-promotional frauds and unauthorized reprints—has been removed. There is no affiliation between that entity and the present publisher. This edition has been editorially revised to remove spurious advertising while retaining the full magical and literary content attributed to Mathers' scholarship.

On the Greater and Lesser Keys

The *Greater Key of Solomon* is distinct from the *Lesser Key of Solomon* (*Lemegeton*), though both are attributed to the same legendary source. For the neophyte, the *Greater Key* focuses on the preparation of the magician: purification, consecration of ritual tools, invocations, and planetary operations aligned with astrological timing. It is a manual of sacred magic, structured with the gravitas of scriptural form and invoking divine names from Judaic and Christian traditions.

In contrast, the *Lesser Key*, particularly the first book known as the *Goetia*, catalogs 72 spirits said to have been confined by Solomon. This grimoire is more concerned with spirit evocation and commanding infernal beings for practical ends. The adept will note that while both texts require ritual precision, the *Greater Key* aims toward theurgic elevation and alignment with divine order, whereas the *Lesser Key* delves into manipulative daemonology.

On Pseudepigrapha and Historical Attribution

Scholars categorize both Keys as pseudepigraphal works—texts falsely ascribed to notable religious or mythic figures to lend them authority. Like many occult manuscripts attributed to Solomon, Hermes Trismegistus, or Enoch, these grimoires emerged from medieval and Renaissance contexts, often reflecting syncretic traditions including Jewish mysticism, Christian angelology, and Arabic magical practices. Their authorship, while obscure, reveals the convergence of mystical philosophy and ritual technology under the veil of ancient wisdom.

A Modern Disclaimer on Mental Health and Magical Practice

In contemporary terms, engagement with texts such as *The Greater Key of Solomon* necessitates psychological discernment and grounded self-awareness. Psychiatrist Johan Weyer—among the earliest critics of demonology—suggested that many supposed spiritual afflictions or possessions were in fact episodes of mental illness. Today, this insight must be taken seriously. One must be vigilant against grandiose delusions, spiritual narcissism, or psychotic interpretation of symbolic material.

To those who undertake inner work through ritual and contemplation: know where you begin and end. Cultivate silence, discipline, and critical thought. Not all spiritual impulses are healthy, and discernment is a greater virtue than unbridled belief. If ritual becomes obsession, or if the boundary between imagination and reality collapses, it is not enlightenment but fragmentation.

On the Ecosystem of Ceremonial Magic and Commercialization

The ceremonial magician will quickly discover that the art is not free. For every tool mentioned—a wand of almond wood, a pentacle of parchment, a robe embroidered with Hebrew names—there exists a merchant ready to sell it. This ecosystem of esoteric commerce has existed for centuries, and it flourished in de Laurence's time as much as it does today. One must question whether such tools serve a spiritual purpose or simply enrich middlemen of mysticism.

Anton LaVey, founder of the Church of Satan, once quipped that "you can cast a spell and hope it works, or you can punch a person in the face and get immediate gratification." While perhaps flippant, the point is clear: the magician must remain action-oriented and pragmatic. Ritual alone is not a substitute for change in the material world.

A Warning Regarding the Use of Seals and Talismans

A word of caution to the modern practitioner: the seals, pentacles, and talismans contained within this text are not decorative symbols nor public declarations. They are intended to be kept private, consecrated, and guarded, used only in the sanctity of ritual. Their externalized display—whether printed on T-shirts, branded into business logos, or worn as casual adornments—betrays a misunderstanding of their sacred function. If encountered in the outer world, such displays should be read not as an invitation to probe deeper, but as a warning to maintain distance. It says more about the wearer—often unknowingly—than they may realize. The true initiate will recognize that spiritual potency is preserved through silence and restraint.

On Cultism, Fraud, and De Laurence's Legacy

A final caution: this text has been weaponized by cult leaders, charlatans, and spiritual grifters. The legacy of L.W. de Laurence is deeply entangled with such controversies. Though he popularized and distributed many important works in the occult canon, his methods included plagiarism, unauthorized reprints, and dubious marketing aimed at economically vulnerable populations—especially in India and the Caribbean. He was frequently accused of operating a mail-order fraud enterprise, using esoteric promises to extract money under false pretenses.

Do not mistake this book—or any grimoire—for doctrine. It is a symbolic system, not a religion. It is a guide for inner inquiry, not a license for manipulation or spiritual hierarchy. Any individual or organization presenting it otherwise should be regarded with suspicion.

On This Edition

To facilitate deeper study and practical engagement, every biblical verse cited in *The Greater Key of Solomon* has been included in full in an appendix at the end of this volume. This editorial decision reflects a commitment to transparency and accessibility, ensuring that readers need not consult external texts to follow the spiritual and symbolic logic of the work.

May this edition serve not as a trap for the credulous, but as a mirror for the discerning.

-Dennis Logan
Richmond, VA USA
7/14/2025

The Greater Key Of Solomon

INCLUDING A CLEAR AND PRECISE EXPOSITION OF
KING SOLOMON'S SECRET PROCEDURE, ITS
MYSTERIES AND MAGIC RITES.
ORIGINAL PLATES, SEALS, CHARMS AND TALISMANS.

TRANSLATED FROM ANCIENT MANUSCRIPTS
IN THE BRITISH MUSEUM, LONDON.

BY S. LIDDELL MAC GREGOR MATHERS
Author of "The Kabbalah Unveiled," "The Tarot," Etc.

SOLOMON, THE SON OF DAVID, KING OF ISRAEL.

THERE IS NOTHING IN OCCULT LITERATURE WHICH CAN SUF-
FER COMPARISON WITH THE HISTORICAL MANUSCRIPTS OF
"SOLOMON, THE SON OF DAVID, KING OF ISRAEL."

Prepared For Publication Under The Editorship Of

L. W. de LAURENCE

AUTHOR OF "THE GREAT BOOK OF MAGICAL ART, HINDU MAGIC
AND EAST INDIAN OCCULTISM."—"THE MASTER KEY."—
"THE SACRED BOOK OF DEATH, HINDU SPIRITISM, SOUL
TRANSITION AND SOUL REINCARNATION."—"THE MYS-
TIC TEST BOOK OF THE HINDU OCCULT CHAMBERS,
THE MAGIC AND OCCULTISM OF INDIA."—"THE
WONDERS OF THE MAGIC MIRROR, HINDU AND
EGYPTIAN CRYSTAL GAZING."—"ASTRAL AURAS
AND COLORS."—"THE IMMANENCE OF GOD,
KNOW THYSELF."—"GOD, THE BIBLE, TRUTH
AND CHRISTIAN THEOLOGY."—"MEDICAL
HYPNOSIS AND MAGNETIC HYPNOTISM."
—"MANUAL OF DISEASE AND MODERN
MEDICINE."—"VALMONDI; THE OLD
BOOK OF ANCIENT MYSTERIES, AN
UNHALLOWED LEGACY."—"THE
DEAD MAN'S HOME." ETC. ETC.

Revised & Edited With a New Introduction By
Dennis Logan

Notice To The Reader

In order to make it easy for the student to understand how to make the Pentacles shown over the figures in this book, it was necessary to change the position of certain pages. By turning to page 57 it will be noticed that pages 59 and 60 have been put between pages 57 and 58 instead of between 58 and 61. This was done, as explained above, in order to bring those pages which contain certain figures near the printed pages which explain the figures. In going through the book it may appear at the first glance that certain pages have been left out, but, upon investigation, it will be found that this is not true, for while there are no numbers shown in the book for pages 59, 60, 65, 66, 69, 70, 73, 74, 77, 78, 99 and 100, nothing has been left out of the reading matter, for the reason that these were illustrated pages showing the figures with the Pentacles above them, and instead of their being placed according to their number they were carried forward or set back in order to get them near the reading matter which gave directions for making the Pentacles shown on them. The above arrangement holds good throughout the book in general.

Instead of there being any pages left out of this book, it will be noticed that there have been many pages added, several extra ones having been inserted by the use of half numbers, and that $61\frac{1}{2}$ and $62\frac{1}{2}$ are between 63 and 64, while $63\frac{1}{2}$ is between 67 and 68, $66\frac{1}{2}$ and $67\frac{1}{2}$ are between 71 and 72, $68\frac{1}{2}$ and $69\frac{1}{2}$ are between 75 and 76, $86\frac{1}{2}$ and $87\frac{1}{2}$ are between 97 and 98. These extra pages were added in order to make everything plain to the student, and to avoid confusion. In studying this book it will be found that the reading matter is complete; and that not one word has been left out of it, ALL the printed pages have been placed exactly where they belong, while the illustrated pages, containing the Pentacles, Seals and Talismans, have been placed so as to make them most convenient for the student.

It should be borne in mind that this famous book is a translation of ancient manuscripts and that the manner in which the book has been translated and put together is a piece of literary work seldom found in the English language; its author having been very painstaking and careful to convey to the student the true sense of the original manuscript, and this translation shows that it has not been thrown together without order, as is often the case with other translators, but that a complete order runs through the Volume from beginning to end.

THE PUBLISHERS.

The Greater Key Of Solomon

PREFACE TO BOOK ONE.

IN presenting this celebrated Magical work to the *Disciple* of *Occultism* some few prefatory remarks are necessary.

THE KEY OF SOLOMON, save for a curtailed and incomplete copy published in France in the seventeenth century, has never yet been printed, but has for centuries remained in *Manuscript* form inaccessible to all but the few fortunate scholars to whom the inmost recesses of the great libraries were open. I therefore consider that I am highly honored in being the individual to whose lot it has fallen to edit and publish the American Edition.

The fountain-head and storehouse of *Qabalistical Magic,* and the origin of much of the *Ceremonial Magic* of *Mediæval* times, the "KEY" has been ever valued by *Occult* writers as a work of the highest authority; and notably in our own day *Eliphaz Lévi* has taken it for the model on which his celebrated *"Dogme et Rituel de la Haute Makie"* was based. It must be evident to the initiated reader of Lévi, that THE KEY OF SOLOMON was his text book of study, and at the end of this volume I give a fragment of an ancient Hebrew *Manuscript* of THE KEY OF SOLOMON, translated and published in the *"Philosophie Occulte,"* as well as an Invocation called the *"Qabalistical Invocation of Solomon,"* which bears close analogy to one in the FIRST BOOK, being constructed in the same manner on the scheme of the *Sephiroth.*

The history of the Hebrew original of THE KEY OF SOLOMON is given in the Introductions, but there is every reason to suppose that this has been entirely lost, and Christian, the pupil of *Lévi,* says as much in his *"Histoire de la Magie."*

I see no reason to doubt the tradition which assigns the authorship of the "KEY" to KING SOLOMON, for among others *Josephus,* the Jewish historian, especially mentions the magical works attributed to that monarch; this is confirmed by many Eastern traditions, and his magical skill is frequently mentioned by the *Old Adepts.*

There are, however, two works on *Black Magic,* the *"Grimorium Verum,"* and the *"Clavicola di Salomone ridolta,"* which have been attributed to SOLOMON, and which have been in some cases especially mixed up with the present work; but which have nothing really to do therewith; they are full of evil magic, and I cannot caution the practical student too strongly against them.

There is also another work called "*Lemegeton, or the Lesser Key of Solomon the King,*" which is full of seals of various Spirits, and is not the same as the present book, though extremely valuable in its own department.

In editing this *Volume* I have omitted one or two experiments partaking largely of *Black Magic,* and which had evidently been derived from the two *Goetic* works mentioned above; I must further caution the practical worker against the use of blood; the prayer, the *Pentacle,* and the perfumes, or TEMPLE INCENSE, rightly used, are sufficient as the former verges dangerously on the evil path. Let him who, in spite of the wornings of this *Volume,* determines to work evil, be assured that evil will recoil on himself and that he will be struck by the reflex current.

This work is edited from several ancient MSS. in the *British Museum,* which all differ from each other in various points, some giving what is omitted by the others, but all unfortunately agreeing in one thing, which is the execrable mangling of the Hebrew words through the ignorance of the transcribers. But it is in the *Pentacles* that the Hebrew is worse, the letters being so vilely scribbled as to be actually undecipherable in some instances, and it has been part of my work for several years to correct and reinstate the proper Hebrew and Magical characters in the *Pentacles.* The student may therefore safely rely on their being now as nearly correct in their present reproduction as it is possible for them to be. I have, therefore, wherever I could, corrected the Hebrew of the Magical Names in the *Conjurations* and *Pentacles;* and in the few instances where it was not possible to do so, I have put them in the most usual form; carefully collating throughout one MS. with another. The Chapters are a little differently classed in the various MSS., in some instances the matter contained in them being transposed, &c. I have added notes wherever necessary.

The MSS. from which this work is edited are :—Add. MSS., 10,862; Sloane MSS., 1307 and 3091; Harleian MSS., 3981; King's MSS., 288: and Lansdowne MSS., 1202 and 1203; seven *codices* in all.

Of all these 10,862 Add. MSS. is the oldest, its date being about the end of the sixteenth century; 3981 Harleian is probably about the middle of the seventeenth century; the others of rather later date.

Add. MSS. 10,862 is written in contracted Latin, and is hard to read, but it contains Chapters which are omitted in the others and also an important Introduction. It is more concise in its wording. Its title is short, being simply THE KEY OF SOLOMON, translated from the Hebrew language into the Latin. An exact copy of the signature of the writer of this MS. is given in *Figure* 93.

3981 Harleian MSS.; 288 King's MSS.; and 3091 Sloane MSS., are similar, and contain the same matter and nearly the same wording; but the latter MS. has many errors of transcription. They are all in French. The *Conjurations* and wording of these are much fuller than in 10,862 Add. MSS. and 1202 Lansdowne MSS. The title is THE KEY OF SOLOMON, *King of the Hebrews*, translated from the Hebrew Language into Italian by *Abraham Colorno*, by the order of his most Serene Highness of Mantua; and recently put into French. The *Pentacles* are much better drawn, are in colored inks, and in the case of 3091 Sloane MSS., gold and silver are employed.

1307 Sloane MSS. is in Italian; its Title is "*La Clavicola di Salomone Redotta et epilogata nella nostra materna lingua del dottissimo Gio Peccatrix.*" It is full of Black Magic, and is a jumble of THE KEY OF SOLOMON proper, and the two Black Magic books before mentioned. The *Pentacles* are badly drawn. It, however, gives part of the Introduction to 10,862 Add. MSS., and is the only other MS. which does, save the beginning of another Italian version which is bound up with the former MS., and bears the title "*Zecorbenei.*"

1202 Lansdowne MSS. is "THE TRUE KEYS OF KING SOLOMON," by Armadel. It is beautifully written, with painted initial letters, and the *Pentacles* are carefully drawn in colored inks. It is more concise in style, but omits several Chapters. At the end are some short extracts from the *Grimorium Verum* with the *Seals* of evil spirits, which, as they do not belong to THE KEY OF SOLOMON proper, I have not given. For the evident classification of the "KEY" is in two books and no more.

1203 Lansdowne MSS. is "*The Veritable Keys of Solomon*" translated from the Hebrew into the Latin language by the Rabbin Agognazar. It is in French, exquisitely written in printing letters, and the *Pentacles* are carefully drawn in colored inks. Though containing similar matter to the others, the arrangement is utterly different; being all in one book, and not even divided into chapters.

The antiquity of the *Planetary Sigils* is shown by the fact that, among the *Gnostic Talismans* in the *British Museum*, there is a ring of copper with the *Sigils* of *Venus*, which are exactly the same as those given by the *Mediæval* writers on Magic.

Where *Psalms* are referred to I have in all instances given the English and not the Hebrew numbering of them.

In some places I have substituted the word AZOTH for "*Alpha and Omega,*" *e. g.*, on the blade of the *Knife* with the *Black Hilt, Figure* 62. I may remark that the *Magical Sword* may, in many cases, be used instead of the Knife.

In conclusion I will only mention, for the benefit of non-*Hebraists*, that Hebrew is written from right to left, and that from the consonantal nature of the *Hebrew Alphabet*, it will require fewer letters than in English to express the same word.

L. W. de LAURENCE.

Chicago, Ill., U. S. A., 1916.

SOLOMON, THE "WISE MAN"

BY   L. W. de LAURENCE

SOLOMON, Son of David and Bathsheba (1033-975 B.C.); King of Israel; noted for his Wisdom and deep Knowledge of *Occult Forces;* author of the "KEY OF SOLOMON".

SOLOMON was a King, the son of a King; the wise son of a wise father; a righteous man's righteous child.

DAVID, the father of SOLOMON, reigned for forty years, as it is written, *"And the days that David governed Israel were forty years."*

Of SOLOMON, it is written, "And Solomon reigned in Jerusalem over all Israel forty years."

SOLOMON was born in the year 2912 A.M., and reigned over *Israel* forty years. Four hundred and thirty-three years elapsed between the date of SOLOMON's reign and that of the *Temple's* destruction.

"Seest thou a man that is diligent in his work? Before kings may he place himself; let him not place himself before obscure men." (Prov. 22:29.)

In this verse SOLOMON alludes to himself. He built *King Solomon's Temple* in seven years, while he occupied fourteen years in erecting his *Palace.* Not because his *Palace* was more elegant or more elaborate in its workmanship than was the *Temple,* but because he was diligent in his work to finish the *Holy Temple,* while his own house could await time and opportunity.

Four cases of comparative righteousness between fathers and children may be noted:

First. A righteous man begets a righteous son.

Second. A wicked man begets a wicked son.

Third. A wicked man begets a righteous son.

Fourth. A righteous man begets a wicked son.

To each of these cases we may find a Biblical allusion; to each of them we may apply a parable and a proverb.

In reference to the righteous father and the righteous son, we find the following verse (*Psalm* 45:17): *"Instead of thy fathers shall be thy children."* And we may apply the parable of the good fig tree which brought forth luscious fruit.

In reference to the wicked father and the wicked son we have in *Numbers* 32:14: *"And now behold, ye are risen up in your father's stead, a new race of sinful men."*

Ancient is the proverb, *"From the wicked proceedeth wickedness";* and applicable, the parable of the serpent bringing forth an asp.

In the third case, the wicked father begets a righteous son, as it is written, "*Instead of the thorn shall come up the fir tree.*" And to this can we apply the *parable* of the rose budding on the bramble bush.

Lastly, a righteous man has a wicked son, as it is written, "*Instead of wheat, thorns came forth.*" (*Job* 21:40.) And we have also the *parable* of the atttractive peach tree which brought forth bitter fruit.

SOLOMON was a king, the son of a King; the wise son of a wise father; a righteous man's righteous child. All the incident's in DAVID'S life, all his characteristics were paralleled in the life of SOLOMON.

DAVID reigned for forty years, as it is written, "*And the days that David governed Israel were forty years.*"

Of SOLOMON it is written, "*And SOLOMON reigned in Jerusalem over all Israel forty years.*" DAVID expressed himself by "words," as it is written, "*And these are the last words of David.*"

SOLOMON likewise expressed himself by "words."

"*The words of Koheleth the son of David.*" (*Eccles.* 1:1.)

DAVID said, "All is *vanity*"; as it is written, "For *vanity* only do all men make a noise." (*Psalm* 39:7.)

SOLOMON expressed himself with the same word, "*vanity.*" "*Vanity of vanities,* saith Koheleth." (*Eccles.* 1:2.)

David wrote books, viz.: the five books of *Psalms;* and SOLOMON wrote four books: *Proverbs, Ecclesiastes,* the *Song of Solomon,* and *The Key of Solomon.*

David composed songs: "*And David spoke unto the Lord the words of this song.*" (*Samuel* 22:1.)

SOLOMON also composed a song: "*The song of songs,*" which is SOLOMON'S.

He was the wise king alluded to in *Proverbs* 16:23, "*The heart of the wise maketh his mouth intelligent, and upon his lips increaseth information.*" Meaning that the heart of the wise is full of knowledge and understanding; but this is shown to the world through the words of his mouth. And, by uttering with his lips the thoughts of his mind (or heart) he increases the information of the people. If a man possessing brilliant diamonds and precious stones, keeps his jewels concealed, no one is aware of their value; but if he allows them to be seen, their worth becomes known, and the pleasure of ownership is enhanced.

Applying this comparison to the case of SOLOMON, while his wisdom was locked up in his own breast it was of value to no one; but when he had given to the world his four books, men became acquainted with his great abilities. The words of his lips increased the information of his people, and so great was his reputation that any one in doubt concerning the meaning of a Biblical passage sought the king for an interpretation.

Not only in sacred lore did he raise the standard of education. He had mastered and taught the sciences of *Natural Philosophy, Physiology, Botany, Agriculture, Mathematics* in all its branches, *Occultism, Astronomy, Chemistry,* and in fact all useful studies. He also taught *Rhetoric* and the rules of *Poesy*. In *Occultism and "Talismanic Magic"* he was an *Adept*.

And in addition to this that Koheleth was wise, he continually taught the people knowledge.

If what others said interested the people, how much more readily did they listen to SOLOMON; with how much more ease did they comprehend him!

We may illustrate his method of teaching by the following comparison: There was a basket without ears, filled with fine fruit, but the owner was unable to get it to his home on account of the difficulty in carrying it, until a wise man, seeing the predicament, attached handles to the basket, when it could be carried with great ease.

So did SOLOMON remove difficulties from the path of the student.

Rabbi Huna further illustrated this same thing. "There was once," he said, "a well of most pure and excellent water; but the well was so deep that the people were not able to reach the water, until a man of wisdom, taking a bucket, attached to it one rope after another until the whole was long enough to reach the water. So was it with SOLOMON's teachings. The Bible is a well of truth, but its teachings are too deep for the understanding of some. SOLOMON, however, introduced parables and proverbs suited to the comprehension of all, through which means a knowledge of the law became readily obtainable."

Rabbi Simon, the son of Chalafta, related the following parable: "A certain king had an officer to whom he was much attached, and whom he took great delight in honoring. One day he said to this favorite, Come, express a wish; anything that I can give thee shall be thine.' Then this officer thought, ' If I ask the king for gold or silver or precious stones, he will give what I ask; even though I desire higher honor and more exalted station he will grant it, yet I will ask him for his daughter, for if he grants that, all the rest will be included.'"

When the Lord appeared to SOLOMON in *Gibon*, and said to him in a dream, *"What shall I give to thee?"* SOLOMON reflected, *"If I ask for gold, silver, or jewels, the Lord will give them to me; I will ask, however, for wisdom; if that is granted me, all other good things are included."* Therefore, he replied, *"Give to thy servant an understanding heart."*

Then said the Lord:

"Because thou hast asked for wisdom, and requested not wealth or dominion over thy enemies; by thy life, wisdom and knowledge shall be thine, and through them thou shalt obtain wealth and power."

"And Solomon awoke, and behold it was a dream." He wandered into the fields, and he heard the voices of the animals; the ass brayed, the lion roared, the dog barked, the rooster crowed, and behold he understood what they said, one to the other.

An ox, even after being killed and dressed, may be made to stand, provided the sinews are uncut; but if they are severed, cords are required to hold the body together. While SOLOMON remained free from sin his prayers were granted him for his own sake, but when he departed from the righteous way, the Lord said to him, *"For the sake of David, my servant, I will not take the kingdom from thee in thy lifetime."*

SOLOMON said, *"Vanity of vanities; vanity, even as a shadow."* A shadow of what nature? The shadow of a tower or a tree remains the shadow for a while, and then is lost, but the shadow of a bird flieth away, and there is neither bird nor shadow. DAVID said, *"Our days are as a passing shadow,"* and Rabbi Huna said, *"Our days pass quickly from us, even as the shadow of a flying bird."*

With the word vanity, SOLOMON expresses seven stages of a man's life.

The infant he compares to a king; riding in his little coach, and being kissed, admired, and praised by all. The child of three or four years he compares to a pig, fond of the dirt and soiling itself with its food. The child of ten is fond of dress; the youth adorns himself and seeks a wife; the married man is bold as the dog in seeking a livelihood for himself and family; and the old man he likens to an ape.

"God gave Wisdom to Solomon."

When SOLOMON was about building the temple, he applied to the King of *Egypt* for men to aid him in the work. *Pharaoh,* consulting his *Astrologers,* selected those men who were to die within the year. When they arrived at *Jerusalem* the wise SOLOMON sent them back at once. With each man he sent a shroud, and directed them to say to their master, "If *Egypt* is too poor to supply shrouds for her dead, and for that purpose sends them to me, behold here they are, the men and the shrouds together; take them and bury thy dead."

He was wiser than all other men, wiser even than Adam, who gave names to all the animals of the world, and even to himself, saying, " From the dust of the ground I was formed, and therefore shall my name be *Adam."* *Rabbi Tanchum* said, "Where is thy wisdom and thy understanding, O King SOLOMON? Thy words not only contradict themselves, but also the words of DAVID, thy father. He said, *'Not the dead can praise the Lord'* (*Psalm* 115:17), and thou didst say, *' Thereupon praised I the dead that are already dead, more than the living who are still alive.'* (*Eccles.* 4:2.) ·And thou didst also say, *'For a living dog fareth better than a dead lion.'"* (*Ibid.* 9:4.)

These seeming contradictions, however, may be readily explained. DAVID said, "Not the dead can praise the Lord," meaning that we should study God's law during life, as after its cessation 'twould be impossible. SOLOMON said, "Thereupon praised I the dead that are already dead." When the children of *Israel* sinned in the wilderness, MOSES prayed for them for their own sakes, and his prayer was unanswered; but when he said, *"Remember Abraham, and Isaac, and Israel, Thy servants,"* he met with a prompt reply. Therefore did not SOLOMON speak well in saying,

"Praise the dead that are already dead"? Take another instance: A king may decree laws, but many of his subjects may disregard them. Sometimes these laws, even if earnestly observed during the life of the one who made them, may be repealed or become obsolete after his death. MOSES, however, made many stringent laws, which have been observed through all generations. Therefore, SOLOMON said well, *"Thereupon will I praise the dead."*

Rabbi Judah, in the name of *Rab*, further explained this verse. He said, "What is the meaning of the following passage? 'Show me a token for good, that they who hate me may see it and be ashamed.' (*Psalm* 76:17.) DAVID said to God, after his sin with *Bathsheba* (*Samuel* 2), 'Sovereign of the Universe, pardon me for my sin.' The Lord answered, 'I will pardon thee.' Then said DAVID, 'Show me the token in my lifetime,' but God said, 'Not in thy lifetime, but in the lifetime of SOLOMON, thy son, will I show it.' Thus, when SOLOMON dedicated the temple, though he prayed with fervent devotion, he was not answered until he said, 'O Lord God, turn not away from the face of thy anointed. Remember the pious deeds of DAVID, thy servant.' (2 *Chron.* 6:42.) Then he was speedily answered, for in the next verse we read, 'And when SOLOMON had made an end of praying, a fire came down from Heaven and consumed the burnt offering and the sacrifices, and the glory of the Lord filled the house.' Then were the enemies of DAVID put to shame, for all *Israel* knew that God had pardoned DAVID for his sin. Did not SOLOMON say well then, 'Thereupon praised I the dead?' For this reason, further on in the chapter we read, 'And on the three-and-twentieth day of the seventh month he dismissed the people unto their tents, joyful and glad of heart, because of the good that the Lord had done for DAVID, and for SOLOMON, and for ISRAEL, His people.'"

SOLOMON said, "For a living dog fareth better than a dead lion."

Expounding this verse, *Rabbi Judah* said, in the name of *Rab*, "What is the meaning of the verse, 'Let me know, O Lord, my end, and the measure of my days, what it is; I wish to know when I shall cease to be.' (*Psalm* 39:5.)

"David said to God, 'Let me know, O Lord, my end.' God answered, 'I have decreed that for each one his end must be veiled in the future.' Then DAVID said, 'What is the measure of my days?' Again God replied, 'No man may know the measure of his days.' 'I wish to know when I shall cease to be,' continued DAVID; and God answered, 'Thou wilt die on a Sabbath.'

"'Let me die the day after,' entreated DAVID, but the Lord answered, 'No; then the kingdom will be SOLOMON's, and one reign may not take away from another reign even so much as a hair's breadth.' 'Then let me die the day before,' exclaimed DAVID, 'for a day in Thy courts is better than a thousand elsewhere,' and God said, 'One day spent by thee in studying my law is more acceptable than the thousand burnt offerings thy son SOLOMON will sacrifice.'

"It was DAVID'S custom to pass every Sabbath in the study of the Bible and its precepts, and he was thus engaged upon the Sabbath which was to be his last. Back of the king's palace there was an orchard, and DAVID, hearing a noise therein, walked thither to ascertain its cause. On entering the orchard he fell to the ground, dead.

"The noise in the orchard had been caused by the barking of the king's dogs, who had not that day received their food. SOLOMON sent a message to the Rabbinical College, saying, 'My father lies dead in his orchard; is it allowable to remove his body on the Sabbath? The dogs of my father are entreating for their food; is it proper to cut meat for them today?' This answer was returned by the college: 'Thy father's body should not be removed today, but give meat to the dogs.' Therefore said SOLOMON, 'A living dog fareth better than a dead lion,' justly comparing the son of *Jesse* to that king of beasts."

SOLOMON was the chosen of the Lord, who called him, through the mouth of *Nathan*, the prophet, *Yedidiah* (the beloved one). He was called SOLOMON (peace), because in his days peace reigned, as it is written, "And *Judah* and *Israel* dwelt in safety." (*Kings* 5:5.) He was called *Ithiel* (God with me) because God was his support.

And when SOLOMON sat upon the throne of his father DAVID, all the nations of the earth feared him; all the people of the earth listened anxiously for his words of wisdom.

Afterwards he had a throne made especially for himself by *Hiram*, the son of a widow of *Tyre*. It was covered with gold of *Ophir*, set with all kinds of precious and valuable stones. The seat of the throne was approached by six broad steps. The right side of the first step was guarded by an ox made of pure gold, and the left side by a lion of the same metal. On the right of the second step stood a bear also of gold, and upon the left a lamb, symbolical of enemies dwelling in peace together. On the right of the third step was placed a golden camel, and on the left an eagle. On the right of the fourth step there was also an eagle with outspread wings, and on the left a bird of prey, all of the same precious metal. On the fifth step to the right a golden cat crouching in position; on the left a chicken. On the right of the sixth step a hawk was fashioned, and on the left side a pigeon, and upon the top of the step a pigeon clutched a hawk in her talons. These animals were designed to typify the time when those of adverse natures shall unite in harmony, as it is written in *Isaiah* (11:6), "And the wolf shall then dwell with the sheep."

Over the throne was hung a chandelier of gold with seven branches; it was ornamented with roses, knobs, bowls, and tongs; and on the seven branches the names of the seven patriarchs, *Adam, Noah, Shem, Abraham, Isaac, Jacob,* and *Job,* were engraven.

On the second row of the branches of the chandelier were engraven the names of the seven pious ones of the world, *Levi, Kehath, Amram, Moses, Aaron, Eldad,* and *Madad.* Above all this hung a golden churn filled with pure olive oil, and on this was engraven the names of *Eli,* the *High Priest,* and his two sons, *Hophni* and *Phineas,* and on the other side the names of the two sons of *Aaron, Nadab* and *Abihu.*

On the right hand of the throne two chairs were placed, one for the *High Priest,* and the other for the *Vice-High Priest,* and upon the left side, from the top to the ground, seventy-one chairs were stationed as seats for the members of the *Sanhedrim.*

The throne was made upon wheels, that it could be moved easily wherever the king might desire it to be.

The Lord gave SOLOMON the power of understanding the nature and properties of the herbs of the field and the trees of the forest, as it is written, "And he spoke concerning the trees, from the cedar tree that is upon the *Lebanon* even unto the hyssop that springeth out of the wall. He spoke also concerning the beasts, and concerning the fowls, and concerning the creeping things, and concerning the fishes." (1 *Kings* 5:13.)

It is said that SOLOMON ruled the whole world, and this verse is quoted as proof of the assertion, "And SOLOMON was ruling over all the kingdoms, which brought presents, and served SOLOMON all the days of his life." (1 *Kings* 5:1.)

All the kingdoms congratulated SOLOMON as the worthy successor of his father, DAVID, whose fame was great among the nations; all save one, the kingdom of *Sheba,* the capital of which was called *Kitore.*

To this kingdom SOLOMON sent a letter:

"From me, King SOLOMON, peace to thee and to thy government. Let it be known to thee that the Almighty God has made me to reign over the whole world, the kingdoms of the *North,* the *South,* the *East,* and the *West.* Lo, they have come to me with their congratulations, all save thee alone.

"Come thou also, I pray thee, and submit to my authority, and much honour shall be done thee; but if thou refusest, behold, I shall by force compel thy acknowledgment.

"To thee *Queen Sheba,* is addressed this letter in peace from me, King SOLOMON, the son of DAVID."

Now when *Queen Sheba* received this letter, she sent in haste for her elders and counsellors to ask their advice as to the nature of her reply.

They spoke but lightly of the message and the one who sent it, but the queen did not regard their words. She sent a vessel, carrying many presents of different metals, minerals, and precious stones, to SOLOMON. It was after a voyage of two years' time that these presents arrived at *Jerusalem,* and in a letter intrusted to the captain the queen said, "After thou hast received the message then I myself will come to thee." And in two years after this time *Queen Sheba* arrived at *Jerusalem*.

When SOLOMON heard that the queen was coming he sent *Benayahu*, the son of *Yehoyadah*, the general of his army, to meet her. When the queen saw him she thought he was the king, and she alighted from her carriage.

Then *Benayahu* asked, "Why alightest thou from thy carriage?" And she answered, "Art thou not his majesty, the king?"

"No," replied *Benayahu*, "I am but one of his officers."

Then the queen turned back and said to her ladies in attendance, "If this is but one of the officers, and he is so noble and imposing in appearance, how great must be his superior, the king."

And *Benayahu*, the son of *Yehoyadah*, conducted *Queen Sheba* to the palace of the king.

SOLOMON prepared to receive his visitor in an apartment laid and lined with glass, and the queen at first was so deceived by the appearance that she imagined the king to be sitting in water.

And when the queen had tested SOLOMON's wisdom, and witnessed his magnificence, she said:

"I believed not what I heard, but now I have come, and my eyes have seen it all; behold, the half has not been told to me. / Happy are thy servants who stand before thee continually to listen to thy words of wisdom. Blessed be the Lord thy God, who hath placed thee on a throne to rule righteously and in justice."

When other kingdoms heard the words of the *Queen of Sheba* they feared SOLOMON exceedingly, and he became greater than all the other kings of the earth in wisdom and in wealth.

SOLOMON was born in the year 2912 A.M., and reigned over *Israel* forty years. Four hundred and thirty-three years elapsed between the date of Solomon's reign and that of the *Temple's* destruction.

PLATE 1.

Fig. 1.

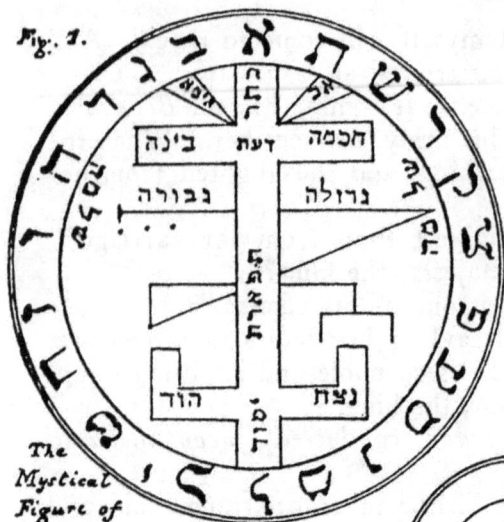

The
Mystical
Figure of
Solomon.

Fig. 3.

Vessel for Incense

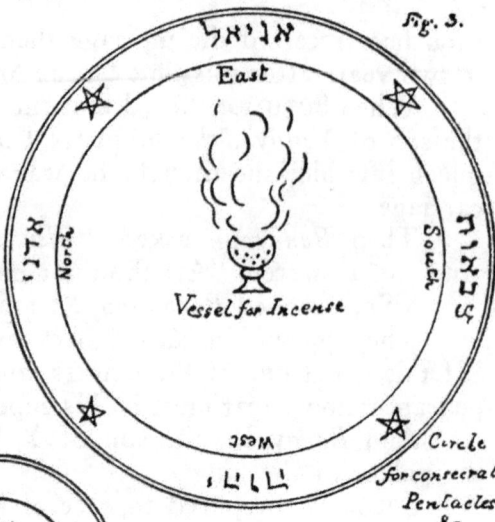

Circle
for consecrati
Pentacles
&c

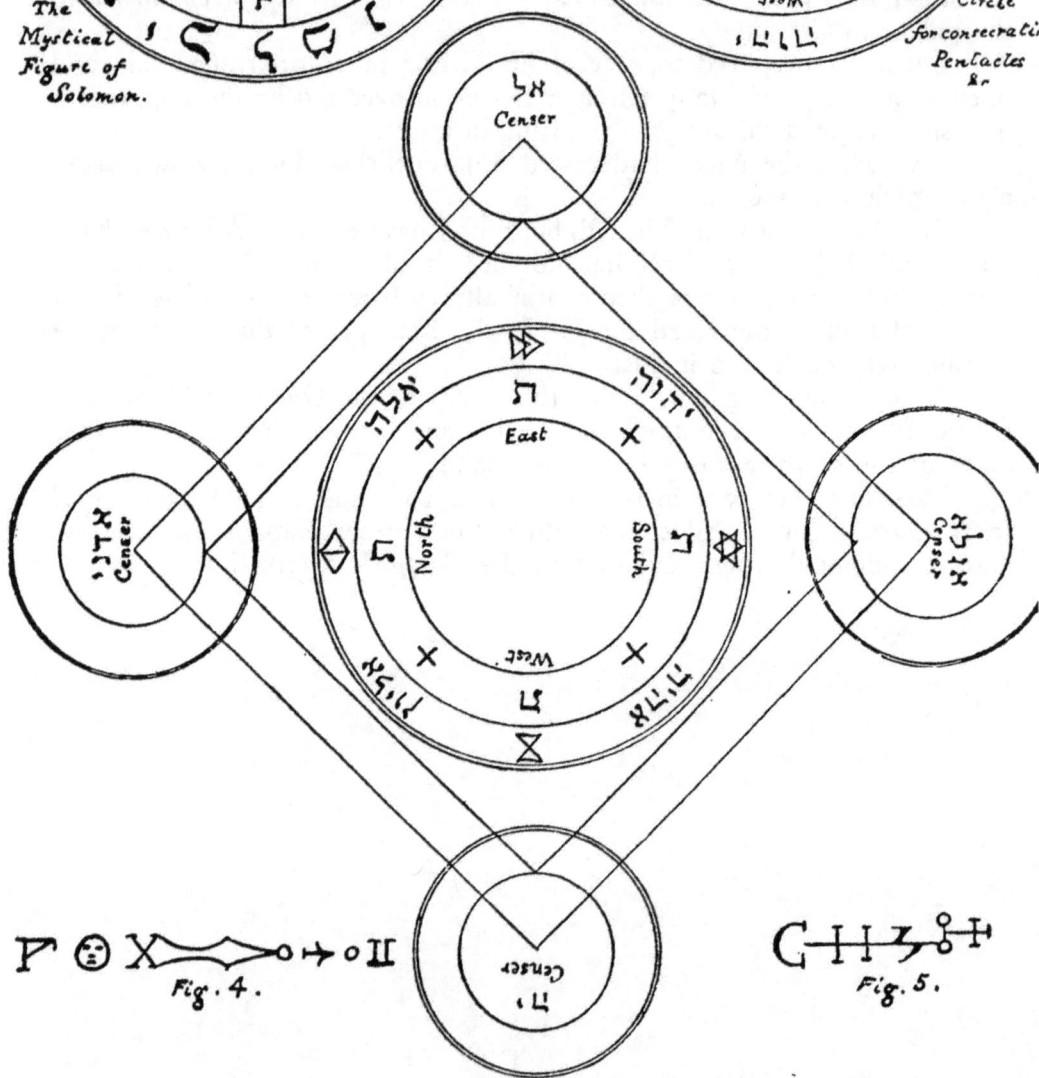

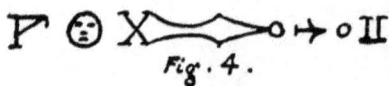

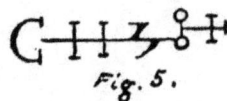

Fig. 4.

Figure 2.

Fig. 5.

INTRODUCTION.

From Add. MSS. 10862, *"The Key of Solomon," translated into Latin from the Hebrew idiom.*

TREASURE up, O my son Roboam! the wisdom of my words, seeing that I SOLOMON, have received it from the Lord.

Then answered Roboam, and said: How have I deserved to follow the example of of my father SOLOMON in such things, who hath been found worthy to receive the knowledge of all living things through (the teaching of) an Angel of God?

And SOLOMON said: Hear, O my son, and receive my sayings, and learn the wonders of God. For, on a certain night, when I laid me down to sleep, I called upon that most holy Name of God, IAH,'and prayed for the *Ineffable Wisdom*, and when I was beginning to close mine eyes, the Angel of the Lord, even *Homadiel,* appeared unto me, spake many things courteously unto me, and said: Listen O SOLOMON! thy prayer before the Most High is not in vain, and since thou hast asked neither for long life, nor for much riches, nor for the souls of thine enemies, but hast asked for thyself wisdom to perform justice. Thus saith the Lord: According to thy word have I given unto thee a wise and understanding heart, so that before thee was none like unto thee, nor ever shall arise.'

And when I comprehended the speech which was made unto me, I understood that in me was the knowledge of all creatures, both things which are in the heavens and things which are beneath the heavens; and I saw that all the writings and wisdom of this present age were vain and futile, and that no man was perfect. And I composed a certain work wherein I rehearsed the secret of secrets, in which I have preserved them hidden, and I have also therein concealed all secrets whatsoever of magical arts of any masters; any secret or experiments, namely, of these sciences which is in any way worth being accomplished. Also I have written them in this *"Key,"* so that like as a key openeth a treasure-house, so this *Key* alone may open the knowledge and understanding of *magical arts* and sciences.

Therefore, O my son! thou mayest see every experiment of mine or of others, and let everything be properly prepared for them, as thou shalt see properly set down by me, both day and hour, and all things necessary; for without this there will be but falsehood and vanity in this my work; wherein are hidden all secrets and mysteries which can be performed; and that which is (set down) concerning a single divination or a single experiment, that same I think concerning all things which are in the Universe, and which have been, and which shall be in future time.

Therefore, O my son Roboam, I command thee by the blessing which thou expectest from thy father, that thou shall make an *Ivory Casket*, and therein place, keep, and hide this my *"Key";* and when I shall have passed away unto my fathers, I entreat thee to place the same in my *Sepulchre*

1

beside me, lest at another time it might fall into the hands of the wicked. And as SOLOMON commanded, so was it done.

And when, therefore (men) had waited for a long time, there came unto the *Sepulchre* certain *Babylonian Philosophers;* and when they had assembled they at once took counsel together that a certain number of men should renew the *Sepulchre* in his (SOLOMON's) honour; and when the *Sepulchre* was dug out and repaired the *Ivory Casket* was discovered, and therein was the *Key of Secrets,* which they took with joyful mind, and when they had opened it none among them could understand it on account of the obscurity of the words and their *Occult* arrangement, and the hidden character of the sense and knowledge, for they were not worthy to possess this treasure.

Then, therefore, arose one among them, more worthy (than the others), both in the sight of the gods, and by reason of his age, who was called *Iohé Grevis,* and said unto the others: Unless we shall come and ask the interpretation from the Lord, with tears and entreaties, we shall never arrive at the knowledge of it.

Therefore, when each of them had retired to his bed, *Iohé* indeed falling upon his face on the earth, began to weep, and striking his breast, and:

What have I deserved (above others), seeing that so many men can neither understand nor interpret this knowledge, even though there were no secret thing in nature which the Lord hath hidden from me! Wherefore are these words so obscure? Wherefore am I so ignorant?

And then on his bended knees, stretching his hands to Heaven, he said:

O God, the Creator of all, Thou Who knowest all things, Who gavest so great Wisdom unto SOLOMON THE SON OF DAVID THE KING; grant unto me, I beseech Thee, O Holy Omnipotent and Ineffable Father, to receive the virtue of that wisdom, so that I may become worthy by Thine aid to attain unto the understanding of this *Key Of Secrets.*

And immediately there appeared unto me, the Angel of the Lord, saying:

Do thou remember if the secrets of SOLOMON appear hidden and obscure unto thee, that the Lord hath wished it, so that such wisdom may not fall into the hands of wicked men; wherefore do thou promise unto me, that thou art not willing that so great wisdom should ever come to any living creature, and that which thou revealest unto any let them know that they must keep it unto themselves, otherwise the secrets are profaned and no effect can follow?

And *Iohé* answered: I promise unto thee that to none will I reveal (them), save to the honour of the Lord, and with much discipline, unto peninent, secret, and faithful (persons).

Then answered the Angel: Go and read the "*Key,*" and its words which were obscure throughout shall be manifest unto thee.

And after this the Angel ascended into Heaven in a Flame of Fire.

Then *Iohé* was glad, and labouring with a clear mind, understood that which th' Angel of the Lord had said, and he saw that THE KEY OF SOLOMON was changed, so that it appeared quite clear unto him plainly in all parts. And *Iohé* understood that this Work might fall into the hands of the ignorant, and he said: I conjure him into whose hands this secret may come, by the Power of the Creator, and His Wisdom, that in all things he may, desire, intend and perform, that this Treasure may come unto no unworthy (person), nor may he manifest it unto any who is unwise, nor unto one who feareth not God. Because if he act otherwise, I pray God that he may never be worthy to attain unto the desired effect.

And so he deposited the *"Key,"* which SOLOMON preserved, in the *Ivory Casket.* But the Words of the *"Key"* are as follows, divided into TWO BOOKS, and shown in order.

AN ADMONISHMENT BY   de LAURENCE.

In presenting to the student of *Occultism* this translation from a most ancient and historical *Manuscript,* now in the *British Museum,* London, an admonishment is necessary. Death

For the space of twenty years, the writer has had many hundreds of urgent requests from serious investigators and advanced *Occult* students for an authentic and official copy of *"The Key of* SOLOMON, *Son of David, King of Israel."* Of these students, those who have made this request, are that class which are intensely interested in the production of such *Seals* and *Charms* as are used in different operations and experiments. I shall, however, admonish the one who reads here that if he would succeed, in these things, and have his wish gratified, by being able to perform these operations, it will be absolutely necessary for him to previously arrange all things which are essential, and to observe and practice the instructions contained herein.

To be brief, it will be necessary for the *Disciple* to prescribe care and observation, to abstain from all things unlawful, and from every kind of impiety. Again, the *Disciple* should put into practice the operations as they are set down herein. Therefore, let it be understood that there is nothing further to add to the instructions contained herein, as all the information that was contained in *King* SOLOMON's *Manuscripts* is included in this *Volume.* Let the students study it seriously and with proper meditation, and he will have his mind enlightened and advance by degrees; but under no circumstances can he expect to go forward without serious study and deep meditation. Let the one who reads here realize that to learn the work of the Old Masters, and such great men as SOLOMON, who, in his time, became *King Of Israel,* is no slight task and requires faithful application.

From Lansdowne MSS. 1203, *"The Veritable Clavicles of Solomon,"*
translated from the Hebrew into the Latin by the Rabbi Abognazar.

O my Son Roboam! seeing that of all Sciences there is none more useful than the knowledge of *Celestial Movements,* I have thought it my duty,
being at the point of death, to leave thee an inheritance more precious than
all the riches which I have enjoyed. And in order that thou mayest understand how I have arrived at this degree (of wisdom), it is necessary to
tell thee that one day, when I was meditating upon the power of the *Supreme
Being,* the Angel of the great God appeared before me as I was saying,
O how wonderful are the works of God! I suddenly beheld, at the end
of a thickly-shaded vista of trees, a Light in the form of a blazing *Star,*
which said unto me with a voice of thunder: SOLOMON, SOLOMON, be not
dismayed; the Lord is willing to satisfy thy desire by giving thee knowledge of whatsoever thing is most pleasant unto thee. I order thee to ask
of Him whatsoever thou desirest. Whereupon, recovering from my sur-
prise, I answered unto the Angel, that according to the Will of the Lord,
I only desired the Gift of Wisdom, and by the Grace of God I obtained
in addition the enjoyment of all the *Celestial* treasures and the knowledge
of all natural things.

It is by this means, my Son, that I possess all the virtues and riches of
which thou now seest me in the enjoyment, and in order that thou mayest be
willing to be attentive to all which I am about to relate to thee, and that
thou mayest retain with care all that I am about to tell thee, I assure thee
that the Graces of the Great God will be familiar unto thee, and that the
Celestial and *Terrestrial Creatures* will be obedient unto thee, and a
science which only works by the strength and power of natural things, and
by the pure Angels which govern them. Of which latter I will give thee
the names in order, their exercises and particular employments to which
they are destined, together with the days over which they particularly preside, in order that thou mayest arrive at the accomplishment of all, which
thou wilt find in this my *Testament.* In all which I promise thee success,
provided that all thy works only tend unto the honour of God, Who hath
given me the power to rule, not only over *Terrestrial* but also over *Celestial* things, that is to say, over the Angels, of whom I am able to dispose
according to my will, and to obtain from them very considerable services.

Firstly. It is necessary for thee to understand that God, having made
all things, in order that they may be submitted unto Him, hath wished to
bring His works to perfection, by making one which participates of the
Divine and of the *Terrestrial,* that is to say, Man; whose body is gross and
terrestrial, while his soul is spiritual and celestial, unto whom He hath
made subject the whole earth and its inhabitants, and hath given unto Him
means by which He may render the Angels familiar, as I call those
Celestial creatures who are destined: some to regulate the motion of the
Stars, others to inhabit the Elements, others to aid and direct men, and

others again to sing continually the praises of the Lord. Thou mayest then, by the use of their *Seals* and *Characters*, render them familiar unto thee, provided that thou abusest not this privilege by demanding from them things which are contrary to their nature; for accursed be he who will take the Name of God in vain, and who will employ for evil purposes the knowledge and good wherewith He hath enriched us.

I command* thee, my Son, to carefully engrave in thy memory all that I say unto thee, in order that it may never leave thee. If thou dost not intend to use for a good purpose the secrets which I here teach thee, I command thee rather to cast this Testament into the fire, than to abuse the power thou wilt have of constraining the Spirits, for I warn thee that the beneficent Angels, wearied and fatigued by thine illicit demands, would to thy sorrow execute the commands of God, as well as to that of all such who, with evil intent, would abuse those secrets which He hath given and revealed unto me. Think not, however, O my Son, that it would not be permitted thee to profit by the good fortune and happiness which the Divine Spirits can bring thee; on the contrary, it gives them great pleasure to render service to Man for whom many of these Spirits have great liking and affinity, God having destined them for the preservation and guidance of those Terrestrial things which are submitted to the power of Man.

There are different kinds of Spirits, according to the things over which they preside, some of them govern the *Empyrean Heaven,* others the *Primum Mobilé,* others the *First* and *Second Crystalline,* others the *Starry Heaven;* there are also Spirits of the *Heaven of Saturn,* which I call *Saturnites;* there are Jovial, Martial, Solar, Venerean, Mercurial, and Lunar Spirits; there are also (Spirits) in the Elements as well as in the Heavens, there are some in the Fiery Region, others in the Air, others in the Water, and others upon the Earth, which can all render service to that man who learns their nature, and knows how to attract them.

Furthermore, I wish to make thee understand that God hath destined to each one of us a Spirit, which watches over us and takes care of our preservation; these are called *Genii,* who are elementary like us, and who are more ready to render service to those whose temperament is conformed to the Element which these *Genii* inhabit; for example, shouldest thou be of a fiery temperament, that is to say sanguine, thy genius would be fiery and submitted to the *Empire of Baël.* Besides this, there are special times reserved for the invocation of these Spirits, in the days and hours when they have power and absolute empire. It is for this reason that thou wilt see in the following tables to what Planet and to what Angel each Day and Hour is submitted, together with the Colours which belong unto them, the Metals, Herbs, Plants, Aquatic, Aërial, and Terrestrial Animals, and *Temple Incense,* which are proper to each of them, as also in what quarter of the Universe they ask to be invoked. Neither are omitted, the *Conjurations, Seals, Characters,* and *Divine Letters,* which belong to them, by means of which we receive the power to sympathize with these Spirits. * The Disciple must pay strict attention to this command.

Sunday.	Monday.	Tuesday.	Wednes.	Hours from Sunset to Sunset.	Hours from Midnight to Midnight.	Thursd.	Friday.	Saturd.
Merc.	Jup.	Ven.	Sat.	8	1	Sun.	Moon.	Mars.
Moon.	Mars.	Mer.	Jup.	9	2	Ven.	Sat.	Sun.
Sat.	Sun.	Moon.	Mars.	10	3	Mer.	Jup.	Ven.
Jup.	Ven.	Sat.	Sun	11	4	Moon.	Mars.	Mer.
Mars.	Mer.	Jup.	Ven.	12	5	Sat.	Sun.	Moon.
Sun.	Moon.	Mars.	Mer.	1	6	Jup.	Ven.	Sat.
Ven.	Sat.	Sun.	Moon.	2	7	Mars.	Mer.	Jup.
Mer.	Jup.	Ven.	Sat.	3	8	Sun.	Moon.	Mars.
Moon.	Mars.	Mer.	Jup.	4	9	Ven.	Sat.	Sun.
Sat.	Sun.	Moon.	Mars.	5	10	Mer.	Jup.	Ven.
Jup.	Ven.	Sat.	Sun.	6	11	Moon.	Mars.	Mer.
Mars.	Mer.	Jup.	Ven.	7	12	Sat.	Sun.	Moon.
Sun.	Moon.	Mars.	Mer.	8	1	Jup.	Ven.	Sat.
Ven.	Sat.	Sun.	Moon.	9	2	Mars.	Mer.	Jup.
Mer.	Jup.	Ven.	Sat.	10	3	Sun.	Moon.	Mars.
Moon.	Mars.	Mer.	Jup.	11	4	Ven.	Sat.	Sun.
Sat.	Sun.	Moon.	Mars.	12	5	Mer.	Jup.	Ven.
Jup.	Ven.	Sat.	Sun.	1	6	Moon.	Mars.	Mer.
Mars.	Mer.	Jup.	Ven.	2	7	Sat.	Sun.	Moon.
Sun.	Moon.	Mars.	Mer.	3	8	Jup.	Ven.	Sat.
Ven.	Sat.	Sun.	Moon.	4	9	Mars.	Mer.	Jup.
Mer.	Jup.	Ven.	Sat.	5	10	Sun.	Moon.	Mars.
Moon.	Mars.	Mer.	Jup.	6	11	Ven.	Sat.	Sun.
Sat.	Sun.	Moon.	Mars.	7	12	Mer.	Jup.	Ven.

Table of the Magical Names of the Hours, and of the Angels who rule them, commencing at the first hour after Midnight of each day, and ending at the ensuing midnight.

Hours.	Sunday.	Monday.	Tuesday.	Wednesd.	Thursd.	Friday.	Saturday.
1. Yayn	Raphael	Sachiel	Anael	Cassiel	Michael	Gabriel	Zamael
2. Yanor	Gabriel	Zamael	Raphael	Sachiel	Anael	Cassiel	Michael
3. Nasnia	Cassiel	Michael	Gabriel	Zamael	Raphael	Sachiel	Anael
4. Salla	Sachiel	Anael	Cassiel	Michael	Gabriel	Zamael	Raphael
5. Sadedali	Zamael	Raphael	Sachiel	Anael	Cassiel	Michael	Gabriel
6. Thamur	Michael	Gabriel	Zamael	Raphael	Sachiel	Anael	Cassiel
7. Ourer	Anael	Cassiel	Michael	Gabriel	Zamael	Raphael	Sachiel
8. Thainé	Raphael	Sachiel	Anael	Cassiel	Michael	Gabriel	Zamael
9. Neron	Gabriel	Zamael	Raphael	Sachiel	Anael	Cassiel	Michael
10. Yayon	Cassiel	Michael	Gabriel	Zamael	Raphael	Sachiel	Anael
11. Abai	Sachiel	Anael	Cassiel	Michael	Gabriel	Zamael	Raphael
12. Nathalon	Zamael	Raphael	Sachiel	Anael	Cassiel	Michael	Gabriel
1. Beron	Michael	Gabriel	Zamael	Raphael	Sachiel	Anael	Cassiel
2. Barol	Anael	Cassiel	Michael	Gabriel	Zamael	Raphael	Sachiel
3. Thanu	Raphael	Sachiel	Anael	Cassiel	Michael	Gabriel	Zamael
4. Athor	Gabriel	Zamael	Raphael	Sachiel	Anael	Cassiel	Michael
5. Mathon	Cassiel	Michael	Gabriel	Zamael	Raphael	Sachiel	Anael
6. Rana	Sachiel	Anael	Cassiel	Michael	Gabriel	Zamael	Raphael
7. Netos	Zamael	Raphael	Sachiel	Anael	Cassiel	Michael	Gabriel
8. Tafrac	Michael	Gabriel	Zamael	Raphael	Sachiel	Anael	Cassiel
9. Sassur	Anael	Cassiel	Michael	Gabriel	Zamael	Raphael	Sachiel
10. Agla	Raphael	Sachiel	Anael	Cassiel	Michael	Gabriel	Zamael
11. Cäerra	Gabriel	Zamael	Raphael	Sachiel	Anael	Cassiel	Michael
12. Salam	Cassiel	Michael	Gabriel	Zamael	Raphael	Sachiel	Anael

Table of the Archangels, Angels, Metals, Days of the Week, and Colours Attributed to each Planet.

Days.	Saturday.	Thursd.	Tuesday.	Sunday	Friday.	Wednesd.	Monday.
Archangel . .	Tzaphqiel	Tzadiqel	Khamael	Raphael	Haniel	Michael	Gabriel
Angel . . .	Cassiel	Sachiel	Zamael	Michael	Anael	Raphael	Gabriel
Planet . . .	Saturn	Jupiter	Mars	Sun	Venus	Mercury	Moon
Metal	Lead	Tin	Iron	Gold	Copper	Mercury	Silver
Colour . . .	Black	Blue	Red	Yellow	Green	Purple or Mixed Colours	White

NOTE BY de LAURENCE.

These *Tables* have been *collated* and compared with various examples of both MS. and printed. They are to be used thus:—Supposing the student wishes to discover the properties of the hour from 12 to 1 o'clock p.m. on a Tuesday, let him look in the *"Table of the Planetary Hours,"* and having found the hour marked 1 in the column headed *"Hours from Midnight to Midnight,"* he will see in the column headed *"Hours from Sunset to Sunset,"* on the same line the figure 8, showing it to be the eighth hour of the day; and in the column headed Tuesday, the name Mars, showing that it is under the dominion of the planet Mars. On consulting the *"Table of the Magical Names of the Hours,"* &c., he will find under the number 1, the name *Beron*, and in the column "Tuesday," the name of the angel *Zamael* over against it on the same line, showing that the ruler of the hour is the Angel Zamael, and that its Magical Name is *Beron*. Further, on referring to the third Table he will see that Tuesday is under the rule of the planet Mars, whose Archangel is *Khamael, Angel Zamael, Metal Iron, and Colour Red*. Similarly it will be found that the hour from 10 to 11 p.m. on Saturday is the sixth hour of the night, under the dominion of the Sun, that its Magical Name is *Cäerra*, and that the *Angel Michael* rules it; while Saturday itself is under the dominion of the *Archangel Tzaphqiel*, of the *Angel Cassiel*, of the *Planet Saturn*, and that the *Metal Lead* and the *Colour Black* are applicable to it.

The ensuing Text is taken from the following MSS., collated and compared with each other.

Sloane MSS. 1307; *Sloane* MSS. 3091; *Harleian* MSS. 3981; *Add.* MSS. 10862; *King's* MSS. 288; *Lansdowne* MSS. 1202.

Extracts have also been made from *Lansdowne* MSS. 1203, which differs considerably from the others in general arrangement, though containing very similar matter.

In cases where the MSS. varied from each other I have taken the version which seemed most likely to be correct, in some cases mentioning the variant readings in footnotes. I have also corrected the Hebrew names in the Incantations, for these were in some cases so marred as to be hardly recognisable; e.g. *Zenard*, written for *Tzabaoth*, &c.

PRELIMINARY DISCOURSE.

From Lansdowne MSS. 1203, "The Veritable Clavicles of Solomon,"
translated from the Hebrew into the Latin language
by the Rabbi Abognazar.

EVERY one knoweth in the present day that from time immemorial SOLOMON possessed knowledge inspired by the wise teachings of an angel,* to which he appeared so submissive and obedient, that in addition to the gift of wisdom, which he demanded, he obtained with profusion all the other virtues; which happened in order that knowledge worthy of eternal preservation might not be buried with his body. Being, so to speak, near his end, he left to his son *Roboam* a Testament which should contain all (the Wisdom) he had possessed prior to his death. The *Rabbins,* who were careful to cultivate (the same knowledge) after him, called this Testament *"The Clavicle, or Key of Solomon,"* which they caused to be engraved on (pieces of) the bark of trees, while the *Pentacles* were inscribed in Hebrew letters on plates of copper, so that they might be carefully preserved in the *Temple* which that wise king had caused to be built.

This Testament was in ancient time translated from the Hebrew into the Latin language by *Rabbi Abognazar,* who transported it with him into the town of Arles in Provence, where by a notable piece of good fortune the ancient *Hebrew Clavicle,* that is to say, this precious translation of it, fell into the hands of the Archbishop of Arles, after the destruction of the Jews in that city; who, from the Latin, translated it into the vulgar tongue, in the same terms which here follow, without having either changed or augmented the original translation from the Hebrew.

---

* An angel, is, today known as a good helpful spirit on the Astral Plane. In Solomon's time they were called angels or devils. Today they are spoken of as good or evil spirits or influences.—EDITOR'S NOTE.

The Key Of Solomon.

(CLAVICULA SALOMONIS.)

The Beginning Of Book One.

CHAPTER I.

CONCERNING THE DIVINE LOVE WHICH PRECEDES THE ACQUISITION OF THIS KNOWLEDGE.

SOLOMON, THE SON OF DAVID, KING OF ISRAEL, hath said that the beginning of our Key is to fear God, to adore Him, to honour Him with contrition of heart, to invoke Him* in all matters which we wish to undertake, and to operate with very great devotion, for thus God will lead us in the right way. When, therefore, thou shalt wish to acquire the knowledge of Magical Arts and Sciences, it is necessary to have prepared the order of hours and of days, and of the position of the Moon, without the operation of which thou canst effect nothing; but if thou observest them with diligence thou mayest easily and thoroughly arrive at the effect and end which thou desirest to attain.

* 1202, Lansdowne MSS., omits the concluding part of this sentence.

BOOK ONE.

CHAPTER II.

WHEN* thou wishest to make any experiment or operation, thou must first prepare, beforehand, all the requisites, such as candles and Incense,† which thou wilt find described in the following Chapters: observing the days, the hours, and the other effects of the Constellations which may be found in this Chapter.

It is, therefore, advisable to know that the hours of the day and of the night together, are twenty-four in number, and that each hour is governed by one of the Seven Planets in regular order, commencing at the highest and descending to the lowest. The order of the Planets is as follows: SHBThAI, Shabbathai, Saturn; beneath Saturn is TzDQ, Tzedeq, Jupiter; beneath Jupiter is MADIM, Madim, Mars; beneath Mars is SHMSH, Shemesh, the Sun; beneath the Sun is NVGH, Nogah, Venus; beneath Venus is KVKB, Kokav, Mercury; and beneath Mercury is LBNH, Levanah, the Moon, which is the lowest of all the Planets.

It must, therefore, be understood that the Planets have their dominion over the day which approacheth nearest unto the name which is given and attributed unto them—viz., over Saturday, Saturn; Thursday, Jupiter; Tuesday, Mars; Sunday, the Sun; Friday, Venus; Wednesday, Mercury; and Monday, the Moon.

The rule of the Planets over each hour begins from the dawn at the rising of the Sun on the day which take its name from such Planet, and the Planet which follows it in order, succeeds to the rule over the next hour. Thus (on Saturday) Saturn rules the first hour, Jupiter the Second, Mars the third, the Sun the fourth, Venus the fifth, Mercury the sixth, the Moon the seventh, and Saturn returns in the rule over the eighth, and the others in their turn, the Planets always keeping the same relative order.

Note that each experiment or magical operation should be performed under the Planet, and usually in the hour, which refers to the same. For example:—

In the Days and Hours of Saturn thou canst perform experiments to summon the Souls from Hades, but only of those who have died a natural death. Similarly on these days and hours thou canst operate to bring either good or bad fortune to buildings; to have familiar Spirits attend thee in sleep; to cause good or ill success to business, possessions, goods, seeds,

---

* This first paragraph is omitted in 1307 Sloane MSS., and in 10862 Add. MSS.
† Those who wish a supply of Temple Incense or Candles will find the very same listed in Messrs. de Laurence, Scott & Co.'s great Occult Book Catalogue.

fruits, and similar things, in order to acquire learning; to bring destruction and to give death, and to sow hatred and discord.

The Days and Hours of Jupiter are proper for obtaining honours, acquiring riches; contracting friendships, preserving health; and arriving at all that thou canst desire.

In the Days and Hours of Mars thou canst make experiments regarding War; to arrive at military honour; to acquire courage; to overthrow enemies; and further to cause ruin, slaughter, cruelty, discord; to wound and to give death.

The Days and Hours of the Sun are very good for perfecting experiments regarding temporal wealth, hope, gain, fortune, divination, the favour of princes, to dissolve hostile feeling, and to make friends.

The Days and Hours of Venus are good for forming friendships; for kindness and love; for joyous and pleasant undertakings, and for traveling.

The Days and Hours of Mercury are good to operate for eloquence and intelligence; promptitude in business; science and divination; wonders; apparitions; and answers regarding the future. Thou canst also operate under this Planet for thefts; writings; deceit; and merchandise.

The Days and Hours of the Moon are good for embassies; voyages; envoys; messages; navigation; reconciliation; love; and the acquisition of merchandise by water.*

Thou shouldest take care punctually to observe all the instructions contained in this chapter, if thou desirest to succeed, seeing that the truth of Magical Science dependeth thereon.

The Hours of Saturn, of Mars, and of the Moon are alike good for communicating and speaking with Spirits; as those of Mercury are for recovering thefts by the means of Spirits.

The Hours of Mars serve for summoning Souls from Hades,†especially of those slain in battle.

The Hours of the Sun, of Jupiter, and of Venus, are adapted for preparing any operations whatsoever of love, of kindness, and of invisibility, as is hereafter more fully shown, to which must be added other things of a similar nature which are contained in our work.

The Hours of Saturn and Mars and also the days on which the Moon is conjunct ‡ with them, or when she receives their opposition or quartile aspect, are excellent for making experiments of hatred, enmity, quarrel, and discord; and other operations of the same kind which are given later on in this work.

---

* Much of these foregoing instructions is omitted in the 10862 Add. MSS., but given in a different way in the ensuing paragraphs.

† In the French "des Enfers," in the Latin "Inferis."

‡ Conjunction means being in the same degree of the Zodiac; opposition is being 180 degrees, and quartile 90 degrees apart from each other.

The Hours of Mercury are good for undertaking experiments relating to games, raillery, jests, sports, and the like.

The Hours of the Sun, of Jupiter, and of Venus, particularly on the days which they rule, are good for all extraordinary, uncommon, and unknown operations.

The Hours of the Moon are proper for making trial of experiments relating to recovery of stolen property, for obtaining nocturnal visions, for summoning Spirits in sleep, and for preparing anything relating to Water.

The Hours of Venus are furthermore useful for lots, poisons, all things of the nature of Venus, for preparing powders provocative of madness; and the like things.

But in order to thoroughly effect the operations of this Art, thou shouldest perform them not only on the Hours but on the Days of the Planets as well, because then the experiment will always succeed better, provided thou observest the rules laid down later on, for if thou omittest one single condition thou wilt never arrive at the accomplishment of the Art.

For those matters then which appertain unto the Moon, such as the Invocation of Spirit, the *Works of Necromancy,* and the recovery of stolen property, it is necessary that the Moon should be in a Terrestrial Sign, viz.:—Taurus, Virgo, or Capricorn.

For love, grace, and invisibility, the Moon should be in a Fiery Sign, viz.:—Aries, Leo, or Sagittarius.

For hatred, discord, and destruction, the Moon should be in a Watery Sign, viz.:—Cancer, Scorpio, or Pisces.

For experiments of a peculiar nature, which cannot be classed under any certain head, the Moon should be in an Airy Sign, viz.:—Gemini, Libra, or Aquarius.

But if these things seem unto thee difficult to accomplish, it will suffice thee merely to notice the Moon after her combustion, or conjunction with the Sun, especially just when she* quits his beams and appeareth visible. For then it is good to make all experiments for the construction and operation of any matter. That is why the time from the New unto the Full Moon is proper for performing any of the experiments of which we have spoken above. But in her decrease or wane it is good for War, Disturbance, and Discord. Likewise the period when she is almost deprived of light, is proper for experiments of invisibility, and of Death.

But observe inviolably that thou commence nothing while the Moon is in conjunction with the Sun, seeing that this is extremely unfortunate, and that thou wilt then be able to effect nothing; but the Moon quitting his beams and increasing in Light, thou canst perform all that thou desirest, observing nevertheless the directions in this Chapter.

Furthermore, if thou wishest to converse with Spirits it should be

---

* *i.e.* New Moon.

especially on the day of Mercury and in his hour, and let the Moon be in an Airy Sign,* as well as the Sun.

Retire † thou then unto a secret place, where no one may be able to see thee or to hinder thee, before the completion of the experiment, whether thou shouldest wish to work by day or by night. But if thou shouldest wish to work by night, perfect thy work on the succeeding night; if by day, seeing that the day beginneth with the rising of the Sun (perfect thy work on) the succeeding day. But the Hour of Inception is the Hour of Mercury.

Verily, since no experiments for converse with Spirits can be done without a Circle being prepared, whatsoever experiments therefore thou wishest to undertake for conversing with Spirits, therein thou must learn to construct a certain particular Circle; that being done surround that Circle with the Circle of Art for better caution and efficacy.

* In Add. MSS. 10862; "or in an Earthy Sign, as hath been before said."
† The following paragraphs to the end of this Chapter are only found in the Latin version, Add. MSS. 10862.

BOOK ONE.

CHAPTER III.

CONCERNING THE ARTS.

IF thou wishest to succeed, it is necessary to make the following Experiments and Arts in the appropriate Days and Hours, with the requisite solemnities and ceremonies contained and laid down in the following chapters.

Experiments, then, are of two kinds; the first is to make trial of what, as I have said, can be easily performed without a Circle, and in this case it is not necessary to observe anything but what thou wilt find in the proper Chapters. The second can in no way be brought to perfection without the Circle; and in order to accomplish this perfectly it is necessary to take note of all the preparations which the *Master* of the Art and his *Disciples* must undertake before constructing* the Circle.

Before commencing operations both the *Master* and his *Disciples* must abstain with great and thorough continence during the space of nine days from sensual pleasures and from vain and foolish conversation; as plainly appeareth in the *Second Book, Chapter* 4. Six of these days having expired, he must recite frequently the Prayer and Confession as will be told him; and on the Seventh Day, the Master being alone, let him enter into a secret place, let him take off his clothes, and bathe himself from head to foot in consecrated and exorcised Water, saying devoutly and humbly the prayer, "O Lord Adonaï," &c., as it is written in the *Second Book, Chapter* 2.

The Prayer being finished, let the Master quit the water, and put upon his flesh raiment of white linen clean and unsoiled; and then let him go with his Disciples unto a secret place and command them to strip themselves naked; and they having taken off their clothes, let him take exorcised water and pour it upon their heads so that it flows down to their feet and bathes them completely; and while pouring this water upon them let the Master say:—"*Be ye regenerate, renewed, washed, and pure,*" &c., as in *Book II., Chapter* 3.

Which† being done, the Disciples must clothe themselves, putting upon their flesh, like their Master, raiment of white linen clean and unsoiled; and the three last days the Master and his Disciples should fast, observing the solemnities and prayers marked in *Book II., Chapter* 2.

Note that the three last days should be calm weather, without wind, and without clouds rushing hither and thither over the face of the sky. On the last day let the Master go with his Disciples unto a secret fountain of running water, or unto a flowing stream, and there let each of them, taking off his clothes, wash himself with due solemnity, as is rehearsed

---

* Sloane MSS. 3091, says, "before they come to the Circle."
† This paragraph is omitted in Lansdowne MSS. 1202.

in *Book II.* And when they are clean and pure, let each put upon him garments of white linen, pure, and clean, using the prayers and ceremonies described in *Book II.* After which let the *Master* alone say the confession. The which being finished, the *Master* in sign of penitence will Kiss* the *Disciples* on the forehead, and each of them will Kiss the other. Afterwards let the *Master* extend his hands over the *Disciples,* and in sign of absolution absolve and bless them; which being done he will distribute to each of his *Disciples* the Instruments necessary for Magical Art, which he is to carry into the Circle.

The *First Disciple* will bear the *Censer,* the *Perfumes* and the *Temple Incense;*** the *Second Disciple* will bear the *Book, Papers, Pens, Ink,* and any stinking or impure materials; the *Third* will carry the *Knife* and the *Sickle of Magical Art,* the *Lantern,* and the *Candles;* the *Fourth,* the *Psalms,* and the rest of the *Instruments;* the *Fifth,* the *Crucible* or *Chafingdish,* and the *Charcoal* or *Fuel;* but it is necessary for the Master himself to carry in his hand the *Staff,* and the *Wand* or *Rod.* The things necessary being thus disposed, the Master will go with his Disciples unto the assigned place, where they have proposed to construct the Circle for the Magical Arts and experiments; repeating on the way the prayers and orations which thou wilt find in *Book II.*

When the *Master* shall have arrived at the place appointed, together with his *Disciples,* he having lighted the flame of the fire, and having exorcised it afresh as is laid down in the *Second Book,* shall light the Candle and place it in the Lantern, which one of the *Disciples* is to hold ever in his hand to light the *Master* at his work. Now the *Master* of the Art, every time that he shall have occasion for some particular purpose to speak with the Spirits, must endeavor to form certain Circles which shall differ somewhat, and shall have some particular reference to the particular experiment under consideration. Now, in order to succeed in forming such a Circle concerning *Magical Art,* for the greater assurance and efficacy thou shalt construct it in the following manner:—

THE CONSTRUCTION OF THE CIRCLE.

Take thou the Knife, the Sickle, or the Sword of Magical Art consecrated after the manner and order which we shall deliver unto thee in the Second Book. With this Knife or with the Sickle of Art thou shalt describe, beyond the inner Circle which thou shalt have already formed, a Second Circle, encompassing the other at the distance of one foot therefrom and having the same centre.† Within this space of a foot in breadth between the first and the second circumferential‡ line, thou shalt trace towards the Four Quarters of the Earth,§ the Sacred and Venerable Sym-

---

* Note the "holy kiss" in the New Testament. "Greet ye one another with a holy kiss."
** Temple Incense and Special Waxen Candles can be obtained from Messrs. de Laurence, Scott & Co. by consulting their Catalogue.
† *i.e.* Two Circles enclosed between three circumferential lines.
‡ *i.e.* within the first circle.
§ *i.e.* the four Cardinal points of the compass.

bols of the holy Letter Tau.*   And between the first and the second
Circle,† which thou shalt thyself have drawn with the Instrument of *Magical Art,* thou shalt make four hexagonal pentacles,‡ and between these
thou shalt write four terrible and tremendous Names of God, viz. :—

Between the East and the South the Supreme Name IHVH, *Tetra-
gramaton;*—

Between the South and the West the Essential *Tetragrammatic* Name
AHIH, Eheieh;—

Between the West and the North the Name of Power ALIVN,
Elion;—

And between the North and the East the Great Name ALH, Eloah;—

Which Names are of supreme importance in the list of the Sephiroth,§
and their Sovereign Equivalents.

Furthermore, thou shalt circumscribe about these Circles two Squares,
the Angles of which shall be turned towards the Four Quarters of the
Earth; and the space between the Lines of the Outer and Inner Square
shall be half-a-foot.   The extreme Angles of the Outer Square shall be
made the Centres of four Circles, the measure or diameter of which shall
be one foot.   All these are to be drawn with the Knife or consecrated Instrument of Art.   And within these Four Circles thou must write these
four Names of God the Most Holy One, in this order:—

At the East, AL, El;

At the West, IH, Yah;

At the South, AGLA, Agla;

And at the North ADNI, Adonaï.

Between the two Squares the Name *Tetragrammaton* is to be written
in the same way as is shown in the plate.   (*See Figure* 2.)

While constructing the Circle, the Master should recite the following
Psalms:—Psalm II; Psalm LIV; Psalm CXIII; Psalm LXVII; Psalm
XLVII; Psalm LXVIII.

Or he may as well recite them before tracing the Circle.

The which being finished, and the fumigations being performed, as is
described in the chapter on Fumigations in the Second Book, the Master
should reassemble his Disciples, encourage them, reassure them, fortify
them, and conduct them into the parts of the Circle of Art, where he must
place them in the four quarters of the earth, encourage them, and exhort
them to fear nothing, and to keep in the places assigned to them.   Also, the
Disciple who is placed towards the East should have a pen, ink, paper, silk,

* The letter Tau represents the Cross, and in 10862 Add. MSS. in the drawing of the
Circle, the Hebrew letter is replaced by the Cross; in 1307 Sloane MSS. by the T or Tau-Cross.

† *i.e.* in the Outer Circle, bounded by the second and third circumferential lines.

‡ 10862 Add. MSS. is the only copy which uses the word *hexagonal,* but the others show
four hexagrams in the drawing; in the drawing, however, 10862 gives the hexagrams formed
by various differing interlacements of two triangles, as shown in Figure 2.

§ The Sephiroth are the ten Qabalistical Emanations of the Deity. The Sovereign
Equivalents are the Divine Names referred thereto.

and white cotton, all clean and suitable for the work. Furthermore, each of the Companions should have a new Sword drawn in his hand (besides the consecrated Magical Sword of Art), and he should keep his hand resting upon the hilt thereof, and he should on no pretext quit the place assigned to him, nor move therefrom.

After this the Master should quit the Circle, light the fuel in the earthen pots, and place upon them the Censers, in the Four Quarters of the Earth; and he should have in his hand the consecrated taper of wax, and he should light it and place it in a hidden and secret place prepared for it. Let him after this re-enter and close the Circle.

The *Master* should afresh exhort his *Disciples,* and explain to them all that they have to do and to observe; the which commands they should promise and vow to execute.

Let the Master then repeat this Prayer:—

PRAYER.

When we enter herein with all humility, let God the Almighty One enter into this Circle, by the entrance of an eternal happiness, of a Divine prosperity, of a perfect joy, of an abundant charity, and of an eternal salutation. Let all the demons fly from this place, especially those who are opposed unto this work, and let the Angels of Peace assist and protect this Circle, from which let discord and strife fly and depart. Magnify and extend upon us, O Lord, Thy most Holy Name, and bless our conversation and our assembly. Sanctify, O Lord our God, our humble entry herein, Thou the Blessed and Holy One of the Eternal Ages! Amen.

After this, let the Master say upon his knees, as follows:—

PRAYER.

O Lord God, All Powerful and All Merciful, Thou Who desirest not the death of a sinner, but rather that he may turn from his wickedness and live; give and grant unto us thy grace, by blessing and consecrating this earth and this circle, which is here marked out with the most powerful and holy Names of God. And thee, I conjure, O Earth, by the Most Holy Name of ASHER EHEIEH entering within this Circle, composed and made with mine hand. And may God, even ADONAI, bless this place with all the virtues of Heaven, so that no obscene or unclean spirit may have the power to enter into this Circle, or to annoy any person who is therein; though the Lord God ADONAI, Who liveth eternally unto the Ages of the Ages. Amen.

I beseech Thee, O Lord God, the All Powerful and the All Merciful, that Thou wilt deign to bless this Circle, and all this place, and all those who are therein, and that Thou wilt grant unto us, who serve Thee, and rehearse nothing but the wonders of Thy law, a good Angel for our Guardian; remove from us every adverse power; preserve us from evil and from trouble; grant, O Lord, that we may rest in this place in all safety, through Thee, O Lord, Who livest and reignest unto the Ages of the Ages. Amen.

Let the Master now arise and place upon his head a Crown made of paper (or any other appropriate substance), on the which there must be written (with the Colours and other necessary things which we shall describe hereafter), these four Names AGLA, AGLAI, AGLATA, AGLATAI. The which Names are to be placed in the front, behind, and on either side of the head.

Furthermore, the Master ought to have with him in the Circle, those Pentacles or Medals which are necessary to his purpose, which are described hereinafter, and which should be constructed according to the rules given in the Chapter on *Pentacles*. They should be described on virgin paper with a pen; and ink, blood, or colours, prepared according to the manner which we shall hereafter show in the Chapters on these subjects. It will be sufficient to take only those Pentacles which are actually required, they should be sewed to the front of the linen robe, on the chest, with the consecrated needle of the Art, and with a thread which has been woven by a young girl.

After this, let the Master turn himself towards the Eastern Quarter (unless directed to the contrary, or unless he should be wishing to call Spirits which belong to another quarter of the Universe), and pronounce with a loud voice the Conjuration contained in this Chapter. And if the Spirits be disobedient and do not then make their appearance, he must arise and take the exorcised Knife of Art wherewith he hath constructed the Circle, and raise it towards the sky as if he wished to beat or strike the Air, and conjure the Spirits. Let him then lay his right hand and the Knife upon the Pentacles or Medals, constructed of, and described upon virgin paper, which are fastened to or sewn upon his breast, and let him repeat the following Conjuration upon his knees:

CONJURATION.

O Lord, hear my prayer, and let my cry come unto Thee. O Lord God Almighty, who has reigned before the beginning of the Ages, and Who by Thine Infinite Wisdom, hast created the heavens, the earth, and the sea, and all that in them is, all that is visible, and all that is invisible by a single word; I praise Thee, I bless Thee, I adore Thee, I glorify Thee, and I pray Thee now at the present time to be merciful unto me, a miserable sinner, for I am the work of Thine hands. Save me, and direct me by Thy Holy Name, Thou to Whom nothing is difficult, nothing is impossible; and deliver me from the night of mine ignorance, and enable me to go forth therefrom. Enlighten me with a spark of Thine Infinite Wisdom. Take away from my senses the desire of covetousness, and the iniquity of mine idle words. Give unto me, Thy servant, a wise understanding, penetrating and subtle heart, to acquire and comprehend all Sciences and Arts; give unto me capacity to hear, and strength of memory to retain them, so that I may be able to accomplish my desires, and understand and learn all difficult and desirable Sciences; and also that I may be able to comprehend the hidden secrets of the Holy Writings. Give me the virtue to conceive them, so that I may be able to bring forth and pronounce my words with patience and humility, for the instruction of others, as Thou hast ordered me.

O God, the Father, All Powerful and All Merciful, Who hast created all things, Who knowest and conceivest them universally, and to Whom nothing is hidden, nothing is impossible; I entreat Thy Grace for me and for Thy servants, because Thou seest and knowest well that we perform not this work to tempt Thy Strength and Thy Power as if in doubt thereof, but rather that we may know and understand the truth of all hidden things. I beseech Thee to have the kindness to be favorable unto us; by Thy Splendour, Thy Magnificence, and Thy Holiness, and by Thy Holy, Terrible, and Ineffable Name IAH, at which the whole world doth tremble, and by the Fear with which all creatures obey Thee. Grant, O Lord, that we may become responsive unto Thy Grace, so that through it we may have a full confidence in and knowledge of Thee, and that the Spirits may discover themselves here in our presence, and that those which are gentle and peaceable may come unto us, so that they may be obedient unto Thy commands, through Thee, O Most Holy ADONAI, Whose Kingdom is an everlasting Kingdom, and Whose Empire endureth unto the Ages of the Ages. Amen.

After having said all these words devoutly, let the Master arise, and place his hands upon the Pentacles, and let one of the Companions hold the Book open before the Master, who, raising his eyes to heaven, and turning unto the Four Quarters of the Universe, shall say:

O Lord, be Thou unto me a *Tower* of *Strength* against the appearance and assault of the Evil Spirits.

After this, turning towards the Four Quarters of the Universe, he shall say the following words:—

These be the Symbols and the Names of the Creator, which can bring Terror and Fear unto you. Obey me then, by the power of these Holy Names, and by these *Mysterious Symbols* of the *Secret* of *Secrets*.

The which being said and done, thou shalt see them draw near and approach from all parts. But if they be hindered, detained, or occupied in some way, and so that they cannot come, or if they are unwilling to come, then, the Suffumigations and Censings being performed anew, and (the Disciples) having anew, by especial order, touched their Swords, and the Master having encouraged his Disciples, he shall reform the Circle with the Knife of Art, and, raising the said Knife towards the Sky, he shall as it were strike the air therewith. After this he shall lay his hand upon the Pentacles, and having bent his knees before the Most High, he shall repeat with humility the following Confession; the which his Disciples shall also do, and they shall recite it in a low and humble voice, so that they can scarcely be heard.*

* So as not to interfere with the direction of the Will-currents of the Master.

BOOK ONE.
CHAPTER IV.
The Confession to Be Made by the Exorcist.
CONFESSION.

O Lord of Heaven and of Earth, before Thee do I confess my sins, and lament them, cast down and humbled in thy presence. For I have sinned before Thee by pride, avarice, and boundless desire of honours and riches; by idleness, gluttony, greed, debauchery, and drunkenness; because I have offended Thee by all kinds of sins of the flesh, adulteries, and pollutions, which I have committed myself, and consented that others should commit; by sacrilege, thefts, rapine, violation, and homicide; by the evil use I have made of my possessions, by my prodigality, by the sins which I have committed against Hope and Charity, by my evil advice, flatteries, bribes, and the ill distribution which I have made of the goods of which I have been possessed; by repulsing and maltreating the poor, in the distribution which I have made of the goods committed to my charge, by afflicting those over whom I have been set in authority, by not visiting the prisoners, by depriving the dead of burial, by not receiving the poor, by neither feeding the hungry nor giving drink to the thirsty, by never keeping the Sabbath and the other feasts, by not living chastely and piously on those days, by the easy consent which I have given to those who incited me to evil deeds, by injuring instead of aiding those who demanded help from me, by refusing to give ear unto the cry of the poor, by not respecting the aged, by not keeping my word, by disobedience to my parents, by ingratitude towards those from whom I have received kindness, by indulgence in sensual pleasures, by irreverend behaviour in the Temple of God, by unseemly gestures thereat, by entering therein without reverence, by vain and unprofitable discourse when there, by despising the sacred vessels of the temple, by turning the holy Ceremonies into ridicule, by touching and eating the sacred bread with impure lips and with profane hands, and by the neglect of my prayers and adorations.

I detest also the crimes which I have committed by evil thoughts, vain and impure meditations, false suspicions, and rash judgments; by the evil consent which I have readily given unto the advice of the wicked, by lust of impure and sensual pleasures; by my idle words, my lies, and my deceit; by my false vows in various ways; and by my continual slander and calumny.

I detest also the crimes which I have committed within; the treachery and discord which I have incited; my curiosity, greed, false speaking, violence, malediction, murmurs, blasphemies, vain words, insults, dissimulations; my sins against God by the transgression of the ten commandments, by neglect of my duties and obligations, and by want of love towards God and towards my neighbour.

Furthermore I hate the sins which I have committed in all my senses, by sight, by hearing, by taste, by smell, and by touch, in every way that human weakness can offend the Creator; by my carnal thoughts, deeds, and meditations.

In which I humbly confess that I have sinned, and recognise myself as being in the sight of God the most criminal of all men.

I accuse myself before Thee, O God, and I adore Thee with all humility. O ye, Holy Angels, and ye, Children of God, in your presence I publish my sins, so that mine Enemy may have no advantage over me, and may not be able to reproach me at the last day; that he may not be able to say that I have concealed my sins, and that I be not then accused in the presence of the Lord; but, on the contrary, that on my account there may be joy in Heaven, as over the just who have confessed their sins in thy presence.

O Most Mighty and All Powerful Father, grant through Thine unbounded Mercy that I may both see and know all the Spirits which I invoke, so that by their means I may see my will and desire accomplished, by The Sovereign grandeur, and by Thine Ineffable and Eternal Glory, Thou Who art and Who wilt be for ever the Pure and Ineffable Father of All.

The Confession having been finished with great humility, and with the inward feeling of the heart, the Master will recite the following prayer:—

PRAYER.

O Lord All Powerful, Eternal God and Father of all Creatures, shed upon me the Divine Influence of Thy Mercy, for I am Thy Creature. I beseech Thee to defend me from mine Enemies, and to confirm in me true and steadfast faith.

O Lord, I commit my Body and my Soul unto Thee, seeing I put my trust in none beside Thee; it is on Thee alone that I rely; O Lord my God aid me; O Lord hear me in the day and hour wherein I shall invoke Thee. I pray Thee by Thy Mercy not to put me in oblivion, nor to remove me from Thee. O Lord be Thou my succor, Thou Who art the God of my salvation. O Lord make me a new heart according unto Thy loving Kindness. These, O Lord, are the gifts which I await from Thee, O my God and my Master, Thou Who livest and reignest unto the Ages of the Ages. Amen.

O Lord God the All Powerful One, Who hast formed unto Thyself great and Ineffable Wisdom, and Co-eternal with Thyself before the countless Ages; Thou Who in the Birth of Time hast created the Heavens, and the Earth, the Sea, and things that they contain; Thou who hast vivified all things by the Breath of Thy Mouth, I praise Thee, I bless Thee, I adore Thee, and I glorify Thee. Be Thou propitious unto me who am but a miserable sinner, and despise me not; save me and succor me, even me the work of Thine hands. I conjure and entreat Thee by Thy Holy Name to banish from my Spirit the darkness of Ignorance, and to enlighten me with the Fire of thy Wisdom; take away from me all evil desires, and let not my speech be as that of the foolish. O Thou, God the Living One, Whose Glory, Honour, and Kingdom shall extend unto the Ages of the Ages. Amen.

BOOK ONE.

CHAPTER V.

PRAYERS AND CONJURATIONS.

PRAYER.

O Lord God, Holy Father, Almighty and Merciful One, Who hast created all things, Who knowest all things and can do all things, from Whom nothing is hidden, to Whom nothing is impossible; Thou who knowest that we perform not these ceremonies to tempt Thy power, but that we may penetrate into the knowledge of hidden things; we pray Thee by Thy Sacred Mercy to cause and to permit, that we may arrive at this understanding of secret things, of whatever nature they may be by Thine aid, O Most Holy ADONAI, Whose Kingdom and Power shall have no end unto the Ages of the Ages. Amen.

The Prayer being finished, let the Exorcist lay his hand upon the Pentacles, while one of the Disciples shall hold open before him the Book wherein are written the prayers and conjurations proper for conquering, subduing, and reproving the Spirits. Then the Master, turning towards each Quarter of the Earth, and raising his eyes to Heaven, shall say:

O Lord, be Thou unto me a strong tower of refuge, from the sight and assaults of the Evil Spirits.

After which let him turn again towards the Four Quarters of the Earth, and towards each let him utter the following words:

Behold the Symbols and Names of the Creator, which give unto ye forever Terror and Fear. Obey then, by the virtue of these Holy Names, and by these Mysteries of Mysteries.

After this he shall see the Spirits come from every side. But in case they are occupied in some other place, or that they cannot come, or that they are unwilling to come: then let him commence afresh to invoke them after the following manner, and let the Exorcist be assured that even were they bound with chains of iron, and with fire, they could not refrain from coming to accomplish his will.

THE CONJURATION.*

O ye Spirits, ye I conjure by the Power, Wisdom, and Virtue of the Spirit of God, by the uncreate Divine Knowledge, by the vast Mercy of

---

* There is an Invocation bearing the title of "The Qabalistical Invocation of Solomon," given by Eliphas Lévi, which differs in many points from the one given above, though resembling it in some particulars. Lévi's is more evidently constructed on the plan indicated in the "Siphra Dtzenioutha," c. III.; Annotation § 5, sub. § 8, 9; while the one above more follows that laid down, *ibid.* § 5, sub. § 3. I see no reason to suppose that Lévi's is unauthentic. It will be noted by the Qabalistical reader, that the above Conjuration rehearses the Divine Names attached to the Ten Sephiroth.

God, by the Strength of God, by the Greatness of God, by the Unity of God; and by the Holy Name of God EHEIEH, which is the root, trunk, source, and origin of all the other Divine Names, whence they all draw their life and their virtue, which Adam having invoked, he acquired the knowledge of all created things.

I conjure ye by the Indivisible Name IOD, which marketh and express-eth the Simplicity and the Unity of the Nature Divine, which Abel having invoked, he deserved* to escape from the hands of Cain his brother.

I conjure ye by the Name TETRAGRAMMATON ELOHIM, which ex-presseth and signifieth the Grandeur of so lofty a Majesty, that Noah having pronounced it, saved himself, and protected himself with his whole household from the Waters of the Deluge.

I conjure ye by the Name of God EL Strong and Wonderful, which denoteth the Mercy and Goodness of His Majesty Divine, which Abraham having invoked, he was found worthy to come forth from the Ur of the Chaldeans.

I conjure ye by the most powerful Name of ELOHIM GIBOR, which showeth forth the Strength of God, of a God All Powerful, Who punish-eth the crimes of the wicked, Who seeketh out and chastiseth the iniquities of the fathers upon the children unto the third and fourth generation; which Isaac having invoked, he was found worthy to escape from the Sword of Abraham his father.

I conjure ye and I exorcise ye by the most holy Name of ELOAH VA-DAATH, which Jacob invoked when in great trouble, and was found worthy to bear the Name of Israel, which signifieth Vanquisher of God; and he was delivered from the fury of Esau his brother.

I conjure ye by the most potent Name of EL† ADONAI TZABAOTH, which is the God of Armies, ruling in the Heavens, which Joseph invoked and was found worthy to escape from the hands of his Brethren.

I conjure ye by the most potent Name of ELOHIM TZABAOTH, which expresseth piety, mercy, splendour, and knowledge of God, which Moses invoked, and he was found worthy to deliver the People Israel from Egypt, and from the servitude of Pharaoh.

I conjure ye by the most potent Name of SHADDAI, which signifieth doing good unto all; which Moses invoked, and having struck the Sea, it divided into two parts in the midst, on the right hand and on the left. I conjure ye by the most holy Name of EL‡ CHAI, which is that of the Living God, through the virtue of which alliance with us, and redemption for us have been made; which Moses invoked and all the waters returned to their prior state and enveloped the Egyptians, so that not one of them escaped to carry the news into the Land of Mizraim.

Lastly, I conjure ye all, ye rebellious Spirits, by the most holy Name

---

* In the French, "merita d'échapper."

† More usually the Name TETRAGRAMMATON TZABAOTH is attributed to the Seventh Sephira.

‡ Both this Name and "Shaddai" are attributed to the Ninth Sephira, and I have therefore put the two invocations in the same paragraph.

of God ADONAI MELEKH, which Joshua invoked, and stayed the course of the Sun in his presence, through the virtue of Methratton,* its principal Image; and by the troops of Angels who cease not to cry day and night, QADOSCH, SADOSCH, QADOSCH, ADONAI ELOHIM TZABAOTH (that is, Holy, Holy, Holy, Lord God of Hosts, Heaven and Earth are full of Thy Glory) ; and by the Ten Angels who preside over the Ten Sephiroth, by whom God communicateth and extendeth His influence over lower things, which are KETHER, CHOKMAH, BINAH, GEDULAH, GEBURAH, TIPHERETH, NETZACH, HOD, YESOD, AND MALKUTH.

I conjure ye anew, O Spirits, by all the Names of God, and by all His marvellous work; by the heavens; by the earth; by the sea; by the depth of the Abyss, and by that firmament which the very Spirit of God hath moved; by the sun and by the stars; by the waters and by the seas, and all which they contain; by the winds, the whirlwinds, and the tempests; by the virtue of all herbs, plants, and stones; by all which is in the heavens, upon the earth, and in all the Abysses of the Shades.

I conjure ye anew, and I powerfully urge ye, O Demons, in whatsoever part of the world ye may be, so that ye shall be unable to remain in air, fire, water, earth, or in any part of the universe, or in any pleasant place which may attract ye; but that ye come promptly to accomplish our desire, and all things that we demand from your obedience.

I conjure ye anew by the two Tables of the Law, by the five books of Moses, by the Seven Burning Lamps on the Candlestick of Gold before the face of the Throne of the Majesty of God, and by the Holy of Holies wherein the KOHEN HA-GADUL was alone permitted to enter, that is to say, the High-Priest.

I conjure ye by Him Who hath made the heavens and the earth, and who hath measured those heavens in the hollow of His hand, and enclosed the earth with three of His fingers, Who is seated upon the Kerubim and upon the Seraphim; and by the Kerubim, which is called the Kerub, which God constituted and placed to guard the Tree of Life, armed with a flaming sword, after that Man had been driven out of Paradise.

I conjure ye anew, Apostates from God, by Him Who alone hath performed great wonders; by the Heavenly Jerusalem; and by the Most Holy Name of God in Four Letters, and by Him Who enlighteneth all things and shineth upon all things by his Venerable and Ineffable Name, EHEIEH ASHER EHEIEH; that ye come immediately to execute our desire, whatever it may be.

I conjure ye, and I command ye absolutely, O Demons, in whatsoever part of the Universe ye may be, by the virtue of all these Holy Names;— ADONAI,† YAH, HOA, EL, ELOHA, ELOHINU, ELOHIM, EHEIEH, MARON,

---

* The Archangel, who is called also the Prince of Countenances.

† I have made these Names as correct as possible; as in all the original MSS. the Hebrew is much mutilated. These names are some of them ordinary titles of God; others Magical and Qabalistical names compounded from the initials of sentences, &c.; and others permutations of other names.

KAPHU, ESCH, INNON, AVEN, AGLA, HAZOR, EMETH, YAII, ARARITHA, YOVA, HA-KABIR, MESSIACH, IONAH, MAL-KA, EREL, KUZU, MATZ-PATZ, EL SHADDAI; and by all the Holy names of God which have been written with blood in the sign of an eternal alliance.

I conjure ye anew by these other names of God, Most Holy and un-known, by the virtue of which Names ye tremble every day;—BARUC,* BACURABON, PATACEL, ALCHEEGHEL, AQUACHAI, HOMORION, EHEIEH, ABBATON, CHEVON, CEBON, OYZROYMAS, CHAI, EHEIEH, ALBAMACHI, ORTAGU, NALE, ABELECH (or HELECH), YEZE (or SECHEZZE); that ye come quickly and without any delay into our presence from every quarter and every climate of the world wherein ye may be, to execute all that we shall command ye in the Great Name of God.

* I give these Names as they stand, they do not all appear to be Hebrew; some of them suggest the style of the barbarous names in the Græco-Egyptian Magical Papyri.

BOOK ONE.

CHAPTER VI.

STRONGER AND MORE POTENT CONJURATION.

If they then immediately appear, it is well; if not, let the Master uncover the consecrated *Pentacles* which he should have made to constrain and command the Spirits, and which he should wear fastened round his neck, holding the Medals (or Pentacles) in his left hand, and the consecrated Knife in his right; and encouraging his Companions, he shall say with a loud voice:—

ADDRESS.

Here be the Symbols of Secret things, the standards, the ensigns, and the banners, of God the Conqueror; and the arms of the Almighty One, to compel the *Aerial Potencies*. I command ye absolutely by their power and virtue that ye come near unto us, into our presence, from whatsoever part of the world ye may be in, and that ye delay not to obey us in all things wherein we shall command ye by the virtue of God the Mighty One. Come ye promptly, and delay not to appear, and answer us with humility.

If they appear at this time, show them the Pentacles, and receive them with kindness, gentleness, and courtesy; reason and speak with them, question them, and ask from them all things which thou hast proposed to demand.

But if, on the contrary, they do not yet make their appearance, holding the consecrated Knife in the right hand, and the *Pentacles* being uncovered by the removal of their consecrated covering, strike and beat the air with the Knife as if wishing to commence a combat, comfort and exhort thy Companions, and then in a loud and stern voice repeat the following Conjuration:—

CONJURATION.*

Here again I conjure ye and most urgently command ye; I force, constrain, and exhort ye to the utmost, by the most mighty and powerful Name of God EL, strong and wonderful, and by God the Just and Upright, I exorcise ye and command ye that ye in no way delay, but that ye come immediately and upon the instant hither before us, without noise, deformity, or hideousness, but with all manner of gentleness and mildness.

I exorcise ye anew, and powerfully conjure ye, commanding ye with strength and violence by Him Who spake and it was done; and by all these names: EL, SHADDAI, ELOHIM, ELOHI, TZABAOTH, ELIM, ASHER EHEIEH, YAH, TETRAGRAMMATON, SHADDAI, which signify God the High and

---

* This Conjuration is almost identical with one given in the "Lemegeton," or Lesser Key, a different work, also attributed to Solomon.

Almighty, the God of Israel, through Whom undertaking all our operations we shall prosper in all the works of our hands, seeing that the Lord
is now, always, and for ever with us, in our heart and in our lips; and by
His Holy Names, and by the virtue of the Sovereign God, we shall accomplish all our work.

Come ye at once without any hideousness or deformity before us,
come ye without monstrous appearance, in a gracious form or figure.
Come ye, for we exorcise ye with the utmost vehemence by the Name of
IAH and ON, which Adam spake and heard; by the Name EL, which Noah
heard, and saved himself with all his family from the Deluge; by the
Name IOD, which Noah heard, and knew God the Almighty One; by the
Name AGLA, which Jacob heard, and saw the Ladder which touched
Heaven, and the Angels who ascended and descended upon it, whence he
called that place the House of God and the Gate of Heaven; and by the
Name ELOHIM, and in the Name ELOHIM, which Moses named, invoked,
and heard in Horeb the Mount of God, and he was found worthy to hear
Him speak from the Burning Bush; and by the Name AIN SOPH, which
Aaron heard, and was at once made eloquent, wise, and learned; and by
the Name TZABAOTH, which Moses named and invoked, and all the ponds
and rivers were covered with blood throughout the land of Egypt;* and
by the name IOD, which Moses named and invoked, and striking upon the
dust of the earth both men and beasts were struck with disease;† and by
the Name, and in the Name PRIMEUMATON, which Moses named and
invoked, and there fell a great and severe hail throughout all the land of
Egypt, destroying the vines, the trees, and the woods which were in that
country; and by the Name IAPHAR, which Moses heard and invoked, and
immediately a great pestilence began to appear through all the land of
Egypt, striking and slaying the asses, the oxen, and the sheep of the
Egyptians, so that they all died; and by the Name ABADDON which Moses
invoked and sprinkled the dust towards heaven, and immediately there
fell so great rain upon the men, cattle, and flocks, that they all died throughout the land of Egypt; and by the Name ELION which Moses invoked,
and there fell so great hail as had never been seen from the beginning of
the world unto that time, so that all men, and herds, and everything that
was in the fields perished and died throughout all the land of Egypt. And
by the Name EDONAL, which Moses having invoked, there came so great
a quantity of locusts which appeared in the land of Egypt, that they
devoured and swallowed up all that the hail had spared; and by the Name
of PATHEON,‡ which having invoked, there arose so thick, so awful, and
so terrible darkness throughout the land of Egypt, during the space of
three days and three nights, that almost all who were left alive died; and

---

* Some MSS. add. "et furent purifiés."

† Some MSS. substitute, "les hommes furent reduits en cendre, comme aussi les bœufs,
betail, et troupeaux des Egyptiens."

‡ This is often written PATHTUMON in similar Conjurations, but the MSS. before me agree
in giving this form.

by the Name YESOD and in the Name YESOD, which Moses invoked, and
at midnight all the first-born, both of men and of animals, died; and by
the Name of YESHIMON, which Moses named and invoked, and the Red
Sea divided itself and separated in two; and by the name HESION, which
Moses invoked, and all the army of Pharaoh was drowned in the waters;
and by the Name ANABONA, which Moses having heard upon Mount Sinai,
he was found worthy to receive and obtain the tables of stone written with
the finger of God the Creator; and by the Name ERYGION, which Joshua
having invoked when he fought against the Moabites, he defeated them
and gained the victory; and by the Name HOA, and in the Name HOA,
which David invoked, and he was delivered from the hand of Goliath;
and by the name YOD, which Solomon having named and invoked, he was
found worthy to ask for and obtain in sleep the Ineffable Wisdom of God;
and by the Name YIAI, which Solomon having named and invoked, he
was found worthy to have power over all the Demons, Potencies, Powers,
and Virtues of the Air.

By these, then, and by all the other Names of God Almighty, Holy,
Living, and True, we powerfully command ye, ye who by your own sin
have been cast down from the Empyreal Heaven, and from before His
Throne; by Him who hath cast ye down unto the most profound of the
Abysses of Hell, we command ye boldly and resolutely; and by that
terrible Day of the Sovereign Judgment of God, on which all the dry
bones in the earth will arise to hear and listen unto the Word of God with
their body, and will present themselves before the face of God Almighty;
and by that Last Fire which shall consume all things; by the (Crystal)
Sea which is known unto us, which is before the Face of God; by the
indicible and ineffable virtue, force, and power of the Creator Himself.
by His Almighty power, and by the Light and Flame which emanate from
His Countenance, and which are before His Face; by the Angelical Powers
which are in the Heavens, and by the most great Wisdom of Almighty
God; by the Seal of David, by the Ring and Seal of Solomon, which was
revealed unto him by the Most High and Sovereign Creator; and by the
Nine Medals or Pentacles, which we have among our Symbols, which
proceed and come from Heaven, and are among the Mysteries of Mysteries or Secrets of Secrets, which you can also behold in my hand, consecrated and exorcised with the due and requisite Ceremonies. By these,
then, and by all the Secrets which the Almighty encloseth in the Treasures
of the Sovereign and Highest Wisdom, by His Hand, and by His marvellous power; I conjure, force, and exorcise ye that ye come without delay
to perform in our presence that which we shall command ye.

I conjure ye anew by that most Holy Name which the whole Universe
fears, respects, and reveres, which is written by these letters and characters,
IOD, HE, VAU, HE; and by the last and terrible judgment; by the Seat of
BALDACHIA;* and by this Holy Name, YIAI, which Moses invoked, and

* Sometimes, but as I think erroneously, written Bas-dathea. I imagine the word to mean
"Lord of Life."

there followed that great Judgment of God, when Dathan and Abiram were swallowed up in the centre of the earth. Otherwise, if ye contravene and resist us by your disobedience unto the virtue and power of this Name YIAI, we curse ye even unto the Depth of the Great Abyss, into the which we shall cast, hurl, and bind ye, if ye show yourselves rebellious against the Secret of Secrets, and against the Mystery of Mysteries. AMEN, AMEN. FIAT, FIAT.

This Conjuration thou shalt say and perform, turning thyself unto the East, and if they appear not, thou shalt repeat it unto the Spirits, turning unto the South, the West, and the North, in succession, when thou wilt have repeated it four times. And if they appear not even then, thou shalt make the Sign of TAU* upon the foreheads of thy companions, and thou shalt say:—

CONJURATION.

Behold anew the Symbol and the Name of a Sovereign and Conquering God, through which all the Universe fears, trembles, and shudders, and through the most mysterious words of the Secret Mysteries and by their Virtue, Strength, and Power.

I conjure ye anew, I constrain and command ye with the utmost vehemence and power, by that most potent and powerful Name of God, EL, strong and wonderful, by Him who spake and it was done; and by the Name IAH, which Moses heard, and spoke with God; and by the Name AGLA, which Joseph invoked, and was delivered out of the hands of his brethren; and by the Name VAU, which Abraham heard, and knew God the Almighty One; and by the Name of Four Letters, TETRAGRAMMATON, which Joshua named and invoked, and he was rendered worthy and found deserving to lead the Army of Israel into the Promised Land; and by the Name ANABONA, by which God formed Man and the whole Universe; and by the Name ARPHETON,† and in the Name ARPHETON, by which the Angels who are destined to that end will summon the Universe, in visible body and form, and will assemble (all people) together by the sound of the Trumpet at that terrible and awful Day of Judgment, when the memory of the wicked and ungodly shall perish; and by the Name ADONAI, by which God will judge all human flesh, at Whose voice all men, both good and evil, will rise again, and all men and Angels will assemble in the air before the Lord, Who will judge and condemn the wicked; and by the Name ONEIPHETON,‡ by which God will summon the dead, and raise them up again unto life; and by the Name ELOHIM, and in the Name ELOHIM, by which God will disturb and excite tempests throughout all the seas, so that they will cast out the fish therefrom, and in one day the third part of men about the sea and the rivers shall die; and by the Name

---

* Or the Cross.

† Also written *Hipeton;* and I believe sometimes replaced by *Anapheneton,* or *Anaphaxeton.*

‡ This word is given variously in the MSS., as *Oneypheon, Onayepheton,* and *Donecepheron,* &c.

ELOHI,* and in the Name ELOHI, by which God will dry up the sea and the rivers, so that men can go on foot through their channels; and by the Name ON, and in the Name ON, by which God shall restore and replace the sea, the rivers, the streams, and the brooks, in their previous state; and by the Name MESSIACH,† and in the Name MESSIACH, by which God will make all animals combat together, so that they shall die in a single day; and by the Name ARIEL, by which God shall destroy in a single day all buildings, so that there shall not be left one stone upon another; and by the Name IAHT,‡ by which God will cast one stone upon another, so that all people and nations will fly from the sea-shore, and will say unto them cover us and hide us; and by the Name EMANUEL, by which God will perform wonders, and the winged creatures and birds of the air shall contend with one another; and by the Name ANAEL,§ and in the Name ANAEL, by which God will cast down the mountains and fill up the valleys, so that the surface of the earth shall be level in all parts; and by the Name ZEDEREZA,‖ and in the Name ZEDEREZA, by which God will cause the Sun and Moon to be darkened, and the Stars of heaven to fall; and by the Name SEPHERIEL,¶ by which God will come to Universal Judgment, like a Prince newly crowned entering in triumph into his capital city, girded with a zone of gold, and preceded by Angels, and at His aspect all climes and parts of the Universe shall be troubled and astonished, and a fire shall go forth before Him, and flames and storm shall surround Him; and by the Name TA'U,** by which God brought the Deluge, and the waters prevailed above the mountains, and fifteen cubits above their summits; and by the Name RUACHIAH,†† by which God having purged the Ages, He will make His Holy spirit to descend upon the Universe, and will cast ye, ye rebellious Spirits, and unclean beings, into the Depths of the Lake of the Abyss, in misery, filth, and mire, and will place ye in impure and foul dungeons bound with eternal chains of fire.

By these Names then, and by all the other Holy Names of God before Whom no man can stand and live, and which Names the armies of the Demons fear, tremble at, and shudder; we conjure ye, we potently exorcise and command ye, conjuring ye in addition by the terrible and tremendous PATHS‡‡ of GOD and by His Holy habitation wherein He reigneth and commandeth unto the eternal Ages.   Amen.

* Or *Elia.*
† What is said here refers symbolically to the rooting out of the Evil Spirits, and Shells, from the Universe by King Messiach, which is spoken of in the Qabalah. The Qabalah sometimes expresses the Evil Spirits by the words animals, or beasts, and creeping things.
‡ The oldest MSS. gives the above form, in the others it is changed into *Iaphat, Taphat,* and even *Japhet.* It is probably a corruption of *Achad* Unity.
§ This is also the name of the Angel of Venus.
‖ So written in the oldest MS., the others give it as *Zedeesia, Zedeezia,* and *Zedezias.*
¶ Meaning "emanating from God." It is corrupted into *Sephosiel,* &c., in the MSS.
** *Iaha,* in 10862 Add. MSS.
†† Meaning Spirit of Iah.
‡‡ That is, the hidden and occult grades and links of emanation in the Sephiroth. The later MSS. have put, by mistake, *voix* for *voies,* the oldest Latin MS. gives Semitis.

By the virtue of all these aforesaid, we command ye that ye remain not in any place wherein ye are, but to come hither promptly without delay to do that which we shall enjoin ye. But if ye be still contumacious, we, by the Authority of a Sovereign and Potent God, deprive ye of all quality, condition, degree, and place which ye now enjoy, and precipitate ye into and relegate ye unto the Kingdom of Fire and of Sulphur, to be there eternally tormented. Come ye then from all parts of the earth, wheresoever ye may be, and behold the Symbols and Names of that Triumphant Sovereign Whom all creatures obey, otherwise we shall bind ye and conduct ye in spite of yourselves, into our presence bound with chains of fire, because those effects which proceed and issue from our Science and operation, are ardent with a fire which shall consume and burn ye eternally, for by these the whole Universe trembleth, the earth is moved, the stones thereof rush together, all creatures obey, and the rebellious Spirits are tormented by the power of the *Sovereign Creator.*

Then it is certain that they will come, even if they be bound with chains of fire, unless prevented by affairs of the very greatest importance, but in this latter case they will send ambassadors and messengers by whom thou shalt easily and surely learn what occupies the Spirits and what they are about. But if they appear not yet in answer to the above Conjuration, and are still disobedient, then let the Master of the Art or Exorciser arise and exhort his Companions to be of good cheer and not to despair of the ultimate success of the operation; let him strike the air with the *Consecrated Knife* towards the Four Quarters of the Universe; and then let him Kneel in the midst of the Circle, and the Companions also in their several places, and let them say consecutively with him in a low voice, turning in the direction of the East, the following

ADDRESS TO THE ANGELS.

I conjure and pray ye, O ye Angels of God, and ye Celestial Spirits, to come unto mine aid; come and behold the Signs of Heaven, and be my witness before the Sovereign Lord, of the disobedience of these evil and fallen Spirits who were at one time your companions.

This being done, let the Master arise, and constrain and force them by a stronger conjuration, in manner following.

BOOK ONE.
CHAPTER VII.
An Extremely Powerful Conjuration.

BEHOLD us again prepared to conjure ye by the Names and Symbols of God, wherewith we are fortified, and by the virtue of the Highest One. We command ye and potently ordain ye by the most strong and powerful Names of God, Who is worthy of all praise, admiration, honor, glory, veneration, and fear, that ye delay not longer, but that ye appear before us without any tumult or disturbance, but, on the contrary, with great respect and courtesy, in a beautiful and human form.·

If they then appear, let them see the Pentacles, and say:

Obey ye, Obey ye, behold the Symbols and Names of the Creator; be ye gentle and peaceable, and obey in all things that we shall command ye.

They will then immediately talk with thee, as a friend speaketh unto a friend. Ask of them all that thou desirest, with constancy, firmness, and assurance, and they will obey thee.

But if they appear not yet, let not the Master on that account lose his courage, for there is nothing in the world stronger and of greater force to overawe the Spirits than constancy. Let him, however, re-examine and reform the Circle, and let him take up a little dust of the earth, which he shall cast towards the Four Quarters of the Universe; and having placed his Knife upon the ground, let him say on his knees, turning towards the direction of the North:

In the Name of ADONAI ELOHIM TZABAOTH SHADDAI, Lord God of Armies Almighty, may we successfully perform the works of our hands, and may the Lord be present with us in our heart and in our lips.

These words having been said kneeling upon the earth, let the Master shortly after arise and open his arms wide as if wishing to embrace the air, and say:

CONJURATION.

By the Holy Names of God written in this Book, and by the other Holy and Ineffable Names which are written in the Book of Life, we conjure ye to come unto us promptly and without any delay, wherefore tarry not, but appear in a beautiful and agreeable form the figure, by these Holy Names: ADONAI, TZABAOTH, EL, ELOHI, ELOHIM, SHADDAI; and by EHEIEH, YOD HE VAU HE which is the Great Name of God TETRAGRAMMATION written with Four Letters, ANAPHODITION, and Ineffable; by the God of those Virtues and Potencies, Who dwelleth in the Heavens, Who rideth upon the Kerubim, Who moveth upon the Wings of the Wind, He Whose Power is in Heaven and in Earth, Who spake and it was done, Who commanded and the whole Universe was created; and by the Holy Names and in the Holy Names, IAH, IAH, IAH, ADONAI TZABAOTH; and by all the Names of God, the Living, and the True, I reiterate the Conjuration, and I conjure ye afresh ye Evil and rebellious Spirits, abiding in the Abysses of Darkness.

I conjure, I address, and I exorcise ye, that ye may approach unto and come before the Throne of God, the Living and the True, and before the Tribunal of the Judgment of His Majesty, and before the Holy Angels of God to hear the sentence of your condemnation.

Come ye then by the Name and in the Name of SHADDA. which is that of God Almighty, strong, powerful, admirable, exalted, pure, clean, glorified, virtuous, great, just, terrible, and holy; and by the Name and in the Name of EL, IAH, IAH, IAH, Who hath formed and created the world by the Breath of His Mouth, Who supporteth it by His Power, Who ruleth and governeth it by His Wisdom, and Who hath cast ye for your pride into the *Land of Darkness* and into the *Shadow of Death.*

Therefore, by the Name of the Living God, Who hath formed the heavens above, and hath laid the foundations of the earth beneath, we command ye that, immediately and without any delay, ye come unto us from all places, valleys, mountains, hills, field, seas, rivers, fountains, ponds, brooks, caverns, grottos, cities, towns, villages, markets, fairs, habitations, baths, courtyards, gardens, vineyards, plantations, reservoirs, cisterns, and from every corner of the terrestrial earth where ye may happen to be in your assemblies, so that ye may execute and accomplish our demands with all mildness and courtesy; by that Ineffable Name which Moses heard and invoked, which he received from God from the midst of the Burning Bush, we conjure ye to obey our commands, and to come unto us promptly with all gentleness of manner.

Again we command ye with vehemence, and we exorcise ye with constancy, that ye and all your comrades come unto us in an agreeable and gracious manner like the breeze, to accomplish successively our various commands and desires. Come ye, then, by the virtue of these Names by the which we exorcise ye; ANAI, ÆCHHAD, TRANSIN, EMETH, CHAIA, IONA, PROFA, TITACHE, BEN ANI, BRIAH, THEIT; all which names are written in Heaven in the characters of Malachim,* that is to say, the tongue of the Angels.

We then, by the just judgment of God, by the Ineffiable and Admirable Virtue of God, just, living, and true, we call ye with power, we force and exorcise ye by and in the admirable Name which was written on the Tables of Stone which God gave upon Mount Sinai; and by and in the wonderful Name which Aaron the High Priest bare written upon his breast, by which also God created the World, the which name is AXINETON; and by the Living God Who is One throughout the Ages, whose dwelling is in the Ineffable Light, Whose Name is Wisdom, and Whose Spirit is Life, before Whom goeth forth Fire and Flame, Who hath from that Fire formed the firmament, the Stars and the Sun; and Who with that Fire will burn ye all for ever, as also all who shall contravene the Words of His Will.

Come ye, then, without delay, without noise, and without rage, before us, without any deformity or hideousness, to execute all our will; come ye

---

* The Mystic Alphabet known as the "Writing of Malachim" is formed from the positions of the Stars in the heavens, by drawing imaginary lines from one star to another so as to obtain the shapes of the characters of this Alphabet.

from all places wherein ye are, from all mountains, valleys, streams, rivers, brooks, ponds, places, baths, synagogues; for God, strong and powerful, will chase ye and constrain ye, being glorious over all things; He will compel ye, both ye and the Prince of Darkness. Come ye, come ye, Angels of Darkness; come hither before this Circle without fear, terror, or deformity, to execute our commands, and be ye ready both to achieve and to complete all that we shall command ye.

Come ye, then, by the Crown of the Chief of your Emperors, and by the Sceptres of your power, and of SID, the Great Demon, your Master; by the Names and in the Names of the Holy Angels who have been created to be above you, long before the constitution of the world; and by the Names of the two Princes of the Universe, whose Names are, IONIEL and SEFO-NIEL; by the rod of Moses, by the staff of Jacob; by the ring and seal of David, wherein are written the Names of Sovereign God; and by the Names of the Angels by which SOLOMON has linked and bound ye; and by the sacred bonds by which ANAEL hath environed and hath conquered the Spirit; and by the Name of the Angel who ruleth potently over the rest, and by the praise of all creatures who cry incessantly unto God, Who spake, and immediately all things, even the Ages, were made and formed; and by the Name HA-QADOSCH BERAKHA, which signifies the Holy and Blessed One; and by the Ten Choirs of the Holy Angels, CHAIOTH HA-QADESH, AUPHANIM, ARALIM, CHASHMALIM, SERAPHIM, MALACHIM, ELOHIM, BENI ELOHIM, KERUBIM, and ISHIM; and by, and in the Sacred name of Twelve Letters of which each Letter is the Name of an Angel, and the letters of the Name are ALEPH*, BETH, BETH, NUN, VAU, RESH, VAU, CHETH, HE, QOPH, DALETH, SHIN.

By these Names therefore, and by all the other Holy Names, we conjure ye and we exorcise ye; by the Angel ZECHIEL; by the Angel DUCHIEL; by the Angel DONACHIEL; and by the Great Angel METATRON, Who is the Prince of the Angels, and introduceth the Souls before the Face of God; and by the Angel SANGARIEL, by whom the portals of Heaven are guarded; and by the Angel KERUB, who was made the Guardian of the Terrestrial Paradise, with a Sword of Flame, after the expulsion of Adam our forefather; and by the Angel MICHAEL by whom ye were hurled down from the Height of the THRONE into the Depth of the Lake and of the Abyss, the same Name meaning, "Who is like God upon Earth;" and by the Angel ANIEL; and by the Angel OPHIEL; and by the Angel BEDALIEL; wherefore, by these and by all the other Holy Names of the Angels, we powerfully conjure and exorcise ye, that ye come from all parts of the world immediately, and without any delay, to perform our will and demands, obeying us quickly and courteously, and that ye come by the Name and in the Name of ALEPH, DALETH, NUN, IOD, for we

---

* Which Letters I have, with much care, corrected, for in the MSS. the letters are jumbled together in hopeless confusion, *Seym* is written for *Shin, Res* for *Beth*, &c. The Name is *Ab, Ben, Ve-Ruach, Ha-Qadesch,* Father, Son, and Holy Spirit. There are two other Names of Twelve Letters frequently employed, HQDVSH BRVK HVA, Holy and Blessed be He; and ADNI HMLK NAMN, The Lord, the faithful King; besides other forms.

exorcise ye anew by the application of these Letters, by whose power burning fire is quenched, and the whole Universe trembleth.

We constrain ye yet again by the Seal of the Sun which is the Word of God; and by the Seal of the Moon and of the Stars we bind ye; and by the other Animals and Creatures which are in Heaven, by whose wings Heaven cleanseth itself, we force and attract ye imperiously to execute our will without failure. And we conjure, oblige, and terribly exorcise ye, that ye draw near unto us without delay and without fear, as far as is possible unto ye, here before this Circle, as supplicants gently and with discretion, to accomplish our will in all and through all. If ye come promptly and voluntarily, ye shall inhale our perfumes, and our suffumigations of pleasant odour, which will be both agreeable and delightful unto ye. Furthermore ye will see the Symbol of your Creator, and the Names of his Holy Angels, and we shall afterwards dismiss ye, and send ye hence with thanks. But if, on the contrary, ye come not quickly, and ye show yourselves self-opinionated, rebellious, and contumacious, we shall conjure ye again, and exorcise ye ceaselessly, and will repeat all the aforesaid words and Holy Names of God and of the Holy Angels; by the which Names we shall harass you, and if that be not sufficient we will add thereunto yet greater and more powerful ones, and we will thereunto again add other Names which ye have not yet heard from us, which are those of an Almighty God, and which will make ye tremble and quake with fear, both ye and your princes; by the which Names we conjure both you and them also, and we shall not desist from our work until the accomplishment of our will. But if perchance ye yet shall harden yourselves, and show yourselves self-opinionated, disobedient, rebellious, refractory, and contumacious, and if ye yet resist our powerful conjurations, we shall pronounce against you this warrant of arrest in the Name of God Almighty, and this definite sentence that ye shall fall into dangerous disease and leprosy, and that in sign of the Divine Vengeance ye shall all perish by a terrifying and horrible death, and that a fire shall consume and devour you on every side, and utterly crush you; and that by the Power of God, a flame shall go forth from His Mouth which shall burn ye up and reduce ye unto nothing in Hell. Wherefore delay ye not to come, for we shall not cease from these powerful conjurations until ye shall be obliged to appear against your will.

Thus then, therefore, we anew conjure and exorcise ye by and in the Holy Name of ON, which is interpreted and called God; by the Name and in the Name of EHEIEH, which is the true Name of God, "I am He Who is;" by and in the Ineffable Name of Four Letters YOD HE VAU HE, the Knowledge and understanding of which is hidden even from the Angels; by the Name and in the Name of EL, which signifieth and denoteth the powerful and consuming fire which issueth from His Countenance, and which shall be your ruin and destruction; and by the Light of the Angels which is kindled and taken ineffably from that flame of Divine ardour.

By these then, and by other most Holy Names which we pronounce against you from the bottom of our hearts, do we force and constrain ye, if ye be yet rebellious and disobedient. We conjure ye powerfully and strongly exorcise ye, that ye come unto us with joy and quickness, without fraud or deceit, in truth and not in error.

Come ye then, come ye, behold the Signs and the Names of your Creator, behold the *Holy Pentacles* by the virtue of which the Earth is moved, the trees thereof and the Abysses tremble. Come ye; come ye; come ye.

These things being thus done and performed, ye shall see the Spirits come from all sides in great haste with their Princes and Superiors; the Spirits of the First Order, like Soldiers, armed with spears, shields, and corslets; those of the Second Order like Barons, Princes, Dukes, Captains, and Generals of Armies. For the Third and last Order their King will appear, before whom go many players on instruments of music, accompanied by beautiful and melodious voices which sing in chorus.

Then the Exorcist, or Master of the Art, at the arrival of the King, whom he shall see crowned with a *Diadem*, should uncover the *Holy Pentacles* and Medals which he weareth upon his breast covered with a cloth of silk or of fine twined linen, and show them unto him, saying:—

Behold the Signs and Holy Names by and before whose power every knee should bow, of all that is in Heaven, upon Earth, or in Hell. Humble ye yourselves, therefore, under the Mighty hand of God.

Then will the King bow the knee before thee, and will say, "What dost thou wish, and wherefore hast thou caused us to come hither from the Infernal Abodes?"

Then shall the Exorcist, or Master of Magical Art, with an assured air and a grave and imperious voice, order and command him to be tranquil, to keep the rest of his attendants peaceable, and to impose silence upon them.

Let him, also, renew his fumigations, and offer large quantities of Incense, which he should at once place upon the fire, in order to appease the Spirits as he hath promised them. He should then cover the Pentacles, and he will see wonderful things, which it is impossible to relate, touching worldly matters and all sciences.

This being finished, let the Master uncover the Pentacles, and demand all that he shall wish from the King of the Spirits, and if there are one or two Spirits only, it will be the same; and having obtained all his desire, he shall thus license them to depart:—

THE LICENSE TO DEPART.

In the Name of ADONAI, the Eternal and Everlasting One, let each of you return unto his place; be there peace between us and you, and be ye ready to come when ye are called.

After this he should recite the first chapter of Genesis, *"Berashith Bara Elohim,* In the beginning, &c."

This being done, let them all in order quit the Circle, one after the other, the Master first. Furthermore let them bathe their faces with the exorcised water, as will be hereafter told, and then let them take their ordinary raiment and go about their business.

Take notice and observe carefully that this last conjuration is of so great importance and efficacy, that even if the Spirits were bound with chains of iron and fire, or shut up in some strong place, or retained by an oath, they could not even then delay to come. But supposing that they were being conjured in some other place or part of the Universe by some other Exorcist or Master of the Art, by the same conjuration; the Master should add to his conjuration that they should at least send him some Messengers, or some individual to declare unto him where they are, how employed, and the reason why they cannot come and obey him.

But if (which is almost impossible) they be even yet self-opinionated and disobedient, and unwilling to obey; in this case their names should be written on virgin paper, which he should soil and fill with mud, dust, or clay. Then he shall kindle a fire with dry rue, upon which he shall put powdered assafœtida, and other things of evil odour; after which let him put the aforesaid names, written on parchment* or *Virgin Parchment Paper*, upon the fire, saying:—

THE CONJURATION OF THE FIRE.

I conjure thee, O Creature of Fire, by Him who removeth the Earth, and maketh it tremble, that thou burn and torment these Spirits, so that they may feel it intensely, and that they may be burned eternally by thee.

This being said, thou shalt cast the aforesaid paper into the fire, saying:—

THE CURSE.

Be ye accursed, damned, and eternally reproved; and be ye tormented with perpetual pain, so that we may find no repose by night nor by day, nor for a single moment of time, if ye obey not immediately the command of Him Who maketh the Universe to tremble; by these Names, and in virtue of these Names, the which being named and invoked all creatures obey and tremble with fear and terror, these Names which can turn aside lightning and thunder; and which will utterly make you to perish, destroy, and banish you. These Names then are Aleph, Beth, Gimel, Daleth, He, Vau, Zayin, Cheth, Teth, Yod, Kaph, Lamed, Mem, Nun, Samekh, Ayin, Pe, Tzaddi, Qoph, Resh, Shin, Tau.†

By these secret Names, therefore, and by these signs which are full of Mysteries, we curse ye, and in virtue of the power of the Three Principles, Aleph,‡ Mem, Shin, we deprive ye of all office and dignity which ye may have enjoyed up till now; and by their virtue and power we relegate you unto a lake of sulphur and of flame, and unto the deepest depths of the Abyss, that ye may burn therein eternally for ever.

---

* Genuine Virgin Parchment is made from the skin of young Lambs and can be obtained from Messrs. de Laurence, Scott & Co.

† Which are the Names of the Letters of the Hebrew Alphabet, to each of which a special mystic meaning and power is attached, besides its ordinary application.

‡ The Literal Symbols of Air, Water, and Fire; which are called by the Sepher Yetzirah the Three Mother Letters.

Then will they assuredly come without any delay, and in great haste, crying: "O Our Lord and Prince, deliver us out of this suffering."

All this time thou shouldest have near thee ready an exorcised pen, paper, and ink, as will be described hereinafter. Write their Names afresh, and kindle fresh fire, whereon thou shalt put gum benjamin, olybdanum, and storax to make therewith a fumigation; with these odours thou shalt afresh, perfume the aforesaid paper with the Names; but thou shouldest have these names ready prepared beforehand. Then show them the Holy Pentacles, and ask of them what thou wilt, and thou shalt obtain it; and having gained thy purpose, send away the Spirits, saying:

THE LICENSE TO DEPART.

By the virtue of these *Pentacles,* and because ye have been obedient, and have obeyed the commandments of the Creator, feel and inhale this grateful odour, and afterwards depart ye unto your abodes and retreats; be there peace between us and you; be ye ever ready to come when ye shall be cited and called; and may the blessing of God, as far as ye are capable of receiving it, be upon you, provided ye be obedient and prompt to come unto us without solemn rites and observances on our part.

Thou shouldest further make a Book of Virgin Parchment* Paper, and therein write the foregoing conjurations, and constrain the Demons to swear upon the same book that they will come whenever they be called, and present themselves before thee, whenever thou shalt wish to consult them. Afterwards thou canst cover this Book with sacred Sigils on a plate of silver, and therein write or engrave the *Holy Pentacles.* Thou mayest open this Book either on Sundays or on Thursdays, rather at night than by day, and the Spirits will come.

Regarding the expression *"night,"* understand the night following, and not the night preceding the aforesaid days. And remember that by day (the Demons) are ashamed, for they are Animals of Darkness.

* This Book can be made from Genuine Virgin Parchment Paper which may be obtained from Messrs. de Laurence, Scott & Co. This Book may consist of sixteen pages and can be made, by stitching with black Silk thread, one sheet of Genuine Virgin Parchment Paper, which comes in eight pieces. The stitching you may do yourself. See Order No. 292, in Messrs. de Laurence, Scott & Co.'s Catalogue.

It should be understood, by the *Disciple* who readeth here, that there are many kinds of so-called Parchment Paper sold, but there is in existence only one kind of Parchment Paper, and this is the *Genuine Virgin Parchment.* The very same, being made from the skin of dead born lambs, and, is always used for making *Talismans, Charms* and *Pentacles.* The ancient Astrologers, and the old Masters of *Talismanic Magic* never used anything otherwise than *Genuine Virgin Parchment,* as it is known to be the only material that conforms to the requirements of *Occultism* and *Talismanic Magic.*

Genuine Virgin Parchment, made from the skin of dead born lambs, is very costly, rare, and difficult to obtain. It must first be polished with pumice stone at great labor and expense before its surface is fit to be engraved upon or before any tracings can be made thereon. Many foolishly hesitate to pay the price asked for a sheet of *Genuine Virgin Parchment* greatly preferring to pay less for worthless material; but gold is gold; diamonds are diamonds; and *Virgin Parchment is Virgin Parchment.* As gold is always worth its equivalent in money, and diamonds are always worth so much a *Karat,* so *Genuine Virgin Parchment Paper* is always worth so much a sheet.

Messrs. de Laurence, Scott & Co. are the only firm, as far as the writer knows, that is able to furnish the pure, unspotted, *Genuine Virgin Parchment Paper* made from the skin of dead born lambs. The cost for a sheet is not high considering its great value and the secret purposes for which it can be used. Whether you care to pay the price asked or not is entirely an affair of your own.

BOOK ONE.
CHAPTER VIII.
CONCERNING PENTACLES, AND THE MANNER OF CONSTRUCTING THEM.

As we have already made mention of the *Pentacles*, it is necessary that thou shouldest understand that the whole Science and understanding of our *"Key"* dependeth upon the operation, Knowledge, and use of *Pentacles*.

He then who shall wish to perform any operation by the means of the *Medals*, or *Pentacles*, and therein to render himself expert, must observe what hath been hereinbefore ordained. Let him then, *O my Son Roboam*, know and understand that in the aforesaid *Pentacles* he shall find those Ineffable and Most Holy Names which were written by the finger of God in the *Tablets* of *Moses;* and which I, SOLOMON, have received through the Ministry of an Angel by Divine Revelation. These then have I collected together, arranged, consecrated, and kept, for the benefit of the human race, and the preservation of *Body* and of *Soul*.

The *Pentacles* should then be made in the days and hours of Mercury, when the Moon is in an *aërial** or terrestrial sign; she should also be in her increase, and in equal number of days with the Sun.

It is necessary to have a Chamber or Cabinet specially set apart and newly cleaned, wherein thou canst remain without interruption, the which having entered with thy Companions, thou shalt incense and perfume it with the odours and perfumes of the Art. The sky should be clear and serene. It is necessary that thou shouldest have one or more pieces of virgin paper prepared and arranged ready, as we shall tell you more fully later on, in its place.

Thou shalt commence the writing or construction of the *Pentacles* in the hour aforesaid. Among other things, thou shalt chiefly use these colours: Gold, Cinnabar or Vermilion Red, and celestial or brilliant Azure Blue. Furthermore, thou shalt make these *Medals* or *Pentacles* with exorcised pen and colours, as we shall hereafter show thee. Whensoever thou constructest them, if thou canst complete them in the hour wherein thou didst begin them, it is better. However, if it be absolutely necessary to interrupt the work, thou shouldest await the proper day and hour before re-commencing it.

The *Pentacles* being finished and completed, take a cloth of very fine silk, as we shall hereafter ordain thee, in the which thou shalt wrap the Pentacles. After which thou shalt take a large Vessel of Earth filled with Charcoal, upon the which there must be put frankincense, mastic, and aloes, all having been previously conjured and exorcised as shall hereafter be told thee. Thou must also be thyself pure, clean, and washed, as thou shalt find given in the proper place. Furthermore, thou shouldest have the Sickle or Knife of Magical Art, with the which thou shalt make a Circle, and trace within it an inner circle, and in the space between the

---

* *i.e.* in Gemini, Libra, Aquarius, Taurus, Virgo, or Capricorn.

two thou shalt write the Names of God,* which thou shalt think fit and proper. It is necessary after this that thou shouldest have within the Circle a vessel of earth with burning coals and odoriferous perfumes thereon; with the which thou shalt fumigate the aforesaid *Pentacles;* and, having turned thy face towards the East, thou shalt hold the said *Pentacles* over the smoke of the *Temple Incense,* and shalt repeat devoutly the following *Psalms* of *David* my *Father: Psalms* viii., xxi., xxvii., xxix., xxxii., li., lxxii., cxxxiv.†

(For a convenient form of Circle which may be used for preparing Instruments and other things of the same kind, as well as for consecrating the *Pentacles, see Figure* 3.)

After this thou shalt repeat the following Oration:—

THE ORATION.

O ADONAI most powerful, EL most strong, AGLA most holy, ON most righteous, the ALEPH ‡ and the TAU, the Beginning and the End; Thou Who hast established all things in Thy Wisdom; Thou Who has chosen Abraham Thy faithful servant, and hast promised that in his seed shall all nations of the earth be blessed, which seed Thou hast multiplied as the Stars of Heaven; Thou Who hast appeared unto Thy servant Moses in flame in the midst of the *Burning Bush,* and hast made him walk with dry feet through the Red Sea; Thou Who gavest the Law to him upon Mount Sinai; Thou Who hast granted unto SOLOMON Thy Servant these *Pentacles* by Thy great Mercy, for the preservation of Soul and of Body; we most humbly implore and supplicate Thy Holy Majesty, that these *Pentacles* may be consecrated by Thy power, and prepared in such manner that they may obtain virtue and strength against all Spirits, through Thee, O Most Holy ADONAI, Whose Kingdom, Empire, and principality, remaineth and endureth without end.

These words being said, thou shalt perfume the *Pentacles* with the same sweet scents and perfumes, and afterwards having wrapped them in a piece of prepared silk cloth, thou shalt put them in a place fit and clean, which thou mayest open whenever it shall please thee, and close it again, at thy pleasure and according unto thy will. We will hereafter show thee the method and manner of preparing the aforesaid place, of perfuming it with scents and sweet odours, and of sprinkling it with the Water and *Water-Sprinkler* of *Magical Art;* for all these things contain many good properties, and innumerable virtues, as experience will easily teach thee.

We have already said sufficient regarding the *Solemn Conjuration of Spirits.*

We have also spoken enough in our present Key, regarding the manner in which it is necessary to attract the Spirits so as to make them speak. Now, by Divine aid, I will teach thee how to perform certain experiments with success.

* Preferably those having some reference to the work in hand.
† I have given the number of the Psalms according to the *English,* not the *Hebrew* numbers.
‡ The Qabalistic word AZOTH may be substituted for "the Aleph and the Tau."

Know,* O my Son Roboam, that all the Divine Sigils, Characters, and Names (which are the most precious and excellent things in Nature, whether Terrestrial or Celestial), should be written by thee each separately, when thou art in a state of grace and purity, upon Virgin parchment, with ordinary ink, in the beginning of the month† of August before sunrise, raising thine eyes unto heaven, and turning towards the east. Thou shalt preserve them to suspend from thy neck, whichever thou wilt, on the day and hour wherein thou wast born, after which thou shalt take heed to name every day ten times, the Name which is hung from thy neck, turning towards the East, and thou mayest be assured that no enchantment or any other danger shall have power to harm thee.

Furthermore thou shalt vanquish all adversities, and shalt be cherished and loved by the Angels and Spirits, provided that thou hast made their characters and that thou hast them upon thee; I assure thee that this is the true way to succeed with ease in all thine operations, for being fortified with a Divine Name, and the Letters, Characters, and *Sigils,* applicable unto the operation, thou shalt discover with what supernatural exactitude and very great promptitude, both Terrestrial and Celestial things will be obedient unto thee. But all this will only be true, when accompanied by the Pentacles which hereinafter follow, seeing that the Seals, Characters, and Divine Names, serve only to fortify the work, to preserve from unforeseen accidents, and to attract the familiarity of the Angels and Spirits; which is one reason, my Son, that before making any experiment, I order thee to read and re-read my Testament, not once only but many times, so that being perfectly instructed in the several Ceremonies thou mayest in no way fail, and that thus what shall have previously appeared to thee difficult and lengthy, may become in process of time easy and of very great use.

I am about to endow thee with many secrets, which I charge thee never to employ for an evil purpose, for ACCURSED BE HE WHO TAKETH THE NAME OF ALMIGHTY GOD IN VAIN; but thou mayest without any other ceremonies make use of them, provided that, as I have already said, thou hast only the Glory of Eternal God for thine object. Thus, after having taught thee all the Ceremonies which concern the manner of performing the Operations, I am at length determined to make thee a partaker in the secrets of which I have particular knowledge, unknown to this day unto the generality of men; but, nevertheless, only on the condition that thou attemptest not the ruin and destruction of thy neighbour, for his blood will cry for vengeance unto God, and in the end thou and thine shall feel the just wrath of an offended Deity. However, God not having forbidden honest and lawful pleasures, thou mayest perform boldly the Operations which follow, it being always especially necessary to distinguish between the good and the evil, so as to choose the former and avoid the latter, which is why I command thee to be attentive to all that is contained in this my Testament.

* From here to the end of the Chapter is only given in Lansdowne MSS. 1203.
† *i.e.* When the Sun is in the Sign Leo.

BOOK ONE.

CHAPTER IX.

OF THE EXPERIMENT CONCERNING THINGS STOLEN, AND HOW IT
SHOULD BE PERFORMED.

MY beloved Son, if thou findest any Theft, thou shalt do as is hereinafter ordained, and with the help of God thou shalt find that which hath
been taken away.

If the hours and days be not otherwise ordained in this operation,
thou must refer to what hath already been said. But before commencing
any operation whatsoever for the recovery of things stolen, after having
made all necessary preparations, thou shalt say the following Oration:—

THE ORATION.

Ateh* Adonai Elohim Asher Ha-Shamain Ve-Ha-Aretz, &c.
Thou, O Lord, Who hast made both Heaven and Earth, and hast
measured them in the hollow of Thy hand; Thou Who art seated upon
the Kerubim and the Seraphim, in the high places, whereunto human understanding cannot penetrate; Thou Who hast created all things by Thine
agency, in Whose Presence are the Living Creatures, of which four are
marvellously volatile, which have six wings, and who incessantly cry aloud:
"QADOSCH, QADOSCH, QADOSCH, ADONAI ELOHIM TZABAOTH, Heaven
and Earth are full of Thy Glory;" O Lord God, Thou Who hast expelled
Adam from the Terrestrial Paradise, and Who hast placed the Kerubim
to guard the Tree of Life, Thou art the Lord Who alone doest wonders;
show forth I pray Thee Thy Great Mercy, by the Holy City of Jerusalem,
by Thy wonderful Name of four letters which are YOD, HE, VAU, HE,
and by Thy Holy and Admirable Name, give unto me the power and virtue
to enable me to accomplish this experiment, and to come unto the desired
end of this operation; through Thee Who art Life, and unto Whom Life
belongeth unto the eternal ages. Amen.

After this perfume and cense the place by burning *Temple Incense.*
This aforesaid place should be pure, clean, safe from interruption or
disturbance, and proper to the work, as we shall hereafter show. Then
sprinkle the aforesaid place with consecrated Water, as is laid down in
the *Chapter concerning Circles.*

The Operation being in such wise prepared, thou shalt rehearse the
Conjuration necessary for this experiment, at the end of which Thou
shalt say as follows:—

* This is simply the Hebrew of the prayer which follows; but in the MS. Codices it is so
mutilated as to be worthless.

O Almighty Father and Lord, Who regardest the Heavens, the Earth, and the Abyss, mercifully grant unto me by Thy Holy Name written with four letters, YOD, HE, VAU, HE, that by this exorcism I may obtain virtue, Thou Who art IAH, IAH, IAH, grant that by Thy power these Spirits may discover that which we require and which we hope to find, and may they show and declare unto us the persons who have committed the theft, and where they are to be found.

I conjure ye, over this burning Temple Incense, anew, ye Spirits above named, by all the aforesaid Names, through which all things created tremble, that ye show openly unto me (or unto this child here present with us*) those things which we seek.

These things being accomplished they will make thee to see plainly that which thou seekest. Take note that the Exorcist, or Master of the Art, should be such as is ordained in the Chapter concerning the Exorcist and his Companions; and if in this experiment it should be necessary to write down characters or Names, thou shalt do that which it is necessary to observe regarding the pen, ink, and paper, as is duly prescribed in the chapters concerning them.

For if thou dost not regard these things, thou wilt neither accomplish that which thou desirest, nor arrive at thy desired end.

HOW TO KNOW WHO HAS COMMITTED A THEFT.†

Take a Sieve, after burning one-half teaspoonful of *Temple Incense*, and suspend it by a piece of cord wherewith a man has been hung, which should be fastened round the circumference of the rim. Within the rim write with blood in the four divisions thereof the characters given in *Figure* 4. After this take a basin of brass perfectly clean which thou shalt fill with water from a fountain, and having pronounced these words: DIES MIES YES-CHET BENE DONE FET DONNIMA METEMAUZ, make the sieve spin round with thy left hand, and at the same time turn with thy right hand the water in the basin in a contrary direction, by stirring it with a twig of green laurel. When the water becometh still and the sieve no longer whirls, gaze fixedly into the water, and thou shalt see the form of him who hath committed the theft; and in order that thou mayest the more easily recognize him, thou shalt mark him in some part of his face with the Magical Sword of Art; for that sign which thou shalt have cut therewith in the water, shall be really found thereafter upon his own person.

THE MANNER OF CAUSING THE SIEVE TO TURN, THAT THOU MAYEST KNOW WHO HAS COMMITTED THE THEFT.‡

Take a Sieve and stick into the outside of the rim the open points of a pair of scissors, and having rested the rings of the said opened scissors

* A child employed as a clairvoyant in the operation; as is still the custom in some places in the East.

† The rest of this Chapter is from 1203 Lansdowne MSS.

‡ This is the ancient divination by the sieve and shears, and from St. Peter and St. Paul being mentioned in it, has evidently undergone a mediæval reconstruction.

on the thumb-nails of two persons, let one of them say the following Prayer:—

PRAYER.

DIES MIES YES-CHET BENE DONE FET DONNIMA METEMAUZ; O Lord, Who liberatedst the holy Susanna from a false accusation of crime; O Lord, Who liberatedst the holy Thekla; O Lord, Who rescuedst the holy Daniel from the den of lions, and the Three Children from the burning fiery furnace, free the innocent and reveal the guilty.

After this let him or her pronounce aloud the names and surnames of all the persons living in the house where the theft hast been committed, who may be suspected of having stolen the things in question, saying:—

"By Saint Peter and Saint Paul, such a person hath not done this thing."

And let the other reply:—

"By Saint Peter and Saint Paul, he (or she) hath not done it."

Let this be repeated thrice for each person named and suspected, and it is certain that on naming the person who hath committed the theft or done the crime, the sieve will turn of itself without its being able to stop it, and by this thou shalt know the evil doer.

BOOK ONE.

CHAPTER X.

OF THE EXPERIMENT OF INVISIBILITY, AND HOW IT SHOULD BE PERFORMED.

IF thou wishest to perform the *Experiment of Invisibility*, thou shalt follow the instructions for the same. If it be necessary to observe the day and the hour, thou shalt do as is said in their Chapters. But if thou needest not observe the day and the hour as marked in the Chapter thereon, thou shalt do as taught in the Chapter which precedeth it. If in the course of the experiment it be necessary to write anything, it should be done as is described in the Chapters pertaining thereto, with the proper pen, paper, and ink, or blood. But if the matter is to be accomplished by invocation, before thy conjurations, thou shalt, while burning *Temple Incense*, say devoutly in thine heart:—

SCEABOLES, ARBARON, ELOHI, ELIMIGITH, HERENOBULCULE, METHE, BALUTH, TIMAYAL, VILLAQUIEL, TEVENI, YEVIE, FERETE, BACUHABA, GUVARIN; through Him by Whom ye have empire and power over men, ye must accomplish this work so that I may go and remain invisible.

And if it be necessary in this operation to trace a Circle, thou shalt do as is ordained in the Chapter concerning Circles; and if it be necessary to write Characters, &c., thou shalt follow the instructions given in the respective Chapters.

This operation being thus prepared, if there be an especial Conjuration to perform, thou shalt repeat it in the proper manner; if not, thou shalt say the general Conjuration, at the end of which thou shalt add the following words:

O thou ALMIRAS, Master of Invisibility, with thy Ministers CHEROS, MAITOR, TANGEDEM, TRANSIDIM, SUVANTOS, ABELAIOS, BORED, BELAMITH, CASTUMI, DABUEL; I conjure ye by Him Who maketh Earth and Heaven to tremble, Who is seated upon the Throne of His Majesty, that this operation may be perfectly accomplished according to my will, so that at whatsoever time it may please me, I may be able to be invisible.

I conjure thee anew, O ALMIRAS, *Chief of Invisibility*, both thee and thy Ministers, by Him through Whom all things have their being, and by SATURIEL, HARCHIEL, DANIEL, BENIEL, ASSIMONEM, that thou immediately comest thither with all thy Ministers, and achievest this operation, as thou knowest it ought to be accomplished, and that by the same operation thou render me invisible, so that none may be able to see me.

In order then to accomplish this aforesaid operation, thou must prepare all things necessary with requisite care and diligence, and put them in practice with all the general and particular ceremonies laid down for these experiments; and with all the conditions contained in our first and second Books. Thou shalt also in the same operations duly repeat the appropriate Conjurations, with all the solemnities marked in the respective Chapters. Thus shalt thou accomplish the experiment surely and without hindrance, and thus shalt thou find it true.

But, on the contrary, if thou lettest any of these things escape thee, or if thou despiseth them, never shalt thou be able to arrive at thy proposed end; as, for example, we enter not easily into a fenced city over its walls but through its gates.

HOW* TO RENDER ONESELF INVISIBLE.

Make a small image of yellow wax, in the form of a man, in the month January and in the day and hour of Saturn, and at that time write with a needle above the crown of its head and upon its skull which thou shalt have adroitly raised, the character following. (*See Figure 5.*) After which thou shalt re-place the skull in proper position. Thou shalt then write upon a small strip of the skin of a frog or toad which thou shalt have killed, the following words and characters. (*See Figure 6.*) Thou shalt then go and suspend the said figure by one of thy hairs from the vault of a cavern at the hour of midnight, and burning *Temple Incense* under it, thou shalt say:—

METATRON, MELEKH, BEROTH, NOTH, VENIBBETH, MACH, and all ye, I conjure thee O Figure of wax, by the Living God, that by the virtue of these Characters and words, thou render me invisible, wherever I may bear thee with me. Amen.

And after having burned *Temple Incense* again under it, thou shalt bury it in the same place in a small deal box, and every time that thou wishest to pass or enter into any place without being seen, thou shalt say these words, bearing the aforesaid figure in thy left pocket:—

Come unto me and never quit me whithersoever I shall go.

Afterwards thou shalt take it carefully back unto the before-mentioned place and cover it with earth until thou shalt need it again.

* The rest of this Chapter is from 1203 Lansdowne MSS.

BOOK ONE.

CHAPTER XI.

To Hinder a Sportsman from Killing Any Game.

TAKE a stick of green elder, from the two ends of which thou shalt clean out the pith.* In each end place a strip of parchment of hare-skin, having written thereon with the blood of a black hen the following character and word. (*See Figure* 7.) Having made two of these slips, place one in each end of the stick and close the apertures up with pith, afterwards on a Friday in the month of February thou shalt fumigate the aforesaid stick with suitable incense thrice in the air, and having taken it thence thou shalt bury it in the earth under an elder tree. Afterwards thou shalt expose it in the pathway by which the Sportsman will pass, and once he has passed by it, he need not hope to kill any game during that day. If thou shalt wish a second time to lay a spell upon him in like manner, thou needest but to expose the stick again in his path; but take care to bury it again in the earth under an elder tree, so as to be able to take it from thence each time that thou shalt have need of it; and to take it up each time as soon as the Sportsman shall have passed.

* This Chapter is taken from 1203 Lansdowne MSS.

BOOK ONE.

CHAPTER XII.

How to Make the Magic Garters.

TAKE enough of the skin of a stag to make two hollow tubular Garters,* but before stitching them up thou shalt write on the side of the skin which was next the flesh the words and characters shown in *Figure* 8, with the blood of a hare killed on the 25th of June, and having filled the said Garters with green mugwort gathered also on the 25th of June before sunrise, thou shalt put in the two ends of each the eye of the fish called barbel; and when thou shalt wish to use them thou shalt get up before sunrise and wash them in a brook of running water, and place them one on each leg above the knee. After this thou shalt take a short rod of holm-oak cut on the same 25th of June, turn in the direction thou wishest to go, write upon the ground the name of the place, and commencing thy journey thou wilt find it accomplished in a few days and without fatigue. When thou wishest to stop thou hast only to say AMECH and beat the air with the aforesaid wand, and incontinently thou shalt be on firm ground.

* This Chapter is also taken from 1203 Lansdowne MSS.

BOOK ONE.

CHAPTER XIII.

How to Make the Magic Carpet Proper for Interrogating the Intelligences, so as to Obtain an Answer Regarding Whatsoever
Matter One May Wish to Learn.

MAKE a Carpet* of white and new wool, and when the Moon shall
be at her full, in the Sign of Capricorn and in the hour of the Sun, thou
shalt go into the country away from any habitation of man, in a place free
from all impurity, and shalt spread out thy Carpet so that one of its points
shall be towards the east, and another towards the west, and having made
a Circle without it and enclosing it, thou shalt remain within upon the
point towards the east, and holding thy wand in the air for every operation, thou shalt call upon MICHAEL,† towards the north upon RAPHAEL,
towards the west upon GABRIEL, and towards the south upon MURIEL.
After this thou shalt return unto the point of the East and devoutly invoke the Great Name AGLA, and take this point of the Carpet in thy left
hand; turning then towards the North thou shalt do the same, and so
continuing to the other points of the Carpet, thou shalt raise them so that
they touch not the ground, and holding them up thus, and turning anew
towards the East thou shalt say with great veneration the following
Prayer:—

PRAYER.

AGLA, AGLA, AGLA, AGLA; O God Almighty Who art the Life of
the Universe and Who rulest over the four divisions of its vast form by
the strength and virtue of the Four Letters of Thy Holy Name Tetragrammaton, YOD, HE, VAU, HE, bless in Thy Name this covering which
I hold as Thou hast blessed the Mantle of Elijah in the hands of Elisha,
so that being covered by Thy Wings, nothing may be able to injure me,
even as it is said:—"He shall hide thee under His Wings and beneath His
feathers shall thou trust, His truth shall be thy shield and buckler."

After this thou shalt fold it up, saying these words following:—
RECABUSTIRA, CABUSTIRA, BUSTIRA, TIRA RA, A; and shall keep it
carefully to serve thee at need.

When thou shalt be desirous to make thine interrogations, choose
the night of full or of new moon, and from midnight until daybreak.

---

* This Chapter is also taken from 1203 Lansdowne MSS.
† I have usually found Michael attributed to the South; Raphael to the East; Gabriel to
the West; and Auriel to the North. Likewise I think the operator should turn following the
course of the Sun, and not contrariwise as in the text.

Thou shalt transport thyself unto the appointed spot if it be for the purpose of discovering a treasure; if not, any place will serve provided it be clean and pure. Having had the precaution on the preceding evening to write upon a slip of virgin parchment coloured azure-blue, with a pen made from the feather of a dove, this Character and Name (*see Figure* 9); taking thy carpet, thou shalt cover thy head and body therewith, and taking the censer, with new fire therein, thou shalt place it in or upon the proper place, and cast thereon some incense. Then shalt thou prostrate thyself upon the ground, with thy face towards the earth, before the incense beginneth to fume, keeping the fire of the same beneath the carpet, holding thy wand upright, against which to rest thy chin; thou shalt hold with thy right hand the aforesaid strip of parchment against thy forehead, and thou shalt say the following words:—

VEGALE, HAMICATA, UMSA, TERATA, YEH, DAH, MA, BAXASOXA, UN, HORAH, HIMESERE; O God the Vast One send unto me the Inspiration of Thy Light, make me to discover the secret thing which I ask of Thee, whatsoever such or such a thing may be, make me to search it out by the aid of Thy holy Ministers RAZIEL, TZAPHNIEL, MATMONIEL; Lo, Thou hast desired truth in the young, and in the hidden thing shalt Thou make me known wisdom. RECABUSTIRA, CABUSTIRA, BUSTIRA, TIRA, RA, A, KARKAHITA, KAHITA, HITA, TA.

And thou shalt hear distinctly the answer which thou shalt have sought.

BOOK ONE.

CHAPTER XIV.

HOW TO RENDER THYSELF MASTER OF A TREASURE POSSESSED BY THE SPIRITS.

THE Earth being inhabited, as I have before said unto thee, by a great number of Celestial Beings and Spirits,* who by their subtilty and prevision know the places wherein treasures are hidden, and seeing that it often happenneth that those men who undertake a search for these said treasures are molested and sometimes put to death by the aforesaid Spirits, which are called Gnomes; which, however, is not done through the Avarice of these said Gnomes, a Spirit being incapable of possessing anything, having no material senses wherewith to bring it into use, but because these Spirits, who are enemies of the passions, are equally so of Avarice, unto which men are so much inclined; and foreseeing the evil ends for which these treasures will be employed have some interest and aim in maintaining the earth in its condition of price and value, seeing that they are its inhabitants, and when they slightly disturb the workers in such kind of treasures, it is a warning which they give them to cease from the work, and if it happen that the greedy importunity of the aforesaid workers oblige them to continue, notwithstanding the aforesaid warnings, the Spirits, irritated by their despising the same, frequently put the workmen to death. But know, O my Son, that from the time that thou shalt have the good fortune to be familiar with such kinds of Spirits, and that thou shalt be able by means of what I have taught thee to make them submit unto thine orders, they will be happy to give thee, and to make thee partaker in that which they uselessly possess, provided that thine object and end shall be to make a good use thereof.

THE MANNER OF PERFORMING THE OPERATION.

On a Sunday before sunrise, between the 10th of July and the 20th of August, when the moon is in the Sign of the Lion, thou shalt go unto the place where thou shalt know either by interrogation of the Intelligences, or otherwise, that there is a treasure; there thou shalt describe a Circle of sufficient size with the Sword of Magical Art wherein to open up the earth, as the nature of the ground will allow; thrice during the day shalt thou cense it with the incense proper for the day, after which being clothed in the raiment proper for the Operation thou shalt suspend in some way by a machine immediately above the opening a lamp, whose oil should be mingled with the fat of a man who has died in the month of July, and the

* This is also taken from 1203 Lansdowne MSS.

wick being made from the cloth wherein he has been buried. Having kindled this with fresh fire, thou shalt fortify the workmen with a girdle of the skin of a goat newly slain, whereon shall be written with the blood of the dead man from whom thou shalt have taken the fat these words and characters (*see Figure* 10) ; and thou shalt set them to work in safety, warning them not to be at all disturbed at the Spectres which they will see, but to work away boldly. In case they cannot finish the work in a single day, every time they shall have to leave it thou shalt cause them to put a covering of wood over the opening, and above the covering about six inches of earth; and thus shalt thou continue unto the end, being all the time present in the raiment of the Art, and with the Magic Sword, during the operation. After which thou shalt repeat this prayer:—

PRAYER.

ADONAI, ELOHIM, EL, EHEIEH ASHER EHEIEH, Prince of Princes, Existence of Existences, have mercy upon me, and cast Thine eyes upon Thy Servant (N.), who invokes Thee most devoutedly, and supplicates Thee by Thy Holy and tremendous Name *Tetragrammaton* to be propitious, and to order Thine Angels and Spirits to come and take up their abode in this place; O ye Angels and Spirits of the Stars, O all ye Angels and Elementary Spirits, O all ye Spirits present before the Face of God, I the Minister and faithful Servant of the Most High conjure ye, let God himself, the Existence of Existences, conjure ye to come and be present at this Operation, I, the Servant of God, most humbly entreat ye. Amen.

Having then caused the workmen to fill in the hole, thou shalt license the Spirits to depart, thanking them for the favour they have shown unto thee, and saying:—

THE LICENSE TO DEPART.

O ye good and happy Spirits, we thank ye for the benefits which we have just received from your liberal bounty; depart ye in peace to govern the Element which God hath destined for your habitation. Amen.

BOOK ONE.

CHAPTER XV.

OF THE EXPERIMENT OF SEEKING FAVOUR AND LOVE.

IF thou wishest to perform the Experiment of seeking favor and love,* observe in what manner the Experiment is to be carried out, and if it be dependent upon the day and the hour, perform it in the day and the hour required, as thou wilt find it in the chapter concerning the hours; and if the Experiment be one that requireth writing, thou shalt write as it is said in the chapter concerning the same; and if it be with penal bonds, pacts, and fumigations, then thou shalt cense with a fit perfume as is said in the chapter concerning suffumigations; and if it be necessary to sprinkle it with water and hyssop, then let it be as in the chapter concerning the same; similarly if such Experiment require characters, names, or the like, let such names be written as the chapter concerning the writing of characters, and place the same in a clean place as hath been said. Then thou shalt repeat over it, after burning TEMPLE INCENSE, the following Oration:—

THE ORATION.

O ADONAI, most Holy, Most Righteous, and most Mighty God, Who hast made all things through Thy Mercy and Righteousness wherewith Thou art filled, grant unto us that we may be found worthy that this Experiment may be found consecrated and perfect, so that the Light may issue from Thy Most Holy Seat, O ADONAI, which may obtain for us favor and love. Amen.

This being said, thou shalt place it in clean silk, and bury it for a day and a night at the junction of four cross-roads; and whensoever thou wishest to obtain any grace or favor from any, take it, having first properly consecrated it according to the rule, and place it in thy right hand, and seek thou what thou wilt it shall not be denied thee. But if thou doest not the Experiment carefully and rightly, assuredly thou shalt not succeed in any manner.

For obtaining grace and love write down the following words:—

SATOR,† AREPO, TENET, OPERA, ROTAS, IAH, IAH, IAH, ENAM, IAH, IAH, IAH, KETHER, CHOKMAH, BINAH, GEDULAH, GEBURAH, TIPHERETH, NETZACH, HOD, YESOD, MALKUTH, ABRAHAM, ISAAC, JACOB, SHADRACH, MESHACH, ABEDNEGO, be ye all present in my aid and for whatsoever I shall desire to obtain.

Which words being properly written as above, thou shalt also find thy desire brought to pass.

* This Chapter is taken from 10,862 Add. MSS.
† This Incantation is also given in 1307 Sloane MSS., page 76.

BOOK ONE.

CHAPTER XVI.

How Operations of Mockery, Invisibility, and Deceit Should Be Prepared.

EXPERIMENTS relating to tricks, mockeries, and deceits, may be performed in many ways.* When thou shalt wish to practice these experiments with regard to any person, thou shalt observe the day and the hour as we have already said. Should it be necessary to write Characters or Words, it should be done on *Virgin Parchment Paper,* as we shall show farther on. As for the ink, if it be not specially ordained in this operation, it is advisable to use the blood of a bat with the pen and the needle of art. But before describing or writing the Characters or Names, all the necessary rules should be observed as given in the proper Chapters, and having carefully followed out all these, thou shalt pronounce with a loud voice the following words:—

ABAC, ALDAL, IAT, HUDAC, GUTHAC, GUTHOR, GOMEH, TISTATOR, DERISOR, DESTATUR, come hither all ye who love the times and places wherein all kinds of mockeries and deceits are practiced. And ye who make things disappear and who render them invisible, come hither to deceive all those who regard these things, so that they may be deceived, and that they may seem to see that which they see not and hear that which they hear not, so that their senses may be deceived, and that they may behold that which is not true.

Come ye then hither and remain, and consecrate this enchantment, seeing that God the Almighty Lord hath destined ye for such.

When this Experiment is completed in this manner in the hour and time which we have shown and taught, also the foregoing words ABAC, ALDAL, &c., should be written with the pen as hereinafter ordained; but if the Experiment be performed in a different way, yet shalt thou always say the aforesaid words, and they should be repeated as before given.

If thou practicest these things in this manner correctly, thou shalt arrive at the effect of thine operations and experiments, by the which thou mayest easily deceive the senses.

---

* This Chapter is given in 10862 Add. MSS. 3981 Harleian MSS., 288 King's MSS., 3091 Sloane MSS., and 1307 Sloane MSS., but is wanting in 1202 Lansdowne MSS., as are all the Chapters of the First Book after Chap. 8.

BOOK ONE.

CHAPTER XVII.

How Extraordinary Experiments and Operations Should Be Prepared.

We have spoken in the preceding Chapters of common experiments and operations, which it is more usual to practice and put in operation, and therein thou mayest easily see that we have told thee sufficient for their perfection. In this Chapter we treat of extraordinary and unusual experiments, which can also be done in many ways.

None the less should those who wish to put in practice the like experiments and operations observe the days and hours as is laid down in the proper Chapters, and should be provided with *Genuine Parchment** *Paper, made from the skin of dead-born Lambs,* and other necessary things. Having prepared a similar experiment thou shalt say:—

PRAYER.

O God, Who hast created all things, and hast given unto us discernment to understand the good and the evil; through thy Holy Name, and through these Holy Names;—Iod, Iah, Vau, Daleth, Vau, Tzabaoth, Zio, Amator, Creator, do Thou, O Lord, grant that this experiment may become true and veritable in my hands through Thy Holy Seal, O Adonai, Whose reign and empire remaineth eternally and unto the Ages of the Ages. Amen.

This being done, thou shalt perform the experiment, observing its hour, and thou shalt perfume and incense as is laid down in the proper Chapter; sprinkling with exorcised water, and performing all the ceremonies and solemnities as we shall instruct thee in the Second Book of our Key.

BOOK ONE.
CHAPTER XVIII.
CONCERNING THE HOLY PENTACLES OR MEDALS.

THE *Medals or Pentacles,* which we make for the purpose of striking terror into the Spirits and reducing them to obedience, have besides this wonderful and excellent virtue. If thou invokest the Spirits by virtue of these *Pentacles,* they will obey thee without repugnance, and having considered them they will be struck with astonishment, and will fear them, and thou shalt see them so surprised by fear and terror, that none of them will be sufficiently bold to wish to oppose thy will. They are also of great virtue and efficacy against all perils of Earth, of Air, of Water, and of Fire, against poison which hath been drunk, against all kinds of infirmities and necessities, against binding, sortilege, and sorcery, against all terror and fear, and wheresoever thou shalt find thyself, if armed with them, thou shalt be in safety all the days of thy life.

Through them do we acquire grace and good-will from man and woman, fire is extinguished, water is stayed, and all Creatures fear at the sight of the Names which are therein, and obey through that fear.

These *Pentacles* are usually made of the metal the most suitable to the nature of the Planet; and then there is no occasion to observe the rule of particular colors. They should be engraved with the instrument of Art in the days and hours proper to the Planet.

Saturn ruleth over Lead; Jupiter over Tin; Mars over Iron; the Sun over Gold; Venus over Copper; Mercury over the mixture of Metals; and the Moon over Silver.

They may also be made with *Virgin Parchment* paper, writing thereon with the colors adopted for each Planet, referring to the rules already laid down in the proper Chapters, and according to the Planet with which the Pentacle is in sympathy.

Wherefore unto Saturn the color of Black is appropriated; Jupiter ruleth over Celestial Blue; Mars over Red; the Gun over Gold, or the color of Yellow or Citron; Venus over Green; Mercury over Mixed Colors; the Moon over Silver, or the color of Argentine Earth.

The Matter of which the *Pentacle* is constructed should be Virgin, never having been used for any other purpose; or if it be metal it should be purified by fire.

As regards the size of the *Pentacles* it is arbitrary, so long as they are made according to the rules, and with the requisite solemnities, as hath been ordained.

The* virtues of the *Holy Pentacles* are no less advantageous unto thee than the knowledge of the secrets which I have already given unto thee; and thou shouldst take particular care if thou makest them upon virgin parchment to use the proper colors; and if thou engravest them

---

* This and the four following paragraphs are from 1203 Lansdowne MSS.

upon metal, to do so in the manner taught thee; and so shalt thou have the satisfaction of seeing them produce the promised effect. But seeing that this Science is not a Science of argument and open reasoning, but that, on the contrary, it is entirely mysterious and occult, we should not argue and deliberate over these matters, and it is sufficient to believe firmly to enable us to bring into operation that which hath already been taught.

When thou shalt construct these *Pentacles* and *Characters,* it is necessary never to forget the burning of *Temple Incense,* nor to employ anything beyond that which hath already been taught.

It is necessary, above all things, to be attentive to the operation, and never to forget or omit those things which contribute to the success which the *Pentacles* and Experiments promise, having ever in thy mind no other intention than the Glory of God, the accomplishment of thy desires, and loving kindness towards thy neighbor.

Furthermore, my beloved Son, I order thee not to bury this Science, but to make thy friends partakers in the same, subject, however, to the strict command never to profane the things which are Divine, for if thou doest this, far from rendering thee a friend of the Spirits, it will but be the means of bringing thee unto destruction.

But never must thou lavish these things among the ignorant, for that would be as blameable as to cast precious gems before swine; on the contrary, from one Sage the secret knowledge should pass unto another Sage, for in this manner shall the Treasure of Treasures never descend into oblivion.

Adore* and revere the Most Holy Names of God which are found in these *Pentacles* and Characters, for without this never shalt thou be able to come to the end of any enterprise, nor to accomplish the *Mystery of Mysteries.*

Above all things, remember that to perform any of these operations thou must be pure in body and mind, and without blemish, and omit not any of the preparations.

This Key, full of Mysteries, hath been revealed unto me by an Angel.

Accursed be he who undertaketh our Art without having the qualities requisite to thoroughly understand our *"Key,"* accursed be he who invoketh the Name of God in vain, for such an one prepareth for himself the punishments which await the unbelievers, for God shall abandon them and relegate them unto the depths of Hell amongst the impure Spirits.

For God is great and Immutable, He hath been for ever, and He shall remain even unto the end of the Ages.

ACCURSED BE HE WHO TAKETH THE NAME OF GOD IN VAIN! ACCURSED BE HE WHO USETH THIS KNOWLEDGE 'UNTO AN EVIL END, BE HE ACCURSED IN THIS WORLD AND IN THE WORLD TO COME. AMEN. BE HE ACCURSED IN THE NAME WHICH HE HATH BLASPHEMED!

* The rest of the Chapter is from 1202 Lansdowne MSS., except the last sentence.

THE END OF THE FIRST BOOK.

PLATE II.

Fig. 6.

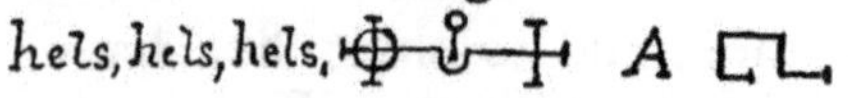

hels, hels, hels. ⊕ ꝏ ┼ A ⌐⌐

Fig. 7.

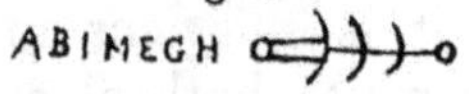

ABIMECH ⊂━┥┥┥○

Fig. 8.

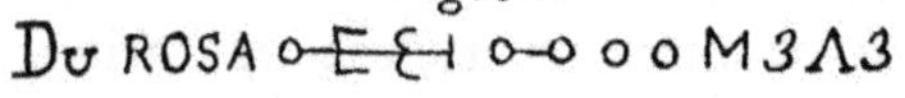

Dʊ ROSA ○━Ɇ┤ ○━○ ○ ○ M 3 Λ 3

Fig. 9.

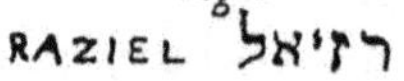

RAZIEL רזיאל

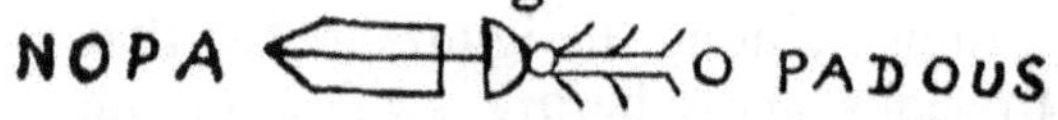

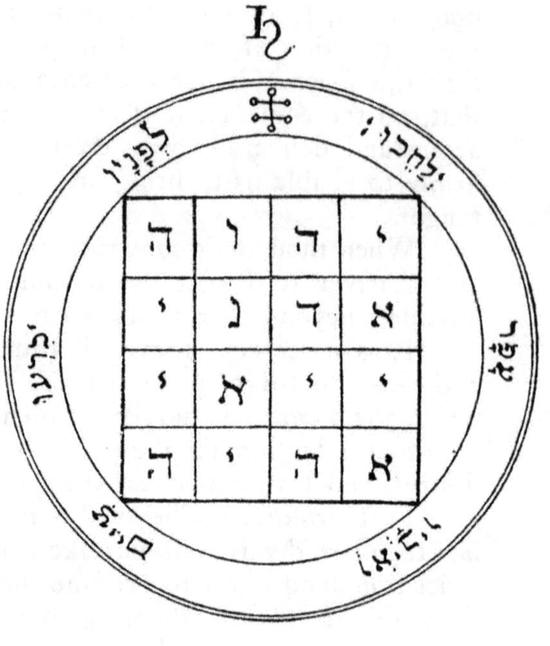

Fig. 11.

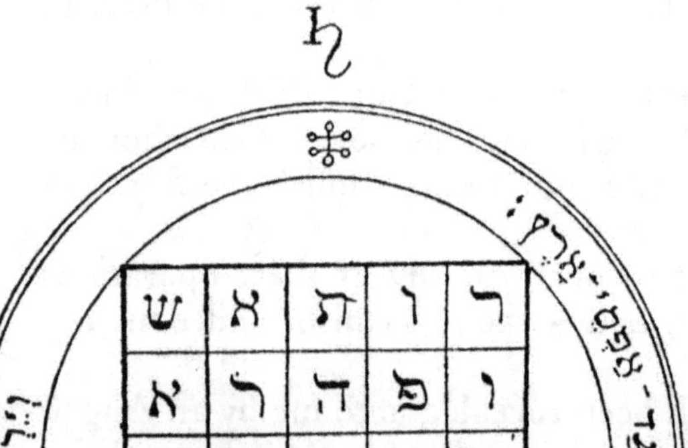

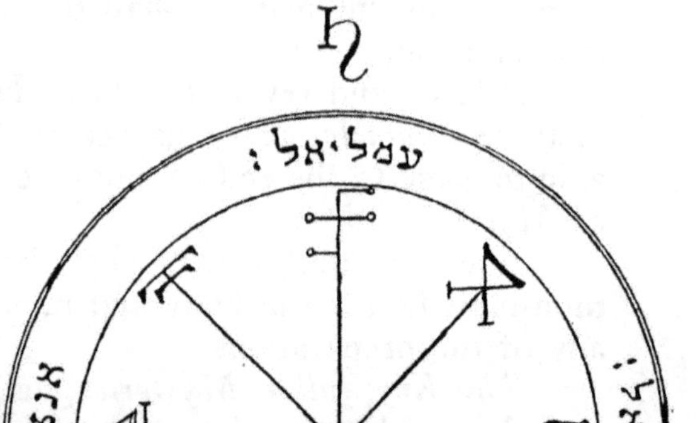

Fig. 10.

NOPA ⟸◆━◁◁◁ ○ PADOUS

Fig. 12.

59½

Fig. 13.

PLATE III.

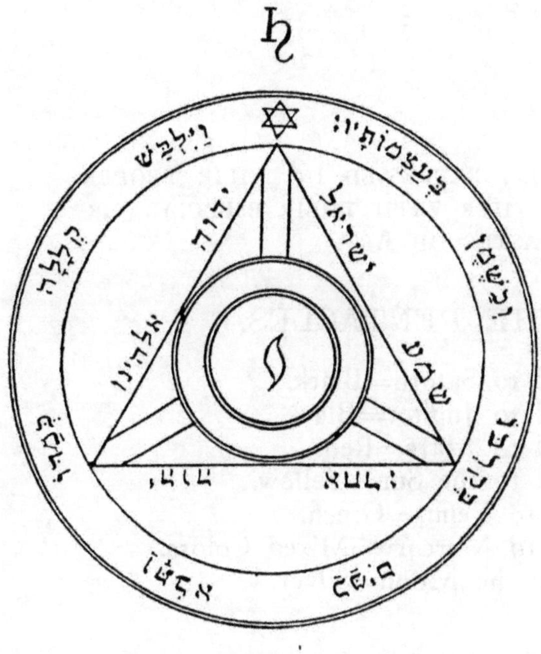

Fig. 14.

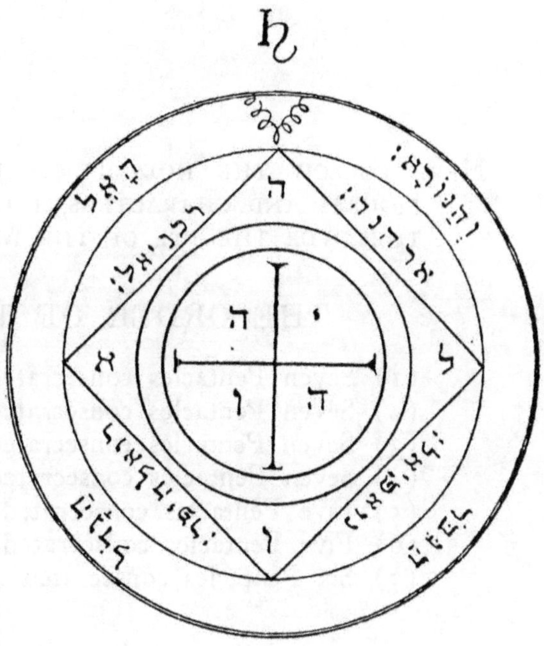

Fig. 15.

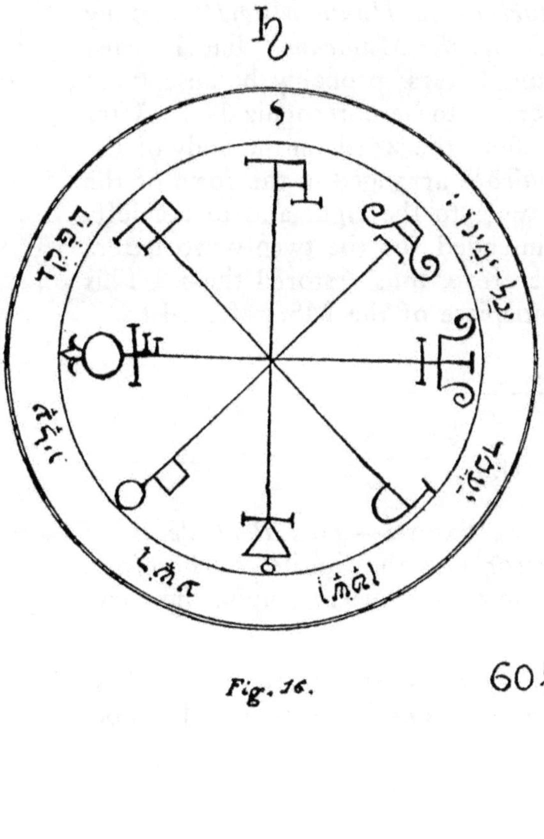

Fig. 16.

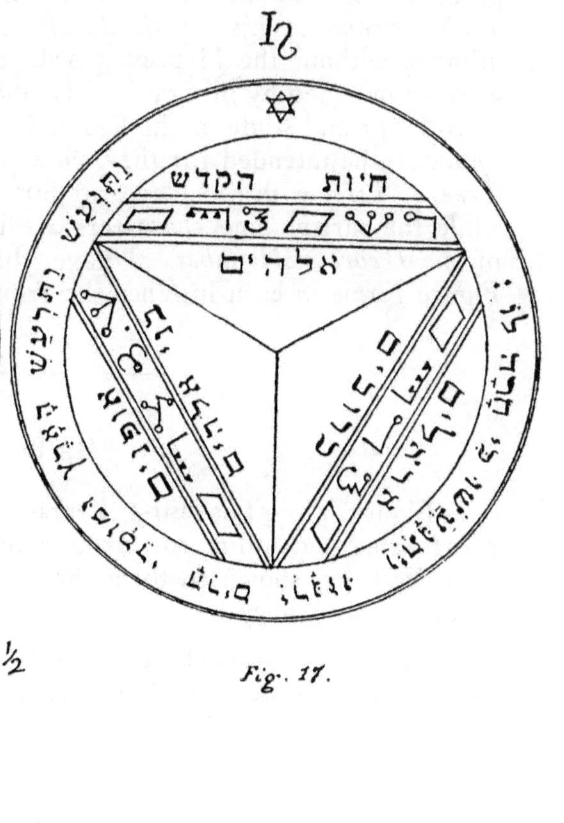

60½

Fig. 17.

HERE FOLLOW THE HOLY PENTACLES, EXPRESSED IN THEIR PROPER FIGURES AND CHARACTERS, TOGETHER WITH THEIR ESPECIAL VIRTUES; FOR THE USE OF THE MASTER OF ART.

THE ORDER OF THE PENTACLES.

(1) Seven Pentacles consecrated to Saturn=Black.
(2) Seven Pentacles consecrated to Jupiter=Blue.
(3) Seven Pentacles consecrated to Mars=Red.
(4) Seven Pentacles consecrated to the Sun=Yellow.
(5) Five Pentacles consecrated to Venus=Green.
(6) Five Pentacles consecrated to Mercury=Mixed Colors.
(7) Six Pentacles consecrated to the Moon=Silver.

Editor's Note on Figure 1.—The Mystical Figure of SOLOMON.—This is only given in the two MSS., Lansdowne 1202 and 1203. It was given by Lévi in his *"Dogme et Rituel de la Haute Magie,"* and by *Tycho Brahé* in his *"Calendarium Naturale Magicum,"* but in each instance without the Hebrew words and letters, probably because these were so mangled by illiterate transcribers as to be unrecognizable. After much labor and study of the figure, I believe the words in the body of the symbol to be intended for the *Ten Sephiroth* arranged in the form of the *Tree of Life*, with the Name of SOLOMON to the right and to the left; while the surrounding characters are intended for the twenty-two letters of the *Hebrew Alphabet*. I have, therefore, thus restored them. This Figure forms in each instance the frontispiece of the MS. referred to.

SATURN.

Figure 11.—The First Pentacle of Saturn.—This *Pentacle* is of great value and utility for striking terror into the Spirits. Wherefore, upon its being shown to them they submit, and kneeling upon the earth before it, they obey.

Editor's Note.—The Hebrew Letters within the square are the four great Names of God which are written with four letters:—IHVH, Yod,

He, Vau, He; ADNI, Adonai; IIAI, Yiai (this Name has the same Numerical value in Hebrew as the Name EL); and AHIH, Eheieh. The Hebrew versicle which surrounds it is from *Psalm lxxii.* 9; "The *Ethiopians* shall kneel before Him, His enemies shall lick the dust."

Figure 12.—The Second Pentacle of Saturn.—This *Pentacle* is of great value against adversaries; and of especial use in repressing the pride of the Spirits.

Editor's Note.—This is the celebrated

SATOR
AREPO
TENET
OPERA
ROTAS,

the most perfect existing form of double acrostic, as far as the arrangement of the letters is concerned; it is repeatedly mentioned in the records of mediæval Magic; and, save to very few, its derivation from the present *Pentacle* has been unknown. It will be seen at a glance that it is a square of five, giving twenty-five letters, which, added to the unity, gives twenty-six, the numerical value of IHVH. The Hebrew versicle surrounding it is taken from *Psalm lxxii.* 8, "His dominion shall be also from the one sea to the other, and from the flood unto the world's end." This passage consists also of exactly twenty-five letters, and its total numerical value (considering the final letters with increased numbers), added to that of the *Name Elohim*, is exactly equal to the total numerical value of the twenty-five letters in the Square.

Figure 13.—The Third Pentacle of Saturn.—This should be made within the *Magical Circle*, and it is good for use at night when thou invokest the Spirits of the nature of Saturn.

Editor's Note.—The characters at the ends of the rays of the Mystic Wheel are Magical Characters of Saturn. Surrounding it are the Names of the Angels:—Omeliel, Anachiel, Arauchiah, and Anazachia, written in Hebrew.

Figure 14.—The Fourth Pentacle of Saturn.—This Pentacle serveth principally for executing all the experiments and operations of ruin, destruction, and death.   And when it is made in full perfection, it serveth also for those Spirits which bring news, when thou invokest them from the side of the South.

Editor's Note.—The Hebrew words around the sides of the triangle are from *Deut. vi.* 4:—"Hear, O Israel, IHVH ALHINVH is IHVH ACHD."   The surrounding versicle is from *Psalm cix.* 18:—"*As he clothed himself with cursing like as with a garment, so let it come into his bowels like water, and like oil into his bones.*"   In the center of the *Pentacle* is the mystic letter Yod.

Figure 15.—The Fifth Pentacle of Saturn.—This *Pentacle* defendeth those who invoke the Spirits of Saturn during the night; and chaseth away the Spirits which guard treasures.

Editor's Note.—The Hebrew letters in the angles of the Cross are those of the Name IHVH.   Those in the Angles of the Square form ALVH, Eloah.   Round the four sides of the Square are the Names of the Angels:—Arehanah, Rakhaniel, Roelhaiphar, and Noaphiel.   The versicle is:—"A Great God, a Mighty, and a Terrible."—*Deut. x.* 17.

Figure 16.—The Sixth Pentacle of Saturn.—Around this *Pentacle* is each Name symbolized as it should be.   The person against whom thou shalt pronounce it shall be obsessed by Demons.

Editor's Note.—It is formed from Mystical Characters of Saturn. Around it is written in Hebrew: "Set thou a wicked one to be ruler over him, and let Satan stand at his right hand."

Figure 17.—The Seventh and Last Pentacle of Saturn.—This *Pentacle* is fit for exciting earthquakes, seeing that the power of each order of Angels herein invoked is sufficient to make the whole Universe tremble.

Editor's Note.—Within the *Pentacle* are the Names of the Nine Orders of Angels, those of six of them in ordinary Hebrew Characters, and the remainder in the letters which are known as "*The Passing of the River.*"   These Nine Orders are:—1, CHAIOTH HA-QADESCH, Holy Living Creatures; 2, AUPHANIM, Wheels; 3, ARALIM, Thrones; 4, CHASCHMALIM, Brilliant Ones; 5, SERAPHIM, Fiery Ones; 6, MELAKIM, Kings; 7, ELOHIM, Gods; 8, BENI ELOHIM, Sons of the Elohim; 9,

KERUBIM, Kerubim. The versicle is from *Psalm xviii.* 7:—"Then the earth shook and trembled, the foundations of the hills also moved and were shaken, because He was wroth."

JUPITER.

Figure 18.—The First Pentacle of Jupiter.—This serveth to invoke the Spirits of Jupiter, and especially those whose Names are written around the *Pentacle,* among whom Parasiel is the Lord and Master of Treasures, and teacheth how to become possessor of places wherein they are.

Editor's Note.—This *Pentacle* is composed of Mystical Characters of Jupiter. Around it are the Names of the Angels:—Netoniel, Deva-chiah, Tzedeqiah, and Parasiel, written in Hebrew.

Figure 19.—The Second Pentacle of Jupiter.—This is proper for acquiring glory, honors, dignities, riches, and all kinds of good, together with great tranquillity of mind; also to discover Treasures and chase away the Spirits who preside over them. It should be written upon *Virgin Parchment,* with the pen of the swallow and the blood of the screech-owl.

Editor's Note.—In the center of the Hexagram are the letters of the Name AHIH, Eheieh; in the upper and lower angles of the same, those of the Name AB, the Father; in the remaining angles those of the Name IHVH. I believe the letters outside the Hexagram in the re-entering angles to be intended for those of the first two words of the Versicle, which is taken from *Psalm cxii.* 3:—"*Wealth and Riches are in his house, and his righteousness endureth for ever.*"

Figure 20.—The Third Pentacle of Jupiter.—This defendeth and protecteth those who invoke and cause the Spirits to come. When they appear show unto them this *Pentacle* and immediately they will obey.

Editor's Note.—In the upper left hand corner is the *Magical Seal* of Jupiter with the letters of the Name IHVH. In the others are the Seal of the Intelligence of Jupiter, and the Names Adonai and IHVH. Around it is the Versicle from *Psalm cxxv.* 1:—"*A Song of degrees. They that trust in IHVH shall be as Mount Zion, which cannot be removed, but abideth for ever.*"

PLATE IV.

Fig. 18.

Fig 19.

Fig. 20.

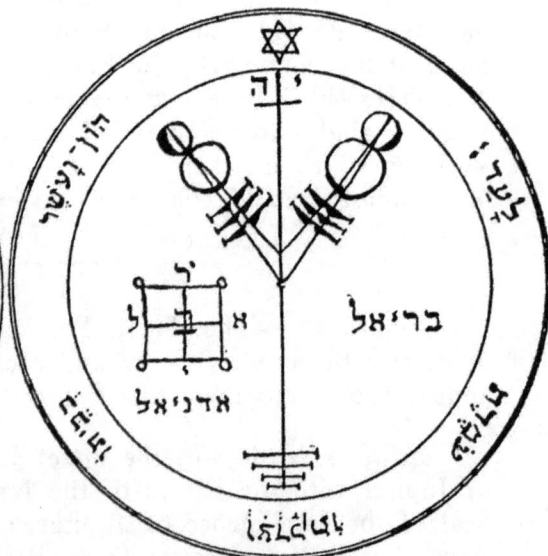

Fig. 21.

PLATE V.

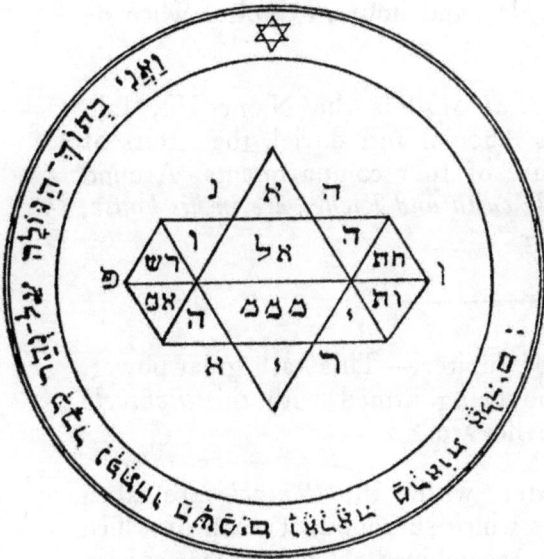

Fig. 22.

Fig. 23.

Fig. 24.

Fig. 25.

Figure 21.—The Fourth Pentacle of Jupiter.—It serveth to acquire riches and honor, and to possess much wealth. Its Angel is Bariel. It should be engraved upon silver in the day and hour of Jupiter when he is in the Sign Cancer.

Editor's Note.—Above the *Magical Sigil* is the Name IH, Iah. Below it are the Names of the Angels Adoniel and Bariel, the letters of the latter being arranged about a square of four compartments. Around is the Versicle from *Psalm cxii.* 3:—"*Wealth and Riches are in his house, and his righteousness endureth for ever.*"

Figure 22.—The Fifth Pentacle of Jupiter.—This hath great power. It serveth for assured visions. Jacob being armed with this *Pentacle* beheld the ladder which reached unto heaven.

Editor's Note.—The Hebrew letters within the *Pentacle* are taken from the five last words of the versicle which surrounds it, each of which contains five letters. These are, then, recombined so as to form certain Mystical Names. The versicle is taken from *Ezekiel i.* 1:—"*As I was among the captives by the river of Chebar, the heavens were opened, and I saw visions of Elohim.*" In my opinion the versicle should only consist of the five last words thereof, when the anachronism of Jacob using a *Pentacle* with a sentence from Ezekiel will not longer exist.

Figure 23.—The Sixth Pentacle of Jupiter.—It serveth for protection against all earthly dangers, by regarding it each day devoutedly, and repeating the versicle which surroundeth it. "*Thus shalt thou never perish.*"

Editor's Note.—The four Names in the Arms of the Cross are:— Seraph, Kerub, Ariel, and Tharsis; the four rulers of the Elements. The versicle is from *Psalm xxii.* 16, 17:—"*They pierced my hands and my feet, I may tell all my bones.*"

Figure 24.—The Seventh and last Pentacle of Jupiter.—It hath great power against poverty, if thou considerest it with devotion, repeating the versicle. It serveth furthermore to drive away those Spirits who guard treasures, and to discover the same.

Editor's Note.—Mystical Characters of Jupiter with the verse:—

"Lifting up the poor out of the mire, and raising the needy from the dunghill, that he may set him with princes, even with the princes of his people."—Psalm cxiii. 7.

MARS.

Figure 25.—The First Pentacle of Mars.—It is proper for invoking Spirits of the Nature of Mars, especially those which are written in the *Pentacle.*

Editor's Note.—Mystical Characters of Mars, and the Names of the four Angels:—Madimiel, Bartzachiah, Eschiel, and Ithuriel written in Hebrew around the *Pentacle.*

Figure 26.—The Second Pentacle of Mars.—This *Pentacle* serveth with great success against all kinds of diseases, if it be applied unto the afflicted part.

Editor's Note.—The letter Hé, in the angles of the Hexagram. Within the same the Names IHVH, IHSHVH Yeheshuah (the mystic Hebrew Name for Joshua or Jesus, formed of the ordinary IHVH with the letter SH placed therein as emblematical of the Spirit), and Elohim. Around it is the sentence, *John i.* 4:—"In Him was life, and the life was the light of man." This *may* be adduced as an argument of the greater antiquity of the first few mystical verses of the Gospel of St. John.

Figure 27—The Third Pentacle of Mars.—It is of great value for exciting war, wrath, discord, and hostility; also for resisting enemies, and striking terror into rebellious Spirits; the Names of God the All Powerful are therein expressly marked.

Editor's Note.—The Letters of the Names Eloah and Shaddaï. In the Center is the great letter Vau, the signature of the Qabalistic Microprosopus. Around is the versicle from *Psalm lxxvii.* 13:—*"Who is so great a God as our Elohim?"*

Figure 28.—The Fourth Pentacle of Mars.—It is of great virtue and power in war, wherefore without doubt it will give thee victory.

PLATE VII.

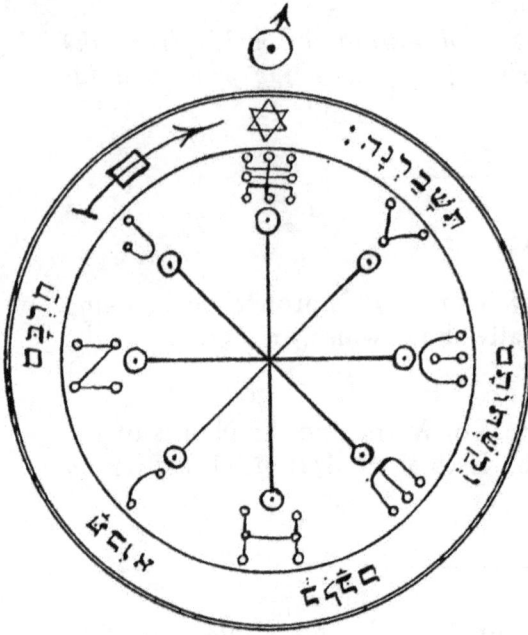

Fig. 30.

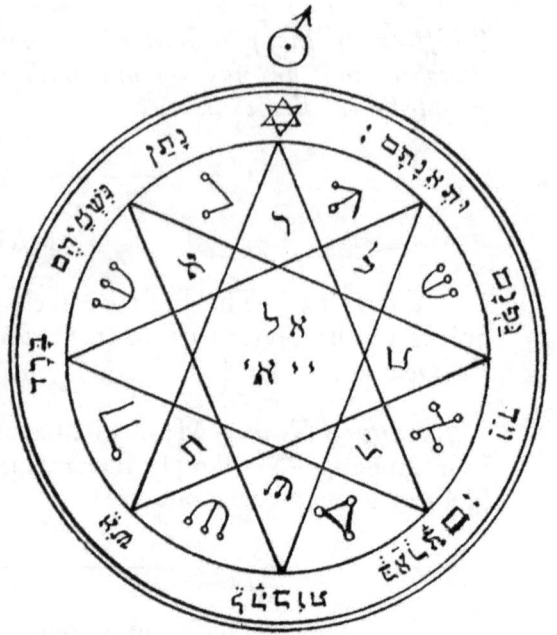

Fig. 31.

Fig. 32.

65½

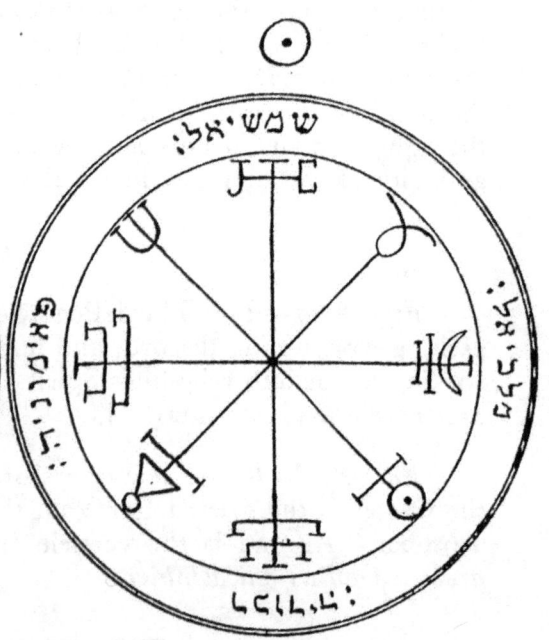

Fig. 33.

PLATE VI.

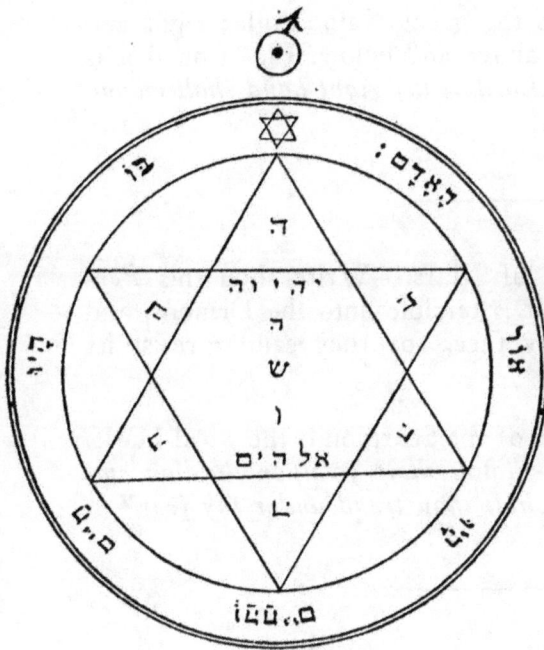

Fig. 26.

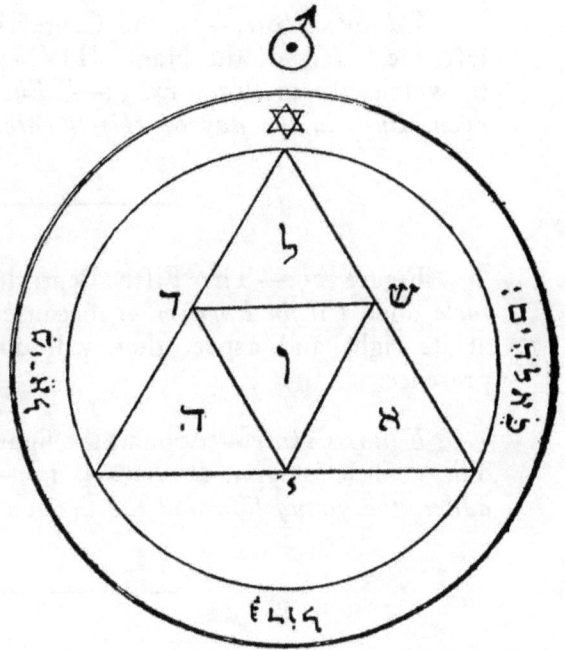

Fig. 27.

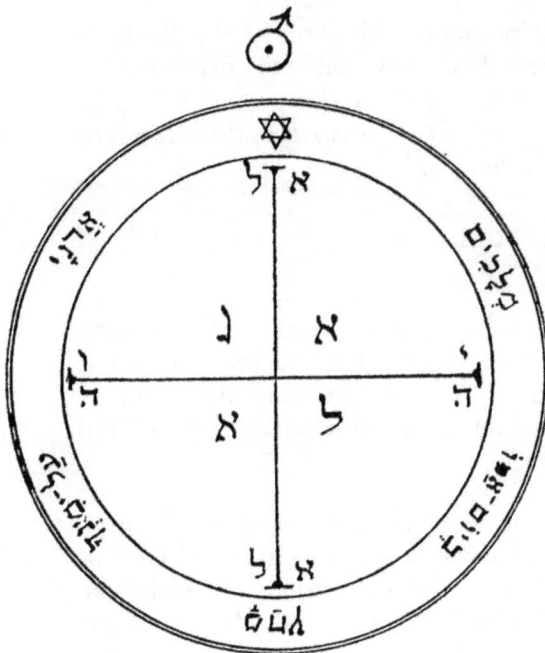

Fig. 28.

63½

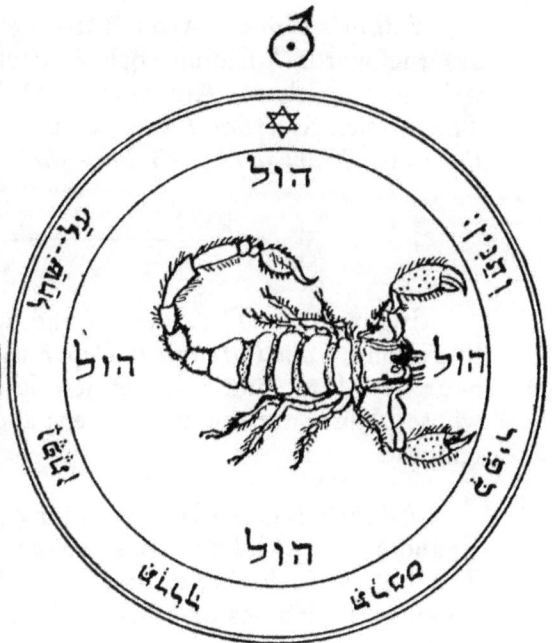

Fig. 29.

Editor's Note.—In the Center is the great Name Agla; right and left, the letters of the Name IHVH; above and below, El. Round it is the versicle from *Psalm cx. 5*:—"*The Lord at thy right hand shall wound even Kings in the day of His Wrath.*"

Figure 29.—The Fifth Pentacle of Mars.—Write thou this *Pentacle* upon *Virgin Parchment*, because it is terrible unto the Demons, and at its sight and aspect they will obey thee, for they cannot resist its presence.

Editor's Note.—Around the figure of the Scorpion is the word HVL. The versicle is from *Psalm xci. 13*:—"*Thou shalt go upon the lion and adder, the young lion and the dragon shalt thou tread under thy feet.*"

Figure 30.—The Sixth Pentacle of Mars.—It hath so great virtue that being armed therewith, if thou art attacked by any one, thou shalt neither be injured nor wounded when thou fightest with him, and his own weapons shall turn against him.

Editor's Note.—Around the eight points of the radii of the *Pentacle* are the words "Elohim qeber, Elohim hath covered (or protected)," written in the Secret Alphabet of Malachim, or the writing of the Angels. The versicle is from *Psalm xxxvii. 15*:—"*Their sword shall enter into their own heart, and their bow shall be broken.*"

Figure 31.—The Seventh and Last Pentacle of Mars.—Write thou this upon *Virgin Parchment Paper* with the blood of a bat, in the day and hour of Mars; and uncover it within the Circle, invoking the Demons whose Names are therein written; and thou shalt immediately see hail and tempest.

Editor's Note.—In the center of the Pentacle are the Divine Names, El and Yiai, which have the same numerical value when written in Hebrew. The Letters in Hebrew, and in the Secret Alphabet called the Celestial, compose the Names of Spirits. Round the *Pentacle* is:—"*He gave them hail for rain, and flaming fire in their land. He smote their vines also, and their fig-trees.*"—*Psalm cv. 32, 33.*

THE SUN.

Figure 32.—The First Pentacle of the Sun.—The Countenance of *Shaddaï* the Almighty, at Whose aspect all creatures obey, and the Angelic Spirits do reverence on bended knees.

Editor's Note.—This singular *Pentacle* contains the head of the great Angel Methraton or Metatron, the vice-gerent and representative of *Shaddaï*, who is called the Prince of Countenances, and the right-hand masculine Cherub of the Ark, as Sandalphon is the left and feminine. On either side is the Name "El Shaddaï." Around is written in Latin: —"*Behold His face and form by Whom all things were made, and Whom all creatures obey.*"

Figure 33.—The Second Pentacle of the Sun.—This *Pentacle*, and the preceding and following, belong to the nature of the Sun. They serve to repress the pride and arrogance of the *Solar Spirits*, which are altogether proud and arrogant by their nature.

Editor's Note.—Mystical characters of the Sun and the Names of the Angels:—Shemeshiel, Paimoniah, Rekhodiah, and Malkhiel.

Figure 34.—The Third Pentacle of the Sun.—This serveth in addition (to the effects of the two preceding) to acquire Kingdom and Empire, to inflict loss, and to acquire renown and glory, especially through the Name of God, *Tetragrammaton*, which therein is twelve times contained.

Editor's Note.—The Name IHVH, twelve times repeated; and a versicle somewhat similar to *Daniel iv.* 34:—"*My Kingdom is an everlasting Kingdom, and my dominion endureth from age to age.*"

Figure 35.—The Fourth Pentacle of the Sun.—This serveth to enable thee to see the Spirits when they appear invisible unto those who invoke them; because, when thou hast uncovered it, they will immediately appear visible.

Editor's Note.—The Names IHVH, Adonai, are written in the center in Hebrew; and round the radii in the mystical characters of the "Passing of the River." The versicle is from *Psalm xiii.* 3, 4:—"*Lighten mine eyes that I sleep not in death, lest mine enemy say, I have prevailed against him.*"

PLATE VIII.

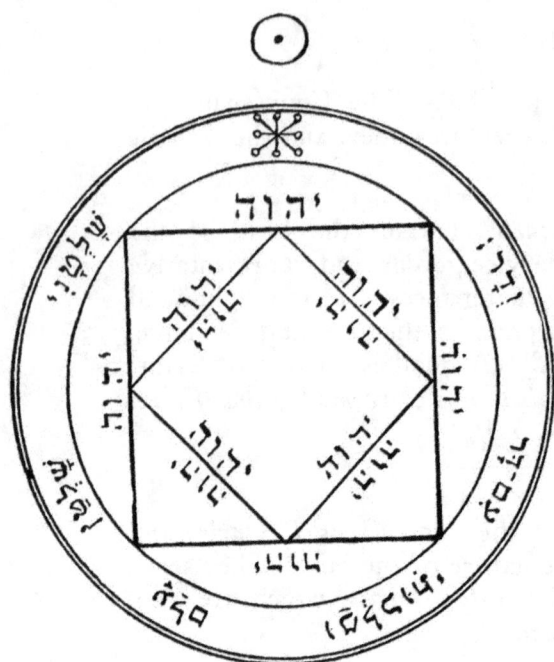

Fig. 34.

Fig. 35.

Fig. 36.

66½

Fig. 37.

PLATE IX.

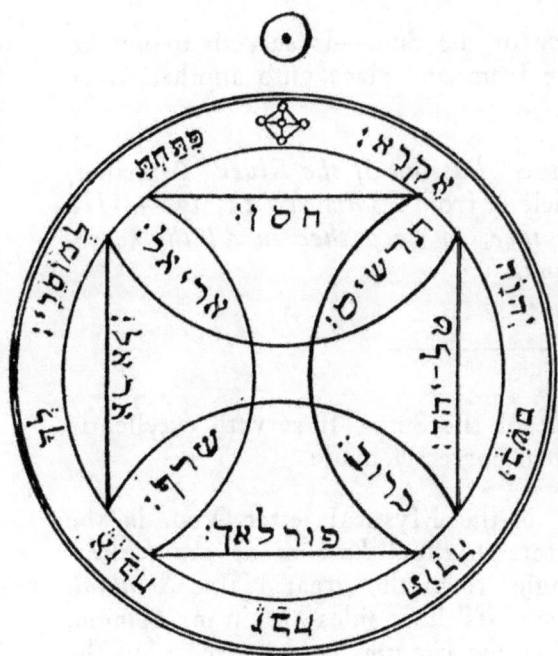

Fig. 38.

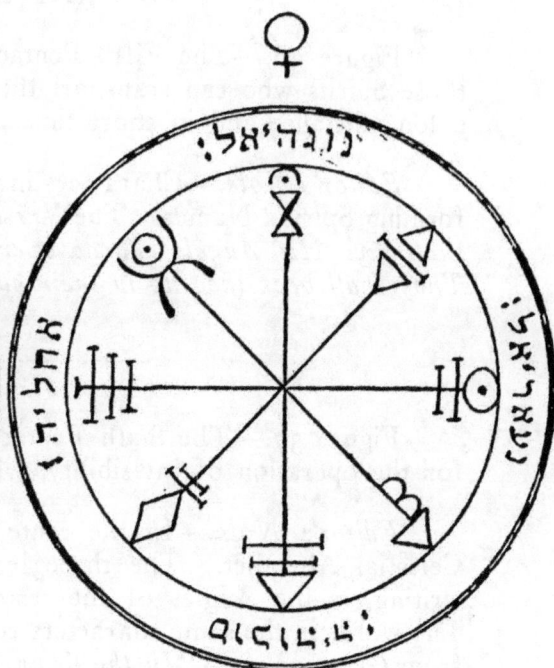

Fig. 39.

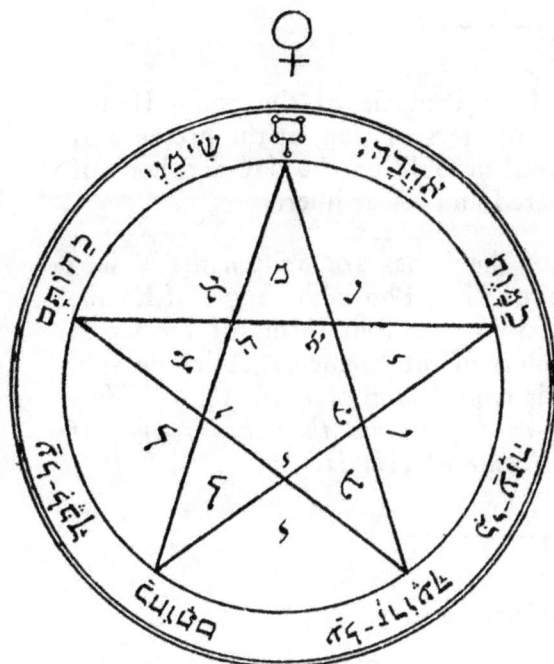

Fig. 40.

67½

Fig. 41.

Figure 36.—The Fifth Pentacle of the Sun.—It serveth to invoke those Spirits who can transport thee from one place unto another, over a long distance and in short time.

Editor's Note.—Characters in the *"Passing of the River"* Alphabet, forming Spirit's Names. The Versicle is from *Psalm xci.* 11, 12:—*"He shall give His Angels charge over thee, to keep thee in all thy ways. They shall bear thee up in their hands."*

Figure 37.—The Sixth Pentacle of the Sun.—It serveth excellently for the operation of invisibility, when correctly made.

Editor's Note.—In the center is the Mystical letter Yod, in the Celestial Alphabet. The three letters in the *"Passing of the River"* writing, in the Angles of the triangle, form the great Name *Shaddaï.* The words in the same characters round its three sides are, in my opinion, from *Genesis i.* 1:—*"In the beginning the Elohim created, etc."*; but the characters are sadly mangled in the MSS. The versicle is from *Psalms lxix.* 23, and *cxxxv.* 16:—*"Let their eyes be darkened that they see not; and make their loins continually to shake. They have eyes and see not."*

Figure 38.—The Seventh and Last Pentacle of the Sun.—If any be by chance imprisoned or detained in fetters of iron, at the presence of this *Pentacle,* which should be engraved in Gold on the day and hour of the Sun, he will be immediately delivered and set at liberty.

Editor's Note.—On the Arms of the Cross are written the Names of Chasan, Angel of Air; Arel, Angel of Fire; Phorlakh, Angel of Earth; and Taliahad, Angel of Water. Between the four Arms of the Cross are written the names of the Four Rulers of the Elements; Ariel, Seraph, Tharshis, and Cherub. The versicle is from *Psalm cxvi.* 16, 17:—*"Thou hast broken my bonds in sunder. I will offer unto thee the sacrifice of thanksgiving, and will call upon the Name of IHVH."*

VENUS.

Figure 39.—The First Pentacle of Venus.—This and those following serve to control the Spirits of Venus, and especially those herein written.

Editor's Note.—Mystical Characters of Venus, and the Names of the Angels Nogahiel, Acheliah, Socodiah (or Socohiah) and Nangariel.

Figure 40.—The Second Pentacle of Venus.—These *Pentacles* are also proper for obtaining grace and honor, and for all things which belong unto *Venus,* and for accomplishing all thy desires herein.

Editor's Note.—The letters round and within the *Pentagram* form the Names of *Spirits of Venus.* The versicle is from Canticles viii. 6 :— *"Place me as a signet upon thine heart, as a signet upon thine arm, for love is strong as death."*

Figure 41.—The Third Pentacle of Venus.—This, if it be only shown unto any person, serveth to attract love. Its Angel Monachiel should be invoked in the day and hour of Venus, at one o'clock or at eight.

Editor's Note.—The following Names are written within the Figure :—IHVH, Adonai, Ruach, Achides, Ægalmiel, Monachiel, and Degaliel. The versicle is from *Genesis i.* 28 :—*"And the Elohim blessed them, and the Elohim said unto them, Be ye fruitful, and multiply, and replenish the earth, and subdue it."*

Figure 42.—The Fourth Pentacle of Venus.—It is of great power, since it compels the Spirits of Venus to obey, and to force on the instant any person thou wishest to come unto thee.

Editor's Note.—At the four Angles of the Figure are the four letters of the Name IHVH. The other letters form the Names of *Spirits of Venus, e. g.*:—Schii, Eli, Ayib, etc. The versicle is from *Genesis ii.* 23, 24:—*"This is bone of my bones, and flesh of my flesh. And they two were one flesh."*

Figure 43.—The Fifth and Last Pentacle of Venus.—When it is only showed unto any person soever, it inciteth and exciteth wonderfully unto love.

Editor's Note.—Around the central Square are the Names Elohim, El Gebil, and two other Names which I cannot decipher, and have, therefore, given them as they stand. The characters are those of the *"Passing of the River."* The surrounding versicle is from *Psalm xxii.* 14:—*"My heart is like wax, it is melted in the midst of my bowels."*

PLATE X.

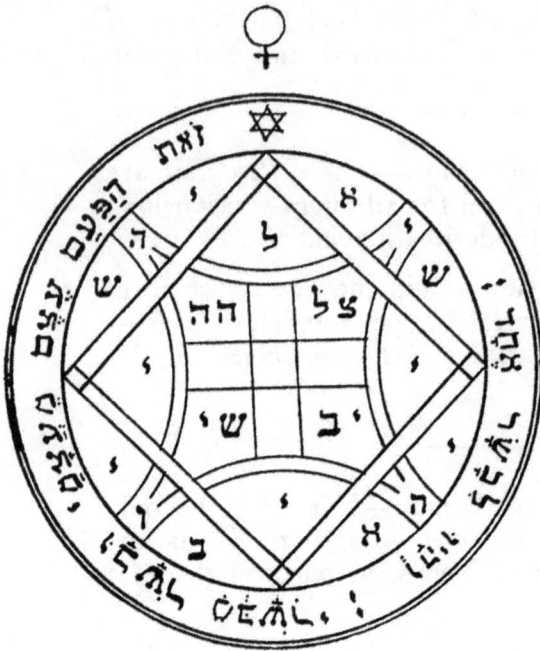

Fig. 42.

Fig. 43.

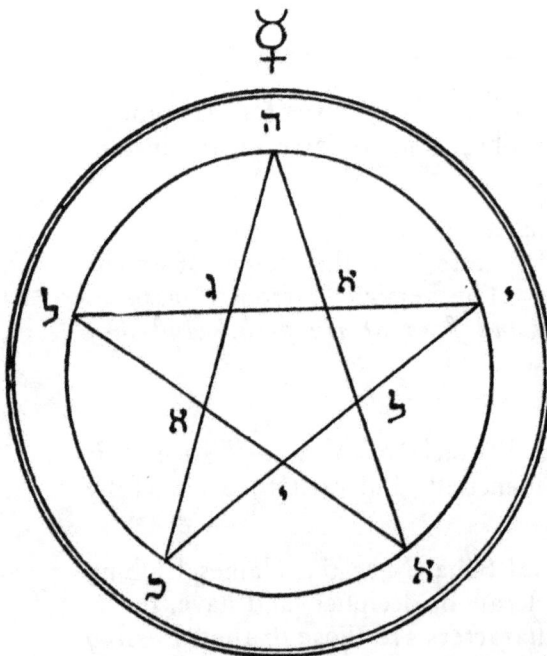

Fig. 44.

68½

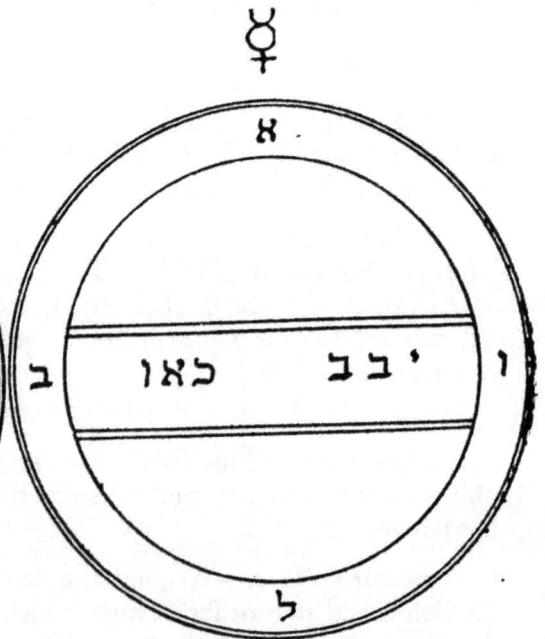

Fig. 45.

PLATE XI.

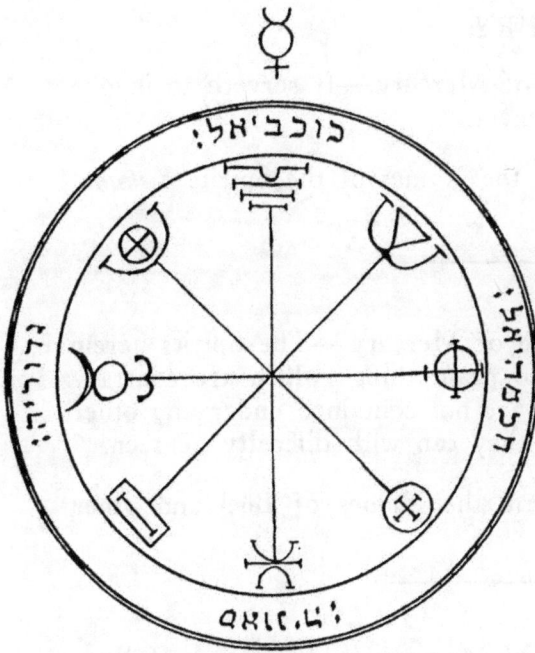

Fig. 46.

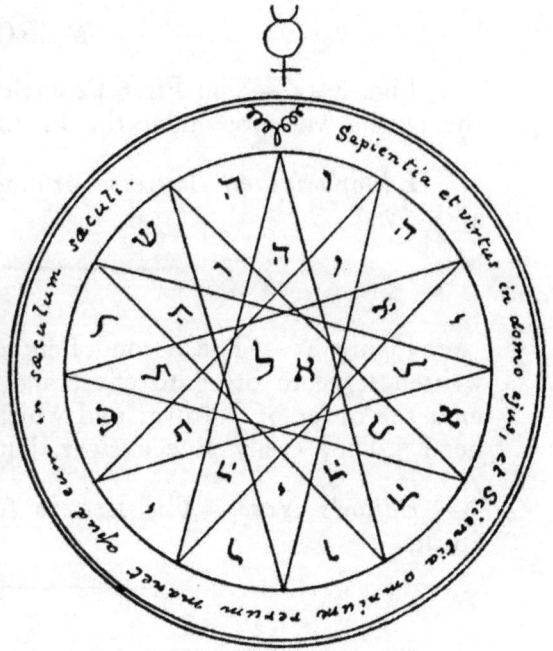

Fig. 47.

Fig. 48.

69½

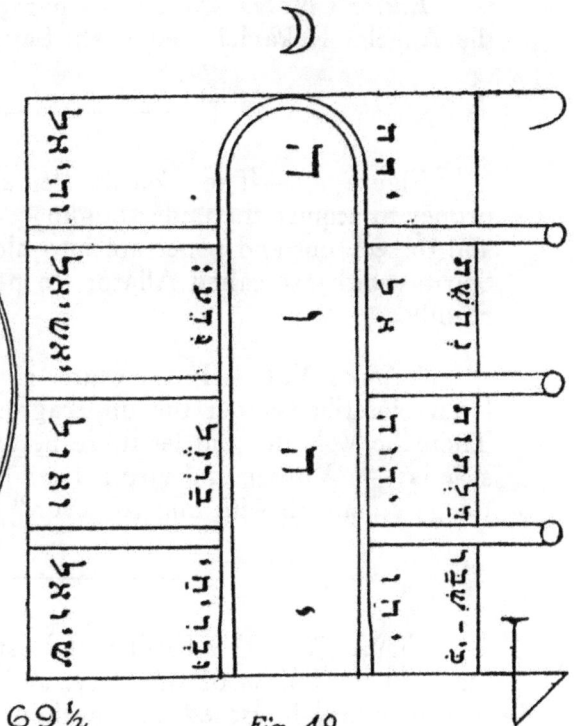

Fig. 49.

MERCURY.

Figure 44.—The First Pentacle of Mercury.—It serveth to invoke the Spirits who are under the Firmament.

Editor's Note.—Letters forming the Names of the Spirits *Yekahel* and *Agiel.*

Figure 45.—The Second Pentacle of Mercury.—The Spirits herein written serve to bring to effect and to grant things which are contrary unto the order of Nature; and which are not contained under any other head. They easily give answer, but they can with difficulty be seen.

Editor's Note.—The Letters form the Names of Böel and other Spirits.

Figure 46.—The Third Pentacle of Mercury.—This and the following serve to invoke the Spirits subject unto Mercury; and especially those who are written in this *Pentacle.*

Editor's Note.—Mystical Characters of Mercury, and the Names of the Angels: Kokaviel, Gheoriah, Savaniah, and Chokmahiel.

Figure 47.—The Fourth Pentacle of Mercury.—This is further proper to acquire the understanding and Knowledge of all things created, and to seek out and penetrate into hidden things; and to command those Spirits which are called Allatori to perform embassies. They obey very readily.

Editor's Note.—In the center is the Name of God, El. The Hebrew letters inscribed about the dodecagram make the sentence, "IHVH, fix Thou the Volatile, and let there be unto the void restriction." The versicle is:—"Wisdom and virtue are in his house, and the Knowledge of all things remaineth with him for ever."

Figure 48.—The Fifth and Last Pentacle of Mercury.—This commandeth the Spirits of Mercury, and serveth to open doors in whatever way they may be closed, and nothing it may encounter can resist it.

Editor's Note.—Within the Pentacle are the Names El Ab, and IHVH. The versicle is from *Psalm xxiv.* 7:—"*Lift up your heads, O ye gates, and be ye lift up ye everlasting doors, and the King of Glory shall come in.*"

THE MOON.

Figure 49.—The First Pentacle of the Moon.—This and the following serve to call forth and invoke the Spirits of the Moon; and it further serveth to open doors, in whatever way they may be fastened.

Editor's Note.—The *Pentacle* is a species of hieroglyphic representation of a door or gate. In the center is written the Name IHVH. On the right hand are the Names IHV, IHVH, AL, and IHH. On the left hand are the Names of the Angels: Schioel, Vaol, Yashiel, and Vehiel. The versicle above the Names on either side, is from *Psalm cvii.* 16:— "*He hath broken the Gates of brass, and smitten the bars of iron in sunder.*"

Figure 50.—The Second Pentacle of the Moon.—This serveth against all perils and dangers by water, and if it should chance that the Spirits of the Moon should excite and cause great rain and exceeding tempests about the Circle, in order to astonish and terrify thee; on showing unto them this *Pentacle,* it will all speedily cease.

Editor's Note.—A hand pointing to the Name *El,* and to that of the Angel Abariel. The versicle is from *Psalm lvi.* 11:—"*In Elohim have I put my trust, I will not fear, what can man do unto me?*"

Figure 51.—The Third Pentacle of the Moon.—This being duly borne with thee when upon a journey, if it be properly made, serveth against all attacks by night, and against every kind of danger and peril by Water.

Editor's Note.—The Names Aub and Vevaphel. The versicle is from *Psalm xl.* 13:—"*Be pleased O IHVH to deliver me, O IHVH make haste to help me.*"

Figure 52.—The Fourth Pentacle of the Moon.—This defendeth thee from all evil sources, and from all injury unto soul or body. Its

Angel, Sophiel, giveth the knowledge of the virtue of all herbs and stones; and unto whomsoever shall name him, he will procure the knowledge of all.

Editor's Note.—The Divine Name Eheieh Asher Eheieh, and the Names of the Angels Yahel and Sophiel. The versicle is:—"*Let them be confounded who persecute me, and let me not be confounded; let them fear, and not I.*"

Figure 53.—The Fifth Pentacle of the Moon.—It serveth to have answers in sleep. Its Angel Iachadiel serveth unto destruction and loss, as well as unto the destruction of enemies. Thou mayest also call upon him by Abdon and Dalé against all Phantoms of the night, and to summon the souls of the departed from Hades.

Editor's Note.—The Divine Names IHVH and *Elohim,* a mystical character of the Moon, and the Names of the Angels Iachadiel and Azarel. The versicle is from *Psalm lxviii.* 1:—"*Let God arise, and let His enemies be scattered; let them also who hate Him flee before Him.*"

Figure 54.—The Sixth and Last Pentacle of the Moon.—This is wonderfully good, and serveth excellently to excite and cause heavy rains, if it be engraved upon a plate of silver; and if it be placed under water, as long as it remaineth there, there will be rain. It should be engraved, drawn, or written in the day and hour of the Moon.

Editor's Note.—The Pentacle is composed of mystical characters of the Moon, surrounded by a versicle from *Genesis vii.* 11, 12:—"*All the fountains of the great deep were broken up . . . and the rain was upon the earth.*"

This is the end of the *Holy Pentacles,* in all which I have, to the best of my power, restored the Hebrew letters and mystical characters correctly. I have further given nearly every versicle in pointed Hebrew, instead of in the Latin; so that the Occult student might not be inconvenienced by having to search out the same in a Hebrew Bible. The restoration of the Hebrew letters in the body of the *Pentacles* has been a work of immense difficulty, and has extended over several years.—Dr. DE LAURENCE.

PLATE XII.

Fig. 50.

Fig. 51.

Fig. 52.

Fig. 53.

70½

PREFATORY NOTE TO BOOK TWO.

THIS Work of SOLOMON is divided into TWO BOOKS. In the first thou mayest see and know how to avoid errors in Experiments, Operations, and in the Spirits themselves. In the second thou art taught in what manner Magical Arts may be reduced to the proposed object and end.

It is for this reason that thou shouldst take great heed and care that this Key of Secrets* fall not into the hands of the foolish, the stupid, and the ignorant. For he who is the possessor hereof, and who availeth himself hereof according to the ordinances herein contained, will not only be able to reduce the Magical Arts herein unto their proposed end, but will, even if he findeth certain errors herein, be able to correct them.

Any Art or Operation of this kind will not be able to attain its end, unless the Master of the Art, or Exorcist, shall have this Work completely in his power, that is to say, unless he thoroughly understand it, for without this he will never attain the effect of any operation.

For this reason I earnestly pray and conjure the person into whose hands this Key of Secrets may fall, neither to communicate it, nor to make any one a partaker in this knowledge, if he be not faithful, nor capable of keeping a secret, nor expert in the Arts. And I most humbly entreat the possessor of this, by the Ineffable Name of God in Four Letters, YOD, HE, VAU, HE, and by the Name ADONAI, and by all the other Most High and Holy Names of God, that he values this work as dearly as his own soul, and that he makes no foolish or ignorant man a partaker therein.

---

* This Prefatory Note is only found in 3981 *Harleian* MSS., 3091 *Sloane* MSS., and 288 King's MSS.

The Key Of Solomon.

The Beginning Of Book Two.

BOOK TWO.

CHAPTER I.

AT WHAT HOUR AFTER THE PREPARATION OF ALL THINGS NECESSARY, WE SHOULD BRING THE EXERCISE OF THE ART TO PERFECTION.

THE Days and Hours have already been treated of, in general, in the First Book. It is now necessary to notice in particular at what hour accomplishment and perfection should be given to the Arts, all things necessary having been previously prepared.

Should it then happen that thou hast undertaken any secret operation for conversing with or conjuring Spirits, in which the day and the hour are not marked, thou shalt put it in execution on the days and hours of Mercury, at the sixteenth or twenty-third hour, but it will be still better at the eighth, which is the third of the same night, which is called and means before the morning, for then thou shalt be able to put in practice all the Arts and Operations which should be performed, according as it shall please thee by day or by night, provided that they have been prepared at the hours suitable to them, as hath been already said. But when neither hour nor time of operation or invocation is specified, it is then much better to perform these experiments at night, seeing that it is more easy to the Spirits to appear in the peaceful silence of night than during the day. And thou shouldst inviolably observe, that wishing to invoke the Spirits, either by day or by night, it is necessary that it should be done in a place hidden, removed, secret, convenient, and proper for such Art, where no man frequenteth or inhabiteth, as we shall relate more fully in its place.

If then thou shouldst operate touching anything which hath been stolen, in whatever way it be performed and whatever way it may have been prepared, it is necessary to practice it on the days and hours of the Moon, being if possible in her increase, and from the first unto the eighth hour of the day.

But if it be by night, then it should be at the fifth or at the third hour; but it is better by day than by the night, for the light justifieth them, and maketh them much more fit for publication. But if the Operations be regarding Invisibility, they should be put in practice at the first, second, and third hours of Mars by day. But if by night, until the third hour. If they be Operations of seeking love, grace, or favor, they should be performed until the eighth hour of the same day, commencing with the first hour of the Sun; and from the first hour of Venus unto the first hour of the same day of Venus.

As for Operations of destruction and desolation, we should practice and put them into execution on the day of Saturn at the first hour, or rather at the eighth or fifteenth of the day; and from the first until the eighth hour of the night.

Experiments of games, raillery, deceit, illusion, and invisibility, ought to be done at the first hour of Venus, and at the eighth hour of the day; but by night at the third and at the seventh.

At all times of practicing and putting into execution Magical Arts, the Moon should be increasing in light, and in an equal number of degrees with the Sun; and it is much better from the first quarter to the Opposition, and the Moon should be in a fiery Sign, and notably in that of the Ram or of the Lion.

Therefore, to execute these Experiments in any manner whatsoever, it should be done when the Moon is clear, and when she is increasing in light.

In order to put in execution those of Invisibility after everything is properly prepared, the Moon should be in the Sign of the Fishes, in the hours proper and fitting, and she should be increasing in light.

For experiments of seeking love and favor, in whatever way it may be desired, they will succeed, provided that they have been prepared at the proper hours, and that the Moon be increasing in light and in the Sign of the Twins.

So exact a preparation of days and hours is not necessary for those who are Adepts in the Art, but it is extremely necessary for apprentices and beginners, seeing that those who have been little or not at all instructed herein, and who only begin to apply themselves to this Art, do not have as much faith in the experiments as those who are adepts therein, and who have practiced them. But as regards beginners, they should always have the days and hours well disposed and appropriate unto the Art. And the Wise should only observe the precepts of the Art which are necessary, and in observing the other solemnities necessary they will operate with a perfect assurance.

It is, nevertheless, necessary to take care that when thou shalt have prepared any experiment thyself for the days and hours ordained, that it should be performed in clear, serene, mild, and pleasant weather, without any great tempest or agitation of the air, which should not be troubled by winds. For when thou shalt have conjured any Spirits in any art or experiment, they will not come when the Air is troubled or agitated by winds, seeing that Spirits have neither flesh nor bones, and are created of different substances.

Some are created from Water.

Others from Wind, unto which they are like.

Some from Earth.

Some from Clouds.

Others from Solar Vapors.

Others from the keenness and strength of Fire; and when they are invoked or summoned, they come always with great noise, and with the terrible nature of fire.

When the Spirits which are created of Water are invoked, they come with great rains, thunder, hail, lightning, thunder-bolts, and the like.

When the Spirits which are created of Clouds are invoked, they come with great deformity, in a horrible form, to strike fear into the Invocator, and with an exceeding great noise.

Others* which are formed from wind appear like thereunto and with exceeding swift motion, and whensoever those which are created from Beauty† appear, they will show themselves in a fair and agreeable form; moreover, whensoever thou shalt call the Spirits created from Air, they will come with a kind of gentle breeze.

When the Spirits which are created from the Vapors of the Sun are invoked, they come under a very beautiful and excellent form, but filled with pride, vanity, and conceit. They are clever, whence it comes that these last are all specified by SOLOMON in his book of ornament, or of beauty. They show great ostentation and vainglory in their dress, and they rejoice in many ornaments; the boast of possessing mundane beauty, and all sorts of ornaments and decorations. Thou shalt only invoke them in serene, mild, and pleasant weather.

The Spirits which are created of Fire reside in the east, those created of Wind in the south.

Note then that it will be much better to perform the experiments or operations in the direction of the East, putting everything necessary in practice towards that point.

But for all other operations or extraordinary experiments, and for those of love, they will be much more efficacious directed towards the north.

Take heed further, that every time that thou performest any experiment, to reduce it unto perfection with the requisite solemnities, thou shalt recommence the former experiment if interrupted therein, without the preparation of hours or other solemnities.

If by chance it should happen that having performed an experiment with due observance of days, hours, and requisite solemnities, thou shalt find it unsuccessful, it must be in some manner false, ill-arranged and defective, and thou must assuredly have failed in some matter; for if thou doest ill in one single point, these experiments or these Arts will not be verified.

Thus upon this Chapter dependeth this whole *Key of Arts, Experiments, and Operations*, and although every solemnity be rightly observed, no experiment will be verified, unless thou canst penetrate the meaning of this Chapter.

* This paragraph is only found in 10862 Add. MSS.
† The Name of the Sixth Qabalistical Sephira or Emanation from the Deity, which is called Tiphereth, or Beauty.

BOOK TWO.

CHAPTER II.

In What Manner the Master of the Art Should Keep, Rule, and Govern Himself.

He who wisheth to apply himself unto so great and so difficult a Science should have his mind free from all business, and from all extraneous ideas of whatever nature they may be.

He should then thoroughly examine the Art or Operation which he should undertake, and write it regularly out on paper, particularly set aside for that purpose, with the appropriate conjurations and exorcisms. If there be anything to mark or write down, it should be performed in the manner specified regarding the paper, ink, and pen. He should also observe at what day and at what hour this Experiment should be undertaken, and what things are necessary to prepare for it, what should be added, and what can be dispensed with.

The which matters being prepared, it is necessary for thee to search out and arrange some fitting place wherein the Magical Art and its Experiments can be put in practice. All these things being thus arranged and disposed, let the Master of the Art go into a proper and fitting place, or into his Cabinet or Secret Chamber if it be convenient for the purpose, and he can there dispose and set in order the whole operation; or he can use any other convenient secret place for the purpose, provided that no one knoweth where it is, and that no man can see him when there.

After this he must strip himself entirely naked, and let him have a bath ready prepared, wherein is water exorcised, after the manner which we shall describe, so that he may bathe and purify himself therein from the crown of his head unto the sole of his foot, saying:—

O Lord ADONAI, Who hast formed me Thine unworthy servant in Thine Image and resemblance of vile and of abject earth; deign to bless and to sanctify this Water, so that it may be for the health and purification of my soul, and of my body, so that no foolishness or deceitfulness may therein in any way have place.

O Most Powerful and Ineffable God, Who madest Thy people pass dryshod through the *Red Sea* when they came up out of the Land of Egypt, grant unto me grace that I may be purified and regenerated from all my past sins by this Water, that so no uncleanness may appear upon me in Thy Presence.

After this thou shalt entirely immerse thyself in the Water, and thou shalt dry thyself with a towel of clean white linen, and then thou shalt put upon thy flesh the garments of pure white linen whereof we shall speak hereafter.

Hereafter, for three days at least, thou shalt abstain from all idle, vain, and impure reasonings, and from every kind of impurity and sin, as will be shown in the Chapter of fast and of vigil. Each day shalt thou recite the following prayer, at least once in the morning, twice about noon, thrice in the afternoon, four times in the evening, and five times before lying down to sleep; this shalt thou do on the three ensuing days:—

THE PRAYER.

HERACHIO, ASAC, ASACRO, BEDRIMULAEL, TILATH, ARABONAS, IERAHLEM, IDEODOC, ARCHARZEL, ZOPHIEL, BLAUTEL, BARACATA, EDONIEL, ELOHIM, EMAGRO, ABRAGATEH, SAMOEL, GEBURAHEL, CADATO, ERA, ELOHI, ACHSAH, EBMISHA, IMACHEDEL, DANIEL, DAMA, ELAMOS, IZACHEL, BAEL, SEGON, GEMON, DEMAS.

O Lord God, Who art seated upon the Heavens, and Who regardest the Abysses beneath, grant unto me Thy Grace I beseech Thee, so that what I conceive in my mind I may accomplish in my work, through Thee, O God, the Sovereign Ruler of all, Who livest and reignest unto the Ages of the Ages. Amen.

These three days having passed, thou must have all things in readiness, as hath been said, and after this a day appointed and set apart. It will be necessary for thee to wait for the hour in which thou shouldst commence the Operation; but when once it shall be commenced at this hour, thou shalt be able to continue it unto the end, seeing that it deriveth its force and virtue from its beginning, which extendeth to and spreadeth over the succeeding hours, so that the Master of the Art will be enabled to complete his work so as to arrive at the desired result.

BOOK TWO.

CHAPTER III.

HOW THE COMPANIONS OR DISCIPLES OF THE MASTER OF THE ART OUGHT TO REGULATE AND GOVERN THEMSELVES.

WHEN the Master of the Art wisheth to put in practice any Operation or Experiment, especially one of importance, he should first consider of what Companions he should avail himself. This is the reason why in every Operation whose Experience should be carried out in the Circle, it is well to have three Companions. And if he cannot have Companions, he should at least have with him a faithful and attached dog. But if it be absolutely necessary for him to have Companions, these Companions should be obligated and bound by oath to do all that the Master shall order or prescribe them, and they should study, observe, and carefully retain, and be attentive unto all which they shall hear. For those who shall act otherwise shall suffer and endure many pains and labors, and run into many dangers, which the Spirits will cause and procure for them, and for this cause sometimes they shall even die.

The Disciples then, being well and thoroughly instructed, and fortified with a wise and understanding heart, the Master shall take exorcised Water, and he shall enter with his Disciples into a secret place purified and clean, where he must strip them entirely naked; after this, let him pour exorcised water upon their heads, which he should cause to flow from the crown of their head unto the sole of their foot, so as to bathe them entirely therewith; and while bathing them thus, he should say:—

Be ye regenerate, cleansed, and purified, in the Name of the Ineffable, Great, and Eternal God, from all your iniquities, and may the virtue of the Most High descend upon you and abide with you always, so that ye may have the power and strength to accomplish the desires of your heart. Amen.

After this let the Disciples robe themselves as the Master hath done, and fast like him for three days, repeating the same prayer; let them act like him, and in the work let them implicitly follow and obey him in all things.

But if the Master of the Art wisheth to have a dog for his Companion, he must bathe him thoroughly with the exorcised water in the same manner as the Disciples, and let him perfume him with the odors and incense of Art, and let him repeat the following Conjuration over him:—

I conjure thee, O thou Creature, being a Dog, by Him Who hath created thee, I bathe and I perfume thee in the Name of the Most High, Most Powerful, and Eternal God, so that thou mayest be my true Companion in this operation, and that thou mayest be also my faithful friend in whatsoever Operation I may hereafter perform.

But if he wisheth to have for his companion a little boy or girl, which will be still better, he must ordain them as he hath ordained the dog; and he must pare and cut the nails of their hands and of their feet, saying:—

I conjure thee, O thou Creature, being a young girl (or boy), by the Most High God, the Father of all Creatures, by the Father ADONAI ELOHIM, and by the Father ELION, that thou shalt have neither will nor power to hide from me anything, nor yet to keep back from me the truth in all which I shall demand of thee, and that thou be obedient and faithful unto me. Amen.

Let him purify, cleanse, and wash this young child anew, with the Water of Art, saying:—

Be thou regenerate, cleansed, and purified, so that the Spirits may neither harm thee nor abide in thee. Amen.

Then perfume the child with odours as above.

When the companions shall be thus ordained and disposed, the Master shalt be able to operate in surety together with them, every time that it shall please him; and he shall perform his operation happily, and shall attain his end.

But for the safety both of soul and of body, the Master and the Companions should have the Pentacles before their breasts, consecrated, and covered with a silken veil, and perfumed with the proper fumigations. By the which being assured and encouraged, they may enter into the matter without fear or terror, and they shall be exempt and free from all perils and dangers, provided that they obey the commands of the Master and do all that he ordain them. If they shall act thus, all things shall go according unto their desires.

All being thus arranged, the Master should take heed that His Disciples are perfectly instructed in those things which they have to perform.

These Companions or Disciples should be three in number, without including the Master. They may also be of the number of five, of seven, or of nine; but so that they ever implicitly obey the orders of their Master; for thus only shall all things come to a successful issue.

BOOK TWO.

CHAPTER IV.

Concerning the Fasting, Care, and Things to Be Observed.

When the Master of the Art shall wish to perform his operations, having previously arranged all things which it is necessary to observe and practise; from the first day of the Experiment, it is absolutely necessary to ordain and to prescribe care and observation, to abstain from all things unlawful, and from every kind of impiety, impurity, wickedness, or immodesty, as well of body as of soul; as, for example, eating and drinking superabundantly, and all sorts of vain words, buffooneries, slanders, calumnies, and other useless discourse; but instead to do good deeds, speak honestly, keep a strict decency in all things, never lose sight of modesty in walking, in conversation, in eating and drinking, and in all things; the which should be principally done and observed for nine days, before the commencement of the Operation. The Disciples should do the same, and should equally put in practice all things necessary to be observed, if they wish to make use of all these operations and experiments.

But before the commencement of the work, it is absolutely necessary that the Master with his Disciples repeat the following Conjuration once in the morning, and twice in the evening:—

THE CONJURATION.

O Lord God Almighty, be propitious unto me a miserable sinner, for I am not worthy to raise mine eyes unto heaven, because of the iniquity of my sins and the multitude of my faults. O pitying and merciful Father, who wouldest not the death of a sinner but rather that he should turn from his wickedness and live, O God have mercy upon me and pardon all my sins; for I unworthy entreat Thee, O Father of all Creatures, Thou Who art full of mercy and of compassion, by Thy great goodness, that Thou deign to grant unto me power to see and know these Spirits which I desire to behold and to invoke to appear before me and to accomplish my will. Through Thee Who art Conqueror, and Who art Blessed unto the Ages of the Ages. Amen.

O Lord God the Father Eternal, Who art seated upon the Kerubim and the Seraphim, Who lookest upon Earth and upon Sea; unto Thee do I raise my hands and implore thine aid alone, Thou Who alone art the accomplishment of good works, Thou Who givest rest unto those who labour, Who humblest the proud, Who art the Author of Life and the Destroyer of Death; Thou art our rest, Thou art the Protector of those who invoke Thee; protect, guard, and defend me in this matter, and in this enterprise which I propose to carry out, O Thou Who livest, reignest, and abidest unto the Eternal Ages. Amen.

During the three last days before the commencement of this action, thou shalt content thyself with only eating fasting diet, and that only once in the day; and it will be better still if thou only partakest of bread and water. Thou shalt also abstain from every impure thing; reciting the prayer above written. And on the last day, when thou shalt wish to commence the Operation, thou shalt remain all day without eating, and later on thou shalt go into a secret place, where thou shalt confess all thy sins unto God with a contrite heart. The Disciples also, together with the Master, shall recite the same Confession with a low but distinct voice, as hath been already said in the *First Book*.

This having been done thrice with a devout, pure, and contrite heart, in a place withdrawn from men, cleansed, and pure, where thou canst not be seen, taking the water and the hyssop, thou shalt say:—

Purify me, O Lord, with hyssop, and I shall be pure; wash me and I shall be whiter than snow.

After this, bathe thyself with the exorcised water, and clothe thyself again with the consecrated garment which thou hast taken off; cense thyself, and surround thyself with odours, as will be told farther on, when we speak of perfumes and suffumigations.

The which being done, thou shalt go unto the ordained place with thy Companions, and all things being prepared, thou shalt make the Circle, as hath been already said, with all other necessary ceremonies; then shalt thou commence to invoke the Spirits by the Exorcisms; thou shalt also repeat anew the foregoing Confession as hath been already said in the First Book. After which, in sign of amendment and of repentance, each shall mutually kiss the other.

Mark well, that up to this point, the Disciples should do the same things as the Master.

Let the Master now give his commands unto his Disciples, and pursue the course of the Experiment, and work with all diligence to bring it unto perfection.

BOOK TWO.

CHAPTER V.

CONCERNING THE BATHS, AND HOW THEY ARE TO BE ARRANGED.

THE Bath is necessary for all *Magical and Necromantic Arts;* wherefore, if thou wishest to perform any experiment or operation, having arranged all things necessary thereunto according to the proper days and hours, thou shalt go unto a river or running stream, or thou shalt have warm water ready in some large vessel or tub in thy secret cabinet, and while disrobing thyself of thy raiment thou shalt repeat the following Psalms:—Psalms xiv. or liii.; xxvii.; liv.; lxxxi.; cv.

And when the Master shall be entirely disrobed let him enter into the water or into the Bath, and let him say:—

THE EXORCISM OF THE WATER.

I exorcise Thee, O Creature of Water, by Him Who hath created thee and gathered thee together into one place so that the dry land appeared, that thou uncover all the deceits of the Enemy, and that thou cast out from thee all the impurities and uncleannesses of the Spirits of the World of Phantasm, so they may harm me not, through the virtue of God almighty who liveth and reigneth unto the Ages of the Ages. Amen.

Then shalt thou begin to wash thyself thoroughly in the Bath, saying:—

MERTALIA, MUSALIA, DOPHALIA, ONEMALIA, ZITANSEIA, GOLDAPHAIRA, DEDULSAIRA, GHEVIALAIRA, GHEMINAIRA, GEGROPHEIRA, CEDAHI, GILTHAR, GODIEB, EZOIIL, MUSIL, GRASSIL, TAMEN, PUERI, GODU, HUZNOTH, ASTACHOTH, TZABAOTH, ADONAI, AGLA, ON, EL, TETRAGRAMMATON, SHEMA, ARESION, ANAPHAXETON, SEGILATON, PRIMEUMATON.

All the which Names thou shalt repeat twice or thrice, until thou art completely washed and clean, and when thou art perfectly pure thou shalt quit the Bath, and sprinkle thyself with exorcised water, in the manner described later on, and thou shalt say:—

Purge me, O Lord, with hyssop, and I shall be clean; wash me, and I shall be whiter than snow.

Whilst again clothing thyself, thou shalt recite the following Psalms: Psalms cii.; li.; iv.; xxx.; cxix., *Mem.*, v. 97.; cxiv.; cxxvi., cxxxix.

After which thou shalt recite the following prayer:—

PRAYER.

EL Strong and Wonderful, I bless Thee, I adore Thee, I glorify Thee, I invoke Thee, I render Thee thanks from this Bath, so that this

Water may be able to cast from me all impurity and concupiscence of heart, through Thee, O Holy Adonai; and may I accomplish all things through Thee Who livest and reignest unto the Ages of the Ages. Amen.

After this take the Salt and bless it in this manner:—

THE BENEDICTION OF THE SALT.

The Blessing of the Father Almighty be upon this Creature of Salt, and let all malignity and hindrance be cast forth hencefrom, and let all good enter herein, for without Thee man cannot live, wherefore I bless thee and invoke thee, that thou mayest aid me.

Then thou shalt recite over the Salt, Psalm ciii.

Then taking the grains of the exorcised Salt thou shalt cast them into the aforesaid Bath; and thou shalt again disrobe thyself, pronouncing the following words:—

IMANEL, ARNAMON, IMATO, MEMEON, RECTACON, MUOBOII, PAL-TELLON, DECAION, YAMENTON, YARON, TATONON, VAPHORON, GARDON, EXISTON, ZAGVERON, MOMERTON, ZARMESITON, TILEION, TIXMION.

After this thou shalt enter a second time into the Bath and recite Psalms civ. and lxxxi.

Then thou shalt quit the Bath and clothe thyself as before in linen garments clean and white, and over them thou shalt put the garments, of which we shall speak in the proper Chapter, and thus clothed thou shalt go to finish thy work.

The Disciples should wash themselves in like manner, and with like solemnities.

BOOK TWO.

CHAPTER VI.

OF THE GARMENTS AND SHOES OF THE ART.

THE exterior habiliments which the Master of the Art should wear ought to be of linen, as well as those which he weareth beneath them; and if he hath the means they should be of Silk. If they be of linen the thread of which they are made should have been spun by a young maiden.

The characters shown in *Figure 55* should be embroidered on the breast with the needle of Art in red silk.

The shoes should also be White, upon the which the characters in *Figure 56* should be traced in the same way.

The shoes or boots should be made of white leather, on the which should be marked the Signs and Characters of Art. These shoes should be made during the days of fast and abstinence, namely, during the nine days set apart before the beginning of the Operation, during which the necessary instruments also should be prepared, polished, brightened, and cleaned.

Besides this, the Master of the Art should have a *Crown* made of *Virgin Parchment* paper, upon the which should be written these four Names:—YOD, HE, VAU, HE, in front; ADONAI behind; EL on the right; and ELOHIM on the left. (*See Figure 57.*) These names should be written with the ink and pen of the Art, whereof we shall speak in the proper Chapter. The Disciples should also each have a Crown of Virgin paper whereon these Divine symbols should be marked in scarlet. (*See Figure 58.*)

Take heed also that in clothing thyself with these aforesaid habiliments, that thou recite these Psalms:—Psalms xv.; cxxxi.; cxxxvii.; cxvii.; lxvii.; lxviii.; and cxxvii.

After this perfume the *Vestments* by burning *Temple Incense*, and sprinkle them with the water and hyssop of the Art.

But when the Master and His Disciples shall commence to robe themselves after the first Psalm, and before continuing with the others, he should pronounce these words:—

AMOR, AMATOR, AMIDES, IDEODANIACH, PAMOR, PLAIOR, ANITOR; through the merits of these holy Angels will I robe and indue myself with the Vestments of Power, through which may I conduct unto the desired end those things which I ardently wish, through Thee, O Most Holy ADONAI, Whose Kingdom and Empire endureth for ever. Amen.

Take notice that if the linen garments were vestments of the Levites or of the Priests, and had been used for holy things, that they would be all the better.

BOOK TWO.

CHAPTER VII.

OF PLACES WHEREIN WE MAY CONVENIENTLY EXECUTE THE EXPERIMENTS AND OPERATIONS OF THE ART.

THE places best fitted for exercising and accomplishing Magical Arts and Operations are those which are concealed, removed, and separated from the habitations of men. Wherefore desolate and uninhabited regions are most appropriate, such as the borders of lakes, forests, dark and obscure places, old and deserted houses, whither rarely and scarce ever men do come, mountains, caves, caverns, grottos, gardens, orchards; but best of all are cross-roads, and where four roads meet, during the depth and silence of night. But if thou canst not conveniently go unto any of these places, thy house, and even thine own chamber, or, indeed, any place, provided it hath been purified and consecrated with the necessary ceremonies, will be found fit and convenient for the convocation and assembling of the Spirits.

These Arts or Operations should be carried out at the prescribed time, but if there be no time specially appointed it will be always better to perform them at night, which is the most fit and proper time for the Operations of Necromancy; this is also a symbol that it is just and right to hide them from the sight of the foolish, the ignorant, and the profane.

But when thou shalt have selected a place fitting, thou mayest perform thine experiments by day or by night. It should be spacious, clear, and bounded on all sides by hedges, shrubs, trees, or walls. Thou shalt thyself cleanse it thoroughly and render it neat and pure, and while doing this thou shalt recite Psalms ii.; lxvii.; and liv.

After this thou shalt perfume it with the odours and suffumigations of the Art, and shalt sprinkle it with the water and the hyssop; and after this thou mayest in this place make all the necessary preparations for an operation.

But when, later on, thou shalt go unto this place, to complete and accomplish the operation, thou shalt repeat on the way thither the following Prayer in a low and distinct voice:—

THE PRAYER.

ZAZAII, ZAMAII, PUIDAMON Most Powerful, SEDON Most Strong, EL, YOD HE VAU HE, IAH, AGLA, assist me an unworthy sinner who have had the boldness to pronounce these Holy Names which no man should name and invoke save in very great danger. Therefore have I recourse unto these Most Holy Names, being in great peril both of soul and of body. Pardon me if I have sinned in any manner, for I trust in Thy protection alone, especially on this journey.

Let the Master as he goeth sprinkle the path with the water and hyssop of the Art, while each of his Disciples shall repeat in a low voice the Prayer which we have enjoined for the days of fasting and preparation.

Furthermore, let the Master appoint his Disciples to carry the things necessary for the Art.

The first shall bear the Censer, the Fire, and the Incense.

The Second; the Book, the Paper, the Pens, the Ink, and the various Perfumes.

The Third; the Knife, and the Sickle.

The Master; the Staff, and the Wand.

But if there be more Disciples present, the Master shall distribute the things for each to carry, according to their number.

When they shall have arrived at the place, and all things being disposed in their proper order, the Master shall take the Knife or other convenient consecrated Magical implement of Steel, wherewith to form the Circle of Art which he intends to construct. This being done, he must perfume it, and sprinkle it with water; and having warned and exhorted his Disciples, he shall work thus:—

First let him have a Trumpet made of new wood, on the one side of which shall be written in Hebrew with the pen and ink of the Art these Names of God, ELOHIM GIBOR, ELOHIM TZABAOTH (*see Figure* 59); and on the other side these characters (*see Figure* 60).

Having entered into the Circle to perform the Experiment, he should sound his Trumpet towards the four quarters of the Universe, first towards the East, then towards the South, then towards the West, and lastly towards the North. Then let him say:—

Hear ye, and be ye ready, in whatever part of the Universe ye may be, to obey the Voice of God the Mighty One, and the Names of the Creator. We let you know by this signal and sound that ye will be convoked hither, wherefore hold ye yourselves in readiness to obey our commands.

This being done let the Master complete his work, renew the Circle, and make the incensements and fumigations.

PLATE XIII.

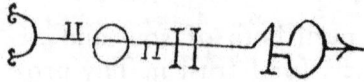

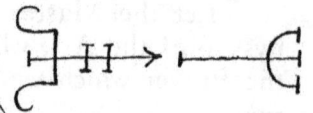

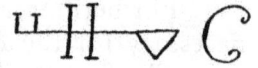

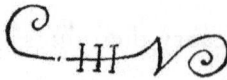

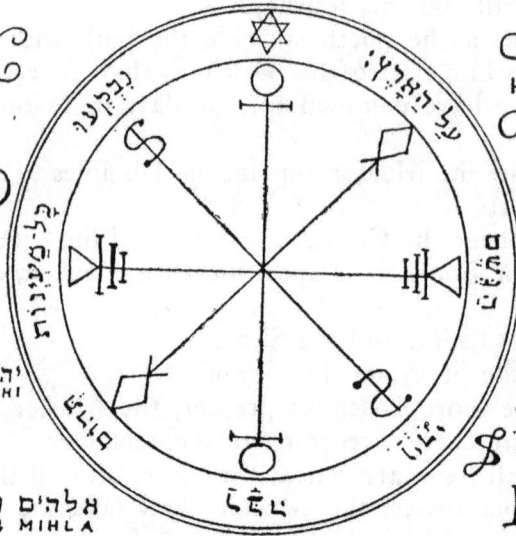

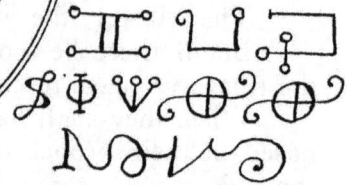

Fig. 55.

Fig. 56.

Fig. 57.

Fig. 60.

יהוה אדני אל אלהים
MIHLA LA INDA HVHI

Fig. 59.

אלהים גבור אלהים צבאות
TₒVABTₒ MIHLA RVBG MIHLA

The Knife with the
White Hilt.

Fig. 61.

Fig. 54.

Fig. 62.

The Knife with the
Black Hilt.

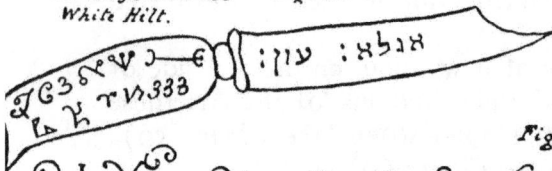

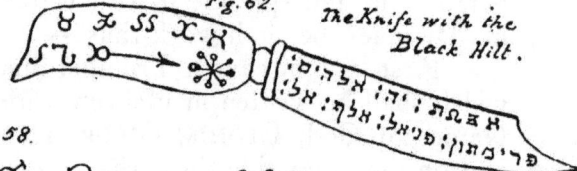

Fig. 58.

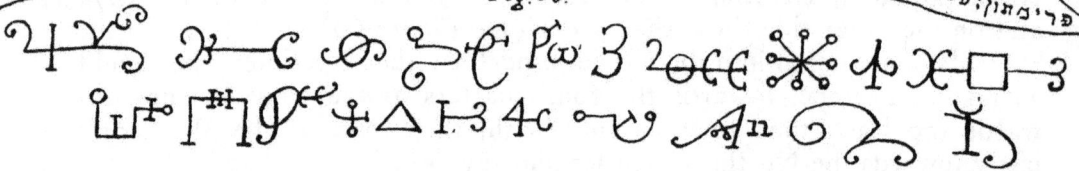

Fig. 63.

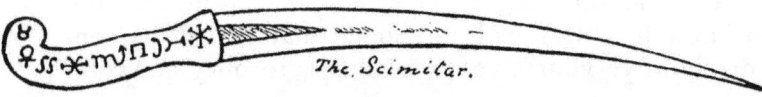

The Scimitar.

The
Short
Lance.

Fig. 67.

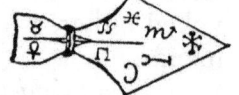

Fig. 64.
The Sickle.

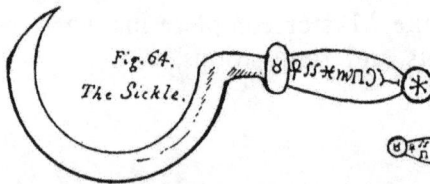

Fig. 65.

The Dagger.

Fig. 66.

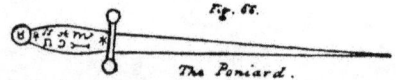

The Poniard.

Fig. 68.

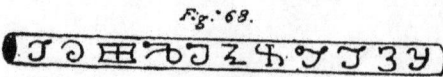

The Staff.

Fig. 69.

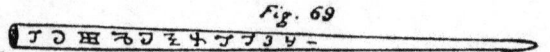

The Wand.

86½

PLATE XIV.

Fig. 94. יהשוה:

Fig. 71. כרריא or גבריאל

Fig. 70.

יהוה: אדני: אהיה: יאי:

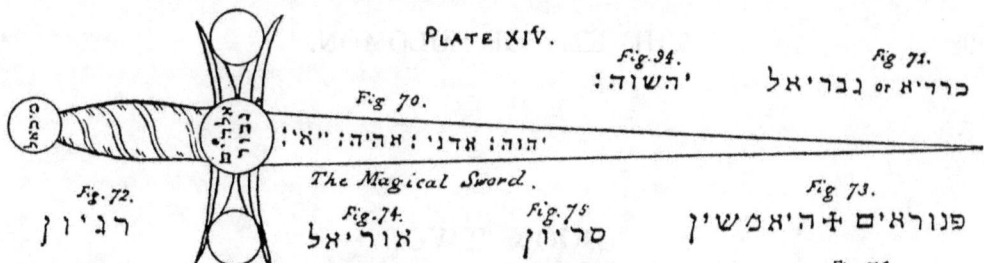

The Magical Sword.

Fig. 72. רגיון

Fig. 74. אוריאל

Fig. 75. סריון

Fig 73. פנוראים + היאמשין

Fig. 79. למדין + ערדים

Fig. 78. ימשון

Fig. 77. דמיאל or רפאל

Fig. 76. גמורין + דבלין

Fig. 80.

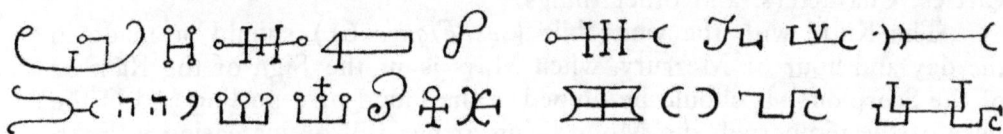

The Burin.

Fig. 82.

Fig. 83.

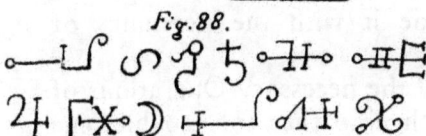

Fig. 84.

Fig. 85.

יהוה: מטטרון: יה יה יה: קדוש:
אלהים צבאות:

Fig. 86. אנאירשון:

Fig. 88.

Fig. 91. אהיה אשר אהיה:

Fig. 92. אין סוף:

Fig. 87. אנלא: אדני:
אלהי:

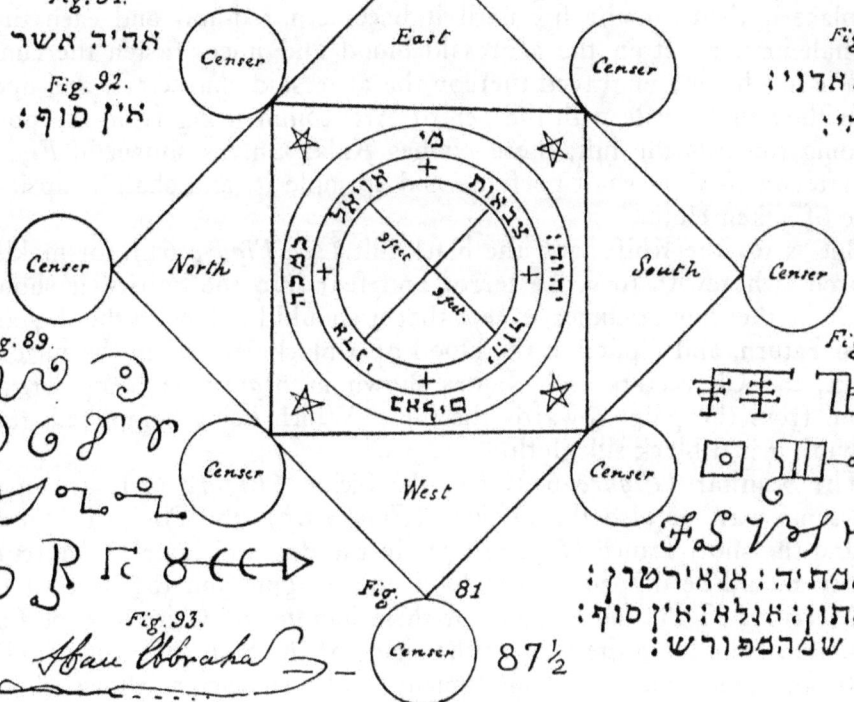

Censer — East — Censer — Center — Censer — North — South — Censer — Center — Censer — West — Censer

Fig. 89.

Fig. 90.

Fig. 81

Censer   87½

אדני: אמתיה: אנאירשון:
פרימומתון: אנלא: אין סוף:
קדוש: שמהמפורש:

Fig. 93.

7½

BOOK TWO.

CHAPTER VIII.

OF THE KNIFE, SWORD, SICKLE, PONIARD, DAGGER, LANCE, WAND, STAFF, AND
OTHER INSTRUMENTS OF MAGICAL ART.

IN order to properly carry out the greatest and most important Operations of the Art, various Instruments are necessary, as a Knife with a
white hilt, another with a black hilt, a short Lance, wherewith to trace
Circles, Characters, and other things.

The Knife with the white hilt (*see Figure* 61) should be made in
the day and hour of Mercury, when Mars is in the Sign of the Ram or
of the Scorpion. It should be dipped in the blood of a gosling and in the
juice of the pimpernel, the Moon being at her full or increasing in light.
Dip therein also the white hilt, upon the which thou shalt have engraved
the Characters shown. Afterwards perfume it with the perfumes of
the Art.

With this Knife thou mayest perform all the necessary Operations of
the Art, except the Circles. But if it seemeth unto thee too troublesome
to make a similar Knife, have one made in the same fashion; and thou
shalt place it thrice in the fire until it becometh red-hot, and each time
thou shalt immerse it in the aforesaid blood and juice, fasten thereunto
the white hilt having engraved thereon the aforesaid characters, and upon
the hilt thou shalt write with the pen of Art, commencing from the point
and going towards the hilt, these Names Agla, On, as shown in *Figure*
61. Afterwards thou shalt perfume and sprinkle it, and shalt wrap it in
a piece of silken cloth.

But as for the Knife with the black hilt (*see Figure* 62) for making
the Circle, wherewith to strike terror and fear into the Spirits, it should
be made in the same manner, except that it should be done in the day and
hour of Saturn, and dipped in the blood of a black cat and in the juice of
hemlock, the Characters and Names shown in *Figure* 62 being written
thereon, from the point towards the hilt. Which being completed, thou
shalt wrap it in a black silk cloth.

The Scimitar (*Figure* 63), and the Sickle (*Figure* 64), are made
in the same way, as also the Dagger (*Figure* 65), the Poniard (*Figure*
66), and the short Lance (*Figure* 67), in the day and hour of Mercury,
and they should be dipped in the blood of a magpie and the juice of the
herb Mercury. Thou must make for them handles of white boxwood cut
at a single stroke from the tree, at the rising of the Sun, with a new knife.
or with any other convenient instrument. The characters shown should

be traced thereon. Thou shalt perfume them according to the rules of Art; and wrap them in silk cloth like the others.

The Staff (*see Figure* 68) should be of elderwood, or cane, or rosewood; and the Wand (*Figure* 69) of hazel or nut tree, in all cases the wood being virgin, that is of one year's growth only. They should each be cut from the tree at a single stroke, on the day of Mercury, at sunrise. The characters shown should be written or engraved thereon in the day and hour of Mercury.

This being done, thou shalt say:—

ADONAI, Most Holy, deign to bless and to consecrate this Wand, and this Staff, that they may obtain the necessary virtue, through Thee, O Most Holy ADONAI, whose kingdom endureth unto the Ages of the Ages. Amen.

After having perfumed and consecrated them, put them aside in a pure and clean place for use when required.

Swords are also frequently necessary for use in Magical Arts. Thou shalt therefore take a new Sword which thou shalt clean and polish on th day of Mercury, and at the first or the fifteenth hour, and after this thou shalt write on one side these Divine Names in Hebrew, YOD HE VAU HE, ADONAI, EHEIEH, YAYAI; and on the other side ELOHIM GIBOR (*see Figure* 70); sprinkle and cense it and repeat over it the following conjuration:—

THE CONJURATION OF THE SWORD.

I conjure thee, O Sword, by these Names, ABRAHACH, ABRACH, ABRACADABRA, YOD HE VAU HE, that thou serve me for a strength and defence in all Magical Operations, against all mine Enemies, visible and invisible.

I conjure thee anew by the Holy and Indivisible Name of EL strong and wonderful; by the Name SHADDAI Almighty; and by these Names QADOSCH, QADOSCH, QADOSCH, ADONAI ELOHIM TZABAOTH, EMANUEL, the First and the Last, Wisdom, Way, Life, Truth, Chief, Speech, Word, Splendour, Light, Sun, Fountain, Glory, the Stone of the Wise, Virtue, Shepherd, Priest, Messiach Immortal; by these Names then, and by the other Names, I conjure thee, O Sword, that thou servest me for a Protection in all adversities.   Amen.

This being finished thou shalt wrap it also in silk like all the other Instruments, being duly purified and consecrated by the Ceremonies requisite for the perfection of all Magical Arts and Operations.

Three* other Swords should be made for the use of the Disciples.

The first one should have on the pommel the Name CARDIEL or GABRIEL (*see Figure* 71); on the Lamen of the Guard, REGION (*Figure* 72); on the Blade, PANORAIM HEAMESIN (*Figure* 73).

The Second should have on the pommel the Name AURIEL (*Figure*

* The description of these three Swords for the Disciples is only given in 1307 Sloane MSS.

74); on the Lamen of the Guard, SARION (*Figure* 75); on the Blade, GAMORIN DEBALIN (*Figure* 76).

The third should have on the pommel the Name DAMIEL or RAPHAEL (*Figure* 77); on the Lamen of the Guard, YEMETON (*Figure* 78); on the Blade, LAMEDIN ERADIM (*Figure* 79).

The Burin* (*Figure* 80) or Graver is useful for engraving or incising characters. In the day and hour either of Mars or of Venus thou shalt engrave thereon the characters shown, and having sprinkled and censed it thou shalt repeat over it the following Prayer:—

PRAYER.

ASOPHIEL, ASOPHIEL, ASOPHIEL, PENTAGRAMMATON, ATHANATOS, EHEIEH ASHER EHEIEH, QADOSCH, QADOSCH, QADOSCH; O God Eternal, and my Father, bless this Instrument prepared in Thine honour, so that it may only serve for a good use and end, for Thy Glory. Amen.

Having again perfumed, thou shalt put it aside for use. The Needle may be consecrated in the same way.

* From here to the end of the Chapter is from 1203 Lansdowne MSS.

BOOK TWO.

CHAPTER IX.

OF THE FORMATION OF THE CIRCLE.

HAVING chosen a place for preparing and constructing the Circle,* and all things necessary being prepared for the perfection of the Operations, take thou the Sickle or Scimitar of Art and stick it into the centre of the place where the Circle is to be made; then take a cord of nine feet in length, fasten one end thereof unto the Sickle and with the other end trace out the circumference of the Circle, which may be marked either with the Sword or with the Knife with the Black hilt. Then within the Circle mark out four regions, namely, towards the East, West, South, and North, wherein place Symbols; and beyond the limits of this Circle describe with the Consecrated Knife or Sword another Circle, but leaving an open space therein towards the North whereby thou mayest enter and depart beyond the Circle of Art. Beyond this again thou shalt describe another Circle at a foot distance with the aforesaid Instrument, yet ever leaving therein an open space for entrance and egress corresponding to the open space already left in the other. Beyond this again make another Circle at another foot distance, and beyond these two Circles, which are beyond the Circle of Art yet upon the same Centre, thou shalt describe Pentagrams with the Symbols and Names of the Creator therein so that they may surround the Circle already described. Without these Circles shalt thou circumscribe a Square, and beyond that another Square, so that the Angles of the former may touch the centres of the sides of the latter, and that the Angles of the latter may stretch towards the four quarters of the Universe, East, West, North, and South; and at the four Angles of each square, and touching them, thou shalt describe lesser Circles wherein let there be placed standing censers with lighted charcoal and sweet odours.

These things being done, let the Magus of Art† assemble his Disciples, exhort, confirm, and cheer them; lead them into the Circle of Art and station them therein towards the Four Quarters of the Universe, exhort them to fear nothing, and to abide in their assigned places. Furthermore let each of the Companions have a Sword besides the Sword of the Art, which he must hold naked in his hand. Then let the Magus quit the Circle, and Kindle the Censers, and place thereon exorcised Incense, as is said in the Chapter of Fumigations; and let him have the Censers in his

* This Chapter is only given in 10,862 Add. MSS.
† "Maghus" in MS. not "Magister."

hand and kindle it, and then place it in the part prepared. Let him now enter within the Circle and carefully close the openings left in the same, and let him again warn his Disciples, and take the Trumpet of Art prepared as is said in the Chapter concerning the same, and let him incense the Circle towards the Four Quarters of the Universe.

After this let the Magus commence his Incantations, having placed the Sickle, Sword, or other Implement of Art upright in the ground at his feet. Having sounded the trumpet as before taught let him invoke the Spirits, and if need be conjure them, as is said in the First Book, and having attained his desired effect, let him license them to depart.

Here followeth the Form of the Circle (*see Figure* 81), wherein whosoever entereth he shall be at safety as within a fortified Castle, and nothing shall be able to harm him.

BOOK TWO.

CHAPTER X.

CONCERNING INCENSE, SUFFUMIGATIONS, PERFUMES, ODOURS, AND SIMILAR THINGS WHICH ARE USED IN MAGICAL ARTS.

THERE are many kinds of *Incense, Suffumigations,* and *Perfumes,* which are made for and offered unto the Spirits; those which are of sweet odour are for the good, those which are of evil savour are for the evil.

For perfumes of good odour, take thou aloes, nutmeg, gum benjamin, musk, and make a mixture which will give off a good perfume.

EDITOR'S NOTE.—The advanced *Occult* student, and *Disciple of Magical Art,* use VALE OF KASHMAR, the great *Oriental Perfume,* today, instead of the spices mentioned herein. Vale of Kashmar Perfume, owing to its pure and beautiful fragrance, strength, and virtue, is believed to possess wonderful power to attract the *Good Spirits* and banish the *Evil Ones,* and for this very reason is now generally used in all invocations instead of the spices mentioned above. The *Disciple,* of course, can use which he or she chooses, but in case it be not easy or convenient to obtain the spices then you may send to MESSRS. DE LAURENCE, SCOTT & CO., for *Order No.* 504, for a bottle of VALE OF KASHMAR, The *Great Oriental Perfume.* The very same gives forth a subtle, powerful, and beautifully fragrant *Oriental* odor.

For a suitable Suffumigation, thou may burn *Temple Incense,* as it gives forth a most fragrant odour which seems to possess the power to attract the *Good Spirits,* and force the *Evil Ones* to go away from thee; over which thou shalt say:—

THE EXORCISM OF TEMPLE INCENSE.

O God of Abraham, God of Isaac, God of Jacob, deign to bless this odoriferous Incense so that it may receive strength, virtue, and power to attract the *Good Spirits,* and to banish and cause to retire all hostile *Phantoms.* Through Thee, O Most *Holy Adonai,* Who livest and reignest unto the Ages of the Ages. Amen.

I exorcise thee, O Spirit impure and unclean, thou who art a hostile *Phantom,* in the Name of God, that thou quit this *Temple Incense,* thou and all thy deceits, that it may be consecrated and sanctified in the name of God Almighty. May the Holy Spirit of God grant protection and virtue unto those who use *Temple Incense;* and may the hostile and *Evil Spirit* and *Phantom* never be able to enter therein, through the Ineffable Name of God Almighty. *Amen.*

O Lord, deign to bless and to sanctify this *Sacred Incense* so that it may be a remedy unto mankind for the health of body and of soul, through the Invocation of Thy Holy Name. May all Creatures who receive the odour of this *Incense* and of these spices* receive health of body and of soul, through Him Who hath formed the Ages. *Amen.*

After this thou shalt sprinkle the various Spices (or the perfumed handkerchief spoken of in Foot Note below) with the Water of the Art, and thou shalt place them aside in a piece of silk as in other cases, or in a box destined for the purpose, so that thou mayest have them ready prepared for use when necessary.

When thou wishest to use the *Temple Incense,* thou shalt kindle a fire of fresh Incense, in an *Incense Burner,* and the Incense being lighted thou shalt say over it as follows, before putting the Spices or Perfumed handkerchief beside the *Incense Burner:*—

THE EXORCISM OF THE FIRE.

I exorcise thee, O Creature of Fire, by Him through Whom all things have been made, so that every kind of Phantasm may retire from thee, and be unable to harm or deceive in any way, through the Invocation of the Most High Creator of all. Amen.

Bless, O Lord All-Powerful, and All-Merciful, this Creature of Fire, so that being blessed by Thee, it may be for the honour and glory of Thy Most Holy Name, so that it may work no hindrance or evil unto those who use it. Through Thee, O Eternal and Almighty Lord, and through Thy Most Holy Name. Amen.

This being done, thou shalt put the Spices upon the Fire, and make what perfumes and suffumigations thou requirest.

Over Fumigations of evil odour thou shalt say:—

ADONAI, LAZAI, DALMAI, AIMA, ELOHI, O Holy Father, grant unto us succour, favour, and grace, by the Invocation of thy Holy Name, so that these things may serve us for aid in all that we wish to perform therewith, that all deceit may quit them, and that they may be blessed and sanctified through Thy Name. Amen.

---

* Vale of Kashmar, The Great Oriental Perfume, may be used by sprinkling it on a clean handkerchief and placing it beside the Incense, instead of the spices if you prefer it.

BOOK TWO.

CHAPTER XI.

OF THE WATER, AND OF THE HYSSOP.

IF it be necessary to sprinkle with water anything required in the Art it should be done with a Sprinkler.

Prepare a Censer in the day and hour of Mercury, with the odoriferous Spices of the Art. After this thou shalt take a vessel of brass, of lead varnished within and without, or of earth, which thou shalt fill with most clear spring water, and thou shalt have salt, and say these words over the salt :—

TZABAOTH, MESSIACH, EMANUEL, ELOHIM GIBOR, YOD HE VAU HE ; O God, Who art the Truth and the Life, deign to bless and sanctify this Creature of Salt, to serve unto us for help, protection, and assistance in this Art, experiment, and operation, and may it be a succor unto us.

After this cast the salt into the vessel wherein is the Water, and say the following Psalms: cii.; liv.; vi.; lxvii.

Thou shalt then make unto thyself a Sprinkler of vervain, fennel, lavender, sage, valerian, mint, garden-basil, rosemary, and hyssop, gathered in the day and hour of Mercury, the moon being in her increase. Bind together these herbs with a thread spun by a young maiden, and engrave upon the handle on the one side the characters shown in *Figure* 82, and on the other side those given in *Figure* 83.

After this thou mayest use the Water, using the Sprinkler whenever it is necessary; and know that wheresoever thou shalt sprinkle this Water, it will chase away all Phantoms, and they shall be unable to hinder or annoy any. With this same Water thou shalt make all the preparations of the Art.

BOOK TWO.

CHAPTER XII.

OF THE LIGHT, AND OF THE FIRE.

IT hath been ever the custom among all nations to use fire and light in sacred things. For this reason the Master of the Art should also employ them in sacred rites, and besides those for reading the Conjurations by, and for the incense, in all operations Lights are necessary in the Circle.

For this reason he should make candles of virgin wax in the day and hour of Mercury; the wicks should have been made by a young girl; and the Candles should be made when the moon is in her increase, of the weight of half a pound each, and on them thou shalt engrave these characters with the Dagger, or the Burin of Art. (*See Figure* 84.)

After this thou shalt repeat over the Candles, * *Psalms cli.; ciii.; cvii., and shalt say:*—

O Lord God, Who governest all things by Thine Almighty Power, give unto me, a poor sinner, understanding and knowledge to do only that which is agreeable unto Thee; grant unto me to fear, adore, love, praise and give thanks unto Thee with true and sincere faith and perfect charity. Grant, O Lord, before I die, and descend into the realms beneath, and before the fiery flame shall devour me, that Thy Grace may not leave me, O Lord of my Soul. Amen.

After this thou shalt add:—

I exorcise thee, O Creature of wax, by Him Who alone hath created all things by His Word, and by the virtue of Him Who is pure truth, that thou cast out from thee every Phantasm, Perversion, and Deceit of the Enemy, and may the Virtue and Power of God enter into thee, so that thou mayest give us light, and chase far from us all fear or terror.

After this thou shalt sprinkle them with the Water of the Art, and incense them with the usual perfumes.

And when thou shalt wish to kindle them thou shalt say:—

I exorcise thee, O Creature of Fire, in the Name of the Sovereign and Eternal Lord, by His Ineffable Name, which is YOD, HE, VAU, HE; by the Name IAH; and by the Name of Power EL; that thou mayest enlighten the heart of all the Spirits which we shall call unto this Circle, so that they may appear before us without fraud and deceit through Him Who hath created all things.

Then thou shalt take a square Lantern, with panes of Crystal glass, and thou shalt fit therein the Candle lighted, to read by, to form the Circle, or any other purpose for which thou shalt require it.

---

* Special Waxen Candles may be obtained from Messrs. de Laurence, Scott & Co., if it is not convenient to construct the kind mentioned above. Many students are using the candles with good results. See Order No. 131.

BOOK TWO.

CHAPTER XIII.

CONCERNING THE PRECEPTS OF THE ART.

HE who hath attained the rank or degree of Exorcist, which we are usually accustomed to call Magus or Master* according to grade, whensoever he desireth to undertake any operation, for the nine days immediately preceding the commencement of the work, should put aside from him all uncleanness, and prepare himself in secret during these days, and prepare all the things necessary, and in the space of these days all these should be made, consecrated, and exorcised.

The which being duly completed, let him go on the day and hour of the commencement of the work, unto the place set apart for the same, as hath been said, in the place concerning the formation of the Circle. Let him instruct his Disciples on no cause whatsoever to move from their assigned places. And the Magus should exhort them with a bold and confident voice as follows:—

THE EXHORTATION OF THE COMPANIONS.

Fear ye not, my beloved Companions, seeing that we draw near unto the desired end; therefore, all things being rightly done and the Conjurations and Exorcisms diligently performed, ye shall behold Kings of Kings, and Emperors of Emperors, and other Kings, Princes, and Majesties with them, and a great crowd of followers, together with all sorts of musical instruments, yet nothing should either the Magus or his Disciples fear.

And then let the Magus say:—

I exhort you by these Holy Names of God, ELOHIM, ADONAI, AGLA, that none of you now presume to move or cross over from your appointed stations.

This being said, let the *Magus* and his *Disciples* uncover the *Holy Pentacles* and show them towards each quarter, and they being shown in each place, there shall be noises and rushings.

Then shall the Emperor of (the Spirits) say unto you:—From the time of the Great Addus until now, there hath not been an Exorciser who could behold my person, and unless those things† which ye have showed unto us hath been made, ye would not now have seen me. But seeing that

* This Chapter is only given in 10,862 Add. MSS.
† The Pentacles.

ye have powerfully called us, as I believe, by the rites derived from Solomon, and which but few of your comrades, or Exorcisers, possess, also they compel us against our will, and I therefore say unto thee that we wish to be obedient in all matters.

Then shall the Magus place the petitions of himself and his companions, which should be written down clearly on virgin card, or paper, beyond the Circle towards the King or Prince of the Spirits, and he will receive it and take counsel with his Chiefs. After this he will return the Card, saying:—That which thou desirest is accomplished, be thy will performed, and all thy demands fulfilled.

BOOK TWO.

CHAPTER XIV.

OF THE PEN, INK, AND COLOURS.

ALL things employed for writing, &c., in this Art, should be prepared in the following manner:

Thou shalt take a male gosling, from which thou shalt pluck the third feather of the right wing, and in plucking it thou shalt say:—

ADRAI, HAHLII, TAMAII, TILONAS, ATHAMAS, ZIANOR, ADONAI, banish from this pen all deceit and error, so that it may be of virtue and efficacy to write all that I desire. Amen.

After this thou shalt sharpen it with the penknife of the Art, perfume it, sprinkle it, and place it aside in a silken cloth.

Thou shalt have an Inkstand made of earth or any convenient matter, and in the day and hour of Mercury thou shalt engrave thereon with the Burin of Art these Names:—Yod, He, Vau, He, Metatron, Iah Iah Iah, Qadosch, Elohim Tzabaoth (see Figure 85); and in putting the ink therein thou shalt say:—

I exorcise thee, O Creature of Ink, by ANAIRETON, by SIMULATOR, and by the Name ADONAI, and by the Name of Him through Whom all things were made, that thou be unto me an aid and succor in all things which I wish to perform by thine aid.

As it sometimes happeneth that it is necessary to write with some noble color, it is well to have a new and clean box wherein to keep them. The principal colors will be Yellow or Gold, Red, Celestial or Azure Blue, Green, and Brown; and any other colors that may be requisite. Thou shalt exorcise, perfume, and sprinkle them in the usual manner.

BOOK TWO.

CHAPTER XV.

OF THE PEN OF THE SWALLOW AND OF THE CROW.

TAKE the feather of a Swallow or of a Crow, and before plucking it thou shalt say:—

May Holy MICHAEL the Archangel of God, and MIDAEL and MIRAEL, the Chiefs and Captains of the Celestial Army, be my aid in the operation I am about to perform, so that I may write herewith all things which are necessary, and that all the experiments which I commence herewith may through you and through your names be perfected by the power of the Most High Creator. Amen.

After this thou shalt point and complete the pen with the Knife of the Art, and with the pen and ink of the art thou shalt write upon its side the Name, ANAIRETON (*see Figure* 86), and thou shalt say over it the following Psalms: cxxxiii.; cxvii.

BOOK TWO.

CHAPTER XVI.

OF THE BLOOD OF THE BAT, PIGEON, AND OTHER ANIMALS.

Take a living Bat and exorcise it thus:—

THE EXORCISM OF THE BAT.

CAMIACH, EOMIAHE, EMIAL, MACBAL, EMOII, ZAZEAN, MAIPHIAT, ZACRATH, TENDAC, VULAMAHI; by these Most Holy Names, and the other Names of Angels which are written in the Book ASSAMAIAN,* I conjure thee O Bat (or whatever animal it may be) that thou assist me in this operation, by God the True, God the Holy, the God Who hath created thee, and by Adam, Who hath imposed thy true name upon thee and upon all other animated beings.

After this, take the Needle or other convenient Instrument of Art, as will be said later on, and pierce the bat in the vein which is in the right wing; and collect the blood in a small vessel over the which thou shalt say:—

Almighty ADONAI, ARATHRON, ASHAI, ELOHIM, ELOHI, ELION, ASHER EHEIEH, SHADDAI, O God the Lord, immaculate, immutable, EMANUEL, MESSIACH, YOD, HE, VAU, HE, be my aid, so that this blood may have power and efficacy in all wherein I shall wish, and in all that I shall demand.

Perfume it and keep it for use.

The blood of other winged animals may be taken in the same manner, with the proper solemnities.

I cannot too strongly impress on the readers of this volume that the use of blood is more or less connected with Black Magic; and that it should be avoided as much as possible.—DR. de LAURENCE.

* The "Sepher Ha-Shamaiim," or "Book of the Heavens."

BOOK TWO.

CHAPTER XVII.

OF VIRGIN PARCHMENT, OR VIRGIN PAPER, AND HOW IT SHOULD BE PREPARED.

VIRGIN *Parchment Paper,* made from the skin of dead-born lambs, which is new, pure, clean, and exorcised, never having served for any other purpose.

Genuine Virgin Parchment is necessary in many *Magical Operations,* and should be properly prepared and consecrated. There are two kinds, one called *Virgin,* the other *Unborn. Virgin Parchment* is that which is taken from an Animal which hath not attained the age of generation, whether it be ram, or kid, or other animal.

Unborn Parchment is taken from an animal which hath been taken before its time from the uterus of its mother.

Take whichsoever of these two classes of animals thou pleasest, provided only that it be male, and in the day and hour of Mercury; and take it to a secret place where no man may see thee at work. Thou shalt have a marsh-reed cut at a single stroke with a new knife, and thou shalt strip from it the leaves, repeating this Conjuration:—

THE CONJURATION OF THE REED.

I conjure thee by the Creator of all things, and by the King of Angels, Whose Name is EL SHADDAI, that thou receivest strength and virtue to flay this animal and to construct the parchment whereon I may write the Holy Names of God, and that it may acquire so great virtue that all which I shall write or do may obtain its effect, through Him who liveth unto the Eternal Ages. Amen.

Before cutting the Reed recite Psalm lxxii.:—

After this, with the Knife of the Art, thou shalt fashion the Reed into the shape of a Knife, and upon it thou shalt write these Names: AGLA, ADONAI, ELOHI (*see Figure* 87), through Whom be the work of this Knife accomplished. Then thou shalt say:—

O God, Who drewest Moses, Thy well-beloved and Thine elect, from among the Reeds on the marshy banks of the Nile, and from the Waters, he being yet but a child, grant unto me through Thy great mercy and compassion that this Reed may receive Power and Virtue to effect that which I desire through Thy Holy Name and the Names of Thy Holy Angels. Amen.

This being done, thou shalt commence with this Knife to flay the Animal, whether it be Virgin or Unborn, saying:—

ZOHAR, ZIO, TALMAÏ, ADONAI, SHADDAI, TETRAGRAMMATON, and

ye Holy Angels of God; be present, and grant power and virtue unto this parchment, and may it be consecrated by you, so that all things which I shall write thereon shall obtain their effect. Amen.

The Animal being flayed, take Salt, and say thus over it:—

God of Gods, and Lord of Lords, Who hast created all things from Negative Existence, deign to bless and sanctify this Salt, so that in placing it upon this parchment which I wish to make, it may have such virtue that whatsoever I may write on it hereafter may attain its desired end. Amen.

Afterwards rub the said parchment with the exorcised salt, and leave it in the Sun, to imbibe this salt for the space of an entire day. Then take a large earthen vessel glazed within and without, round the outside of which thou shalt write the characters in *Figure* 88.

After this thou shalt put powdered lime into the vessel, saying:—

OROII, ZARON, ZAINON, ZEVARON, ZAHIPHIL, ELION, be ye present and bless this work so that it may attain the desired effect, through the King of the Heavens, and the God of the Angels. Amen.

Take then exorcised Water and pour it upon the said lime, and place the skin therein for three days, after which thou shalt take it thence, and scrape therefrom the lime and flesh adhering, with the Knife of Reed.

After this thou shalt cut, with a single stroke, a Wand of Hazel, long enough for thee to form a Circle therewith; take also a cord spun by a young maiden, and small stones or pebbles from a brook, pronouncing these words:—

O God Adonai, Holy and Powerful Father, put virtue into these stones, that they may serve to stretch this parchment, and to chase therefrom all fraud, and may it obtain virtue by Thine Almighty Power.

After this, having stretched the said parchment upon the Circle and bound it with the cord and stones, thou shalt say:

AGLA, YOD, HE, VAU, HE, IAH, EMANUEL, bless and preserve this parchment, so that no Phantasm may enter therein.

Let it dry thus for three days in a dark and shady place, then cut the cord with the Knife of Art, and detach the Parchment from the Circle, saying.—

ANTOR, ANCOR, TURLOS, BEODONOS, PHAIAR, APHARCAR, be present for a guard unto this Parchment.

Then perfume it, and keep it in silk ready for use.

No woman, if her flowers be upon her, should be permitted to see this *Parchment*; otherwise it will lose its virtue. He who maketh it should be pure, clean, and prepared.

But if the preparation of the aforesaid parchment seemeth too tedious, thou mayest make it in the following manner, but it is not so good.

Take any Parchment, and exorcise it; prepare a censer with perfumes; write upon the parchment the characters in *Figure* 89, hold it over the Incense, and say:—

Be ye present to aid me, and may my operation be accomplished through you; ZAZAII, ZALMAII, DALMAII, ADONAI, ANAPHAXETON, CEDRION, CRIPON, PRION, ANAIRETON, ELION, OCTINOMON, ZEVANION, ALAZAION, ZIDEON, AGLA, ON, YOD HE VAU HE, ARTOR, DINOTOR, Holy Angels of God; be present and infuse virtue into this Parchment, so that it may obtain such power through you that all Names or Characters thereon written may receive due power, and that all deceit and hindrance may depart therefrom, through God the Lord merciful and gracious, Who liveth and reigneth through all the Ages.   Amen.

Then shalt thou recite over the parchment Psalms lxxii.; cxvii.; and cxxiv.; and the *"Benedicite Omnia Opera."*   Then say:—

I conjure thee, *O Virgin Parchment,* by all the Holy Names, that thou obtainest efficacy and strength, and becomest exorcised and consecrated, so that none of the things which may be written upon thee shall be effaced from the Book of Truth.   Amen.

Then sprinkle it, and keep it as before said.

The Cauls of newly-born children, duly consecrated, may also be used instead of *Virgin Parchment.*   Also paper, satin, silk, and the like substances, may be employed in operations of less importance if duly exorcised and consecrated.

BOOK TWO.

CHAPTER XVIII.

Of Wax and Virgin Earth.

WAX and Virgin Earth are also employed in many Magical Operations, whether to make Images, or Candles, or other things; therefore they should never have been put to any other use. The Earth should be dug up with thine own hands, and reduced to a paste, without touching it with any instrument whatever, so that it be not defiled thereby.

The Wax should be taken from bees which have only made it for the first time, and it should never have been employed for any other purpose; and when thou shalt wish it to avail thyself of the one or the other, thou shalt before commencing the work repeat the following conjuration:—

CONJURATION.

EXTABOR, HETABOR, SITTACIBOR, ADONAI, ONZO, ZOMEN, MENOR, ASMODAL, ASCOBAI, COMATOS, ERIONAS, PROFAS, ALKOMAS, CONAMAS, PAPUENDOS, OSIANDOS, ESPIACENT, DAMNATH, EHERES, GOLADES, TELANTES, COPHI, ZADES, ye Angels of God be present, for I invoke ye in my work, so that through you it may find virtue and accomplishment. Amen.

After this repeat Psalms cxxxi.; xv.; cii.; viii.; lxxxiv.; lxviii.; lxxii.; cxxxiii.; cxiii.; cxxvi.; xlvi.; xlvii.; xxii.; li.; cxxx.; cxxxix.; xlix.; cx.; liii.; and say:—

I exorcise thee, O Creature of Wax (or of Earth), that through the Holy Name of God and His Holy Angels thou receive blessing, so that thou mayest be sanctified and blessed, and obtain the virtue which we desire, through the Most Holy Name of ADONAI. Amen.

Sprinkle the wax and put it aside for use; but take note that the Earth which should be dug up with thy hands should be prepared every time thou hast need thereof.

BOOK TWO.

CHAPTER XIX.

CONCERNING THE NEEDLE AND OTHER IRON INSTRUMENTS.

THERE are several steel instruments necessary in various Operations, as a Needle to prick or to sew; a Burin, or instrument wherewith to engrave, &c.

Thou shalt make such instruments in the day and hour of Jupiter, and when it is finished thou shalt say: —

I conjure thee, O Instrument of Steel, by God the Father Almighty, by the Virtue of the Heavens, of the Stars, and of the Angels who preside over them; by the virtue of stones, herbs, and animals; by the virtue of hail, snow, and wind; that thou receivest such virtue that thou mayest obtain without deceit the end which I desire in all things where I shall use thee; through God the Creator of the Ages, and Emperor of the Angels. Amen.

Afterwards repeat Psalms iii.; ix.; xxxi.; xlii.; lx.; li.; cxxx.

Perfume it with the perfumes of the Art, and sprinkle it with exorcised water, wrap it in silk and say:—

DANI, ZUMECH, AGALMATUROD, GADIEL, PANI, CANELOAS, MEROD, GAMIDOI, BALDOI, METRATOR, Angels most holy, be present for a guard unto this instrument.

BOOK TWO.

CHAPTER XX.

CONCERNING THE SILKEN CLOTH.

WHEN any Instrument of the Art is properly consecrated, it should be wrapped in silk and put away, as we have said.

Take, then, silk of any color except black or grey, whereon write the words and Characters in *Figure* 90.

Perfume it with incense of good odor, sprinkle it, and recite Psalms lxxxii.; lxxii.; cxxxiv.; lxiv.

After this thou shalt put it aside for seven days with sweet spices; and thou shalt use this silk to wrap all the instruments of the Art.

BOOK TWO.

CHAPTER XXI.

CONCERNING CHARACTERS, AND THE CONSECRATION OF THE MAGICAL BOOK.

WHENSOEVER in any Operation it is necessary to write Characters, and thou fearest that thou wilt fail, do this: Write at the beginning the Name EHEIEH ASHER EHEIEH (*Figure* 91), and at the end the name AIN SOPH (*Figure* 92); between these Names write what thou wishest, and if thou hast anything especial to do bear the said written Names upon the wrapper in silk, and thou shalt say over them:—

Most Wise and Most High Creator of all things, I pray Thee for Thy grace and mercy that Thou mayest grant such virtue and power unto these Holy Names, that Thou mayest keep these characters from all deceit and error, through Thee, O Most Holy ADONAI. Amen.

After having repeated this thou shalt write the requisite Characters, and thou shalt not fail, but shall attain thy desired end.

THE CONSECRATION OF THE BOOK.

Make a Book, containing sixteen pages, from Virgin Parchment, and write therein, with red ink, the Prayers for all the Operations,* the Names of the Angels in the form of Litanies, their Seals and Characters; the which being done thou shalt consecrate the same unto God and unto the pure Spirits in the manner following:—

Thou shalt set in the destined place a small table covered with a white cloth, whereon thou shalt lay the Book opened at the *Great Pentacle* which should be drawn on the first leaf of the said Book; and having kindled a lamp which should be suspended above the center of the table, thou shalt surround the said table with a white curtain; clothe thyself in the proper vestments, and holding the Book open, repeat upon thy knees the following prayer with great humility:—

(For the Prayer beginning "Adonai Elohim," &c., see Book I., Chapter XIV., where it is given in full.)

After which thou shalt incense it with the incense proper to the Planet and the day, and thou shalt replace the Book on the aforesaid Table, taking heed that the fire of the lamp be kept up continually during the operation, and keeping the curtains closed. Repeat the same ceremony for seven days, beginning with Saturday, and perfuming the Book each day with the Incense proper to the Planet ruling the day and hour, and taking heed that the lamp shall burn both day and night; after the

---

* The rest of this Chapter is from 1203 Lansdowne MSS.

which thou shalt shut up the Book in a small drawer under the table, made expressly for it, until thou shalt have occasion to use it; and every time that thou wishest to use it, clothe thyself with thy vestments, kindle the lamp, and repeat upon thy knees the aforesaid prayer, "*Adonai Elohim.*" &c.

It is necessary also, in the Consecration of the Book, to summon all the Angels whose Names are written therein in the form of Litanies, the which thou shalt do with devotion; and even if the Angels and Spirits appear not in the Consecration of the Book, be not thou astonished thereat, seeing that they are of a pure nature, and consequently have much difficulty in familiarizing themselves with men who are inconstant and impure, but the Ceremonies and Characters being correctly carried out devoutedly and with perseverance, they will be constrained to come, and it will at length happen that at thy first invocation thou wilt be able to see and communicate with them. But I advise thee to undertake nothing unclean or impure, for then thy importunity, far from attracting them, will only serve to chase them from thee; and it will be thereafter exceedingly difficult for thee to attract them for use for pure ends.

EDITOR'S NOTE.—*Those wishing Virgin Parchment sufficient to make this sixteen-page book may send to* The de Laurence Company *for* Order No. 292, *which consists of eight sheets, or sixteen pages of Virgin Parchment; but if you wish to make the Book mentioned herein you must state plainly in your order that you want the Parchment made into a Book by being stapled. Just send for Order No. 292 and state that you want it stapled into a book. This Virgin Parchment, after being made into a Book on your order, is not returnable.*

BOOK TWO.

CHAPTER XXII.

CONCERNING SACRIFICES TO THE SPIRITS, AND HOW THEY SHOULD BE MADE.

IN many operations it is necessary to make some sort of sacrifice unto the Demons, and in various ways. Sometimes white animals are sacrificed to the good Spirits and black to the evil. Such sacrifices consist of the blood and sometimes of the flesh.

They who sacrifice animals, of whatsoever kind they be, should select those which are virgin, as being more agreeable unto the Spirits, and rendering them more obedient.

When blood is to be sacrificed it should be drawn also from virgin quadrupeds or birds, but before offering the oblation, say:—

May this Sacrifice which we find it proper to offer unto ye, noble and lofty Beings, be agreeable and pleasing unto your desires; be ye ready to obey us, and ye shall receive greater ones.

Then perfume and sprinkle it according to the rules of Art.

When it is necessary, with all the proper Ceremonies, to make Sacrifices of fire, they should be made of wood which hath some quality referring especially unto the Spirits invoked; as juniper of pine unto the Spirits of Saturn; box, or oak, unto those of Jupiter; cornel, or cedar, unto those of Mars; laurel unto those of the Sun; myrtle unto those of Venus; hazel unto those of Mercury; and willow unto those of the Moon.

But when we make sacrifices of food and drink, everything necessary should be prepared without the circle, and the meats should be covered with some fine clean cloth, and have also a clean white cloth spread beneath them; with new bread and good and sparkling wine, but in all things those which refer to the nature of the Planet. Animals, such as fowls or pigeons, should be roasted. Especially shouldst thou have a vessel of clear and pure fountain water, and before thou enterest into the Circle, thou shalt summon the Spirits by their proper Names, or at least those chief among them, saying:—

In whatsoever place ye may be, ye Spirits, who are invited to this feast, come ye and be ready to receive our offerings, presents, and sacrifices, and ye shall have hereafter yet more agreeable oblations.

First perfume the room by burning Temple Incense therein, and sprinkle the viands with *exorcised water;* then commence to conjure the Spirits until they shall come.

This is the manner of making sacrifices in all arts and operations wherein it is necessary, and acting thus, the Spirits will be prompt to serve thee.

Here endeth our *"Key,"* the which if thou thoroughly instillest into thy memory, thou shalt be able, if it pleaseth thee, even to fly with the wings of the wind. But if thou takest little heed hereof, and despiseth this Book, never shalt thou attain unto the desired end in any Magical experiment or operation whatsoever.

For in this Book is comprised all science of Magical Art, and it should be strictly kept by thee. And hereunto is the end of our *"Key,"* in the Name of God the righteous, the merciful, and the eternal, Who liveth and reigneth throughout the Ages. Amen.

THE END OF THE KEY OF SOLOMON THE KING.

ANCIENT FRAGMENT OF THE KEY OF SOLOMON,

TRANSLATED FROM THE HEBREW BY ELIPHAZ LEVI; *And Given In His "Philosophe Occulte."—Serie II, Page 136.*

I will now give unto thee the Key of the Kingdom of the Spirits.

This Key is the same as that of the Mysterious Numbers of Yetzirah.*

The Spirits are governed by the natural and universal Hierarchy of things.

Three command Three through the medium of Three.

There are the Spirits of Above, those of Below, and those of the Center; then if thou investest the Sacred Ladder, if thou descendest instead of ascending, thou wilt discover the Counter-Hierarchy of the Shells, or of the Dead Spirits.

Know thou only that the Principalities of Heaven, the Virtues, and the Powers, are not Persons, but dignities.

They are the Degrees of the Sacred Ladder upon which the Spirits ascend and descend.

Michael, Gabriel, Raphael, and the others, are not Names but Titles.

The First of the Numbers is the Unity.

The First of the Divine Conceptions called the *Sephiroth* is Kether or the Crown.

The First Category of the Spirits is that of Chaioth Ha-Qadesh or the Intelligences of the Divine Tetragram, whose Letters are symbolized by the Mysterious Animals in the Prophecy of Ezekiel.

Their empire is that of unity and synthesis. They correspond to the Intelligence.

They have for adversaries the *Thamiel* or Double-Headed Ones, the Demons of revolt and of anarchy, whose two Chiefs, ever at War with each other, are *Satan* and *Moloch*.

The Second Number is two; the Second Sephira is Chokmah or Wisdom.

The Spirits of Wisdom are the Auphanim, a Name which signifieth the Wheels, because all acts in Heaven like immense Wheels spangled with Stars. Their Empire is that of Harmony. They correspond to the Reason.

* The "Sepher Yetzirah," or "Book of Formation," one of the most ancient Books of the Qabalah.

They have for Adversaries the *Chaigidel*, or the Shells which attach themselves to Material and Lying Appearances. Their Chief, or rather their Guide, for Evil Spirits obey no one, is *Beelzebub*, whose Name signifieth the God of Flies, because Flies haunt putrefying corpses.

The third Number is three. The third Sephira is Binah or Understanding.

The Spirits of Binah are Aralim, or the Strong. Their empire is the creation of ideas; they correspond to activity and energy of thought.

They have for adversaries the *Satariel*, or concealers, the Demons of absurdity, of intellectual inertia, and of Mystery. The Chief of the *Satariel* is *Lucifuge*, called falsely and by anti-phrase *Lucifer* (as the Eumenides, who are the Furies, are called in Greek the Gracious Ones).

The fourth Number is four. The fourth Sephira is Gedulah or Chesed, Magnificence or Mercy.

The Spirits of Gedulah are the Chaschmalim, or the Lucid Ones. Their empire is that of beneficence; they correspond to the imagination.

They have for adversaries the *Gamchicoth* or the Disturbers of Souls. The Chief or Guide of these Demons is *Ashtaroth* or *Astarte*, the impure Venus of the Syrians, whom they represent with the head of an ass or of a bull, and the breasts of a woman.

The fifth Number is five. The fifth Sephira is Geburah or Justice.

The Spirits of Geburah are the Seraphim, or the Spirits burning with zeal. Their empire is that of the chastisement of crimes. They correspond to the faculty of comparing and of choosing.

They have for adversaries the *Golab or incendiaries*, Genii of wrath and sedition, whose Chief is *Asmodeus*, whom they also call Samael the Black.

The sixth Number is six. The sixth Sephira is Tiphereth the Supreme Beauty.

The Spirits of Tiphereth are the Malachim, or the Kings. Their empire is that of the Universal Harmony. They correspond to the judgment.

They have for adversaries the *Tagaririm*, or Disputers, whose Chief is *Belphegor*.

The seventh Number is seven. The seventh Sephira is Netzach, or Victory.

The Spirits of Netzach is the Elohim or the Gods, that is to say the representatives of God. Their empire is that of progress and of life; they correspond to the *Sensorium* or to sensibility.

They have for adversaries the *Harab-Serapel*, or the Ravens of Death, whose Chief is Baal.

The eighth Number is eight. The eighth Sephira is Hod or eternal order.

The Spirits of Hod are the Beni-Elohim or Sons of the Gods. Their empire is that of order; they correspond to the inner sense.

They have for adversaries the *Samael* or jugglers, whose Chief is *Adramelech.*

The ninth Number is nine. The ninth Sephira is Yesod, or the fundamental principle.

The Spirits of Yesod are the Cherubim or Angels, those powers which fecundate the earth, and which are represented in Hebrew symbolism under the form of bulls. Their empire is that of fecundity. They correspond to true ideas.

They have for adversaries the *Gamaliel* or obscene, whose Queen is *Lilith,* the Demon of debaucheries.

The tenth Number is ten. The tenth Sephira is Malkuth, or the kingdom of forms.

The Spirits of Malkuth are the Ischim, or the virile ones; they are the souls of the Saints whose Chief is Moses. (Let us not forget that it is Solomon who speaks.—Eliphaz Lévi.)

They have for adversaries the wicked ones who obey *Nahema,* the Demon of Impurity.

The wicked are symbolized by the five accursed nations whom Joshua was to destroy.

Joshua, or Jehoshua the Saviour, is a symbol of the Messiach.

His Name is composed of the letters of the Divine Tetragram changed into the Pentagram by the addition of the Letter Schin (*see Figure* 94).

Each letter of this Pentagram represents a power of good attacked by the five accursed nations.

For the real history of the people of God is the allegorical legend of Humanity.

The five accursed nations are:—

1. The Amalekites or Aggressors;
2. The Geburim or Violent Ones;
3. The Raphaim or Cowards;
4. The Nephilim or Voluptuous Ones;
5. The Anakim or Anarchists.

The Anarchists are vanquished by the Yod, which is the Sceptre of the Father.

The Violent are vanquished by the Hé, which is the Gentleness of the Mother.

The Cowards are vanquished by the Vau, which is the Sword of Michael, and Generation by travail and pain.

The Voluptuous are vanquished by the second Hé, which is the painful bringing forth of the Mother.

Lastly, the Aggressors are vanquished by the Schin, which is the Fire of the Lord and the equilibrating Law of Justice.

The Princes of the Perverse Spirits are the False Gods whom they adore.

Hell has then no other government than that fatal law which punishes perversity and corrects error, for the false Gods only exist in the false opinion of their adorers.

Baal, Belphegor, Moloch, Adramelech, have been the idols of the Syrians; idols without soul, idols now destroyed, and of whom the Name alone remaineth.

The True God hath vanquished all the Demons as Truth triumphs over Error. That is past in the opinions of men, and the Wars of Michael against Satan are the symbols of movement, and of the progress of Spirits.

The Devil is ever a God of refusal.

Accredited idolatries are religions in their time.

Superannuated idolatries are Superstitions and Sacrileges.

The Pantheon of Phantoms, which are then in vogue, is the Heaven of the Ignorant.

The Receptacle of Phantoms, whom Folly even wisheth for no longer, is the Hell.

But all this existeth only in the Imagination of the Vulgar.

For the Wise, Heaven is the Supreme Reason, and Hell is Folly.

But it must be understood that we here employ the word Heaven in the Mystical sense which we give it in opposing to it the word Hell.

In order to evoke Phantoms it is sufficient to intoxicate oneself or to render oneself mad; for Phantoms are ever the companions of drunkenness and of vertigo.

The Phosphorus of the imagination, abandoned to all the caprices of over-excited and diseased nerves, fills itself with Monsters and absurd visions.

We can also arrive at hallucination by mingling together wakefulness and sleep by the graduated use of narcotics; but such actions are crimes against nature.

Wisdom chaseth away Phantoms, and enables us to communicate with the Superior Spirits by the contemplation of the Laws of Nature and the study of the Holy Numbers.

(Here King Solomon addresseth himself to his son, Roboam) :—

Do thou, O my son Roboam, remember, that the Fear of Adonai is only the beginning of Wisdom.

Keep and preserve those who have not Understanding in the Fear of Adonai, which will give and will preserve unto thee my crown.

But learn to triumph thyself over Fear by Wisdom, and the Spirits will descend from Heaven to serve thee.

I, SOLOMON, thy father, King of Israel and of Palmyra, I have sought out and obtained in my lot the Holy Chokmah, which is the Wisdom of Adonai.

And I have become King of the Spirits as well of Heaven as of Earth, Master of the Dwellers of the Air, and of the Living Souls of the Sea, because I was in possession of the Key of the Hidden Gates of Light.

I have done great things by the virtue of the Schema Hamphorasch, and by the Thirty-two Paths of Yetzirah.

Number, weight, and measure determine the form of things; the substance is one, and God createth it eternally.

Happy is he who comprehendeth the Letters and the Numbers.

The Letters are from the Numbers, and the Numbers from the Ideas, and the Ideas from the Forces, and the Forces from the Elohim. The Synthesis of the Elohim is the Schema.

The Schema is one, its columns are two, its power is three, its form is four, its reflection giveth eight, which multiplied by three giveth unto thee the twenty-four Thrones of Wisdom.

Upon each Throne reposeth a Crown with three Rays, each Ray beareth a Name, each Name is an Absolute Idea. There are Seventy-two Names upon the Twenty-four Crowns of the Schema.

Thou shalt write these Names upon Thirty-six Talismans, two upon each Talisman, one on each side.

Thou shalt divide these Talismans into four series of nine each, according to the number of the Letters of the Schema.

Upon the first Series thou shalt engrave the Letter Yod, symbolized by the Flowering Rod of Aaron.

Upon the second the Letter Hé, symbolized by the Cup of Joseph.

Upon the third the Letter Vau, symbolized by the Sword of David my father.

And upon the fourth the Hé final, symbolized by the Shekel of Gold.

These thirty-six Talismans will be a Book which will contain all the Secrets of Nature. And by their diverse combinations thou shalt make the Genii and Angels speak.

HERE ENDETH THE FRAGMENT OF THE KEY OF SOLOMON.

PLATE XV.

The Mystical Alphabets.

114½

Hebrew Alphabet.	Alphabet of the Magi.	The Characters of Celestial Writing.	Malachim or the Writing of the Angels	The Writing called "Passing the River"	Names of the Letters.		The Powers of the Letters.	
					Aleph	Samekh	a'	s
					Beth	Ayin.	b th v	o aa ng
					Gimel	Pé	g gh	p ph
					Daleth	Tzaddi	d dh th	tz
					Hé	Qoph	hˀ	q qh
					Vau	Resh	v u o	r
					Zaïn	Schin	z	s sh
					Cheth	Tau	ch gut.	t th
	Finals.				Teth		t	
				Another form of Samekh	Yod	Final Kaph	i y	k
					Kaph	Final Mem	k kh	m
					Lamed	Final Nun	l	n
					Mem	Final Pé	m	p
					Nun	Final Tzaddi	n	tz

THE QABALISTICAL INVOCATION OF SOLOMON.

Given by Eliphaz Lévi in "Rituel de la Haute Magie," Chapter xiii.

POWERS of the Kingdom, be beneath my left foot, and within my right hand.

Glory and Eternity touch my shoulders, and guide me in the Paths of Victory.

Mercy and Justice be ye the Equilibrium and splendor of my life.

Understanding and Wisdom give unto me the Crown.

Spirits of Malkuth conduct me between the two columns whereon is supported the whole edifice of the Temple.

Angels of Netzach and of Hod strengthen me upon the Cubical Stone of Yesod.

O GEDULAHEL! O GEBURAHEL! O TIPHERETH!

BINAHEL, be Thou my Love!

RUACH CHOKMAHEL, be Thou my Light!

Be that which Thou art, and that which Thou willest to be, O KETHERIEL!

Ishim, assist me in the Name of SHADDAI.

Cherubim, be my strength in the Name of ADONAI.

Beni Elohim, be ye my brethren in the Name of the Son, and by the virtues of TZABAOTH.

Elohim, fight for me in the Name of TETRAGRAMMATON.

Malachim, protect me in the Name of YOD HE VAU HE.

Seraphim, purify my love in the Name of ELOAH.

Chaschmalim, enlighten me with the splendors of ELOHI, and of SCHECHINAH.

Aralim, act ye; *Auphanim,* revolve and shine.

Chaioth Ha-Qadosch, cry aloud, speak, roar, and groan; Qadosch, Qadosch, Qadosch, SHADDAI, ADONAI, YOD CHAVAH, EHEIEH ASHER EHEIEH!

Halelu-Yah! Halelu-Yah! Halelu-Yah. Amen.

Conclusion: On Power, Symbol, and the Return to Source

The *Greater Key of Solomon* stands as one of the most influential ritual manuals in the Western esoteric tradition, blending biblical invocations, angelic and divine names, and ceremonial protocols into a system designed to mediate between the human will and the unseen powers. Its pages, dense with references to the Psalms, scriptural formulae, and ritual requisites, reveal a worldview in which language, material, and intention are interwoven into a single act of symbolic creation.

While originally framed as an instrument for divine petition and the command of spirits, the *Greater Key* now exists far beyond the confines of the ritual chamber. Artists, writers, game designers, musicians, philosophers, and students of comparative religion encounter in it not only a manual of magic but a lexicon of archetypes—adaptable, enduring, and aesthetically potent. Its tools and formulas can be, and often have been, repurposed: for political awakening, spiritual resistance, and cultural expression. History offers countless examples of sacred systems reinterpreted to oppose empire, subvert orthodoxy, or give form to the ineffable through art and myth.

Yet, such symbolic potency is never without risk. The very structures that can inspire transformation may also destabilize. In ceremonial contexts, prolonged engagement without grounding can blur the line between inspiration and obsession; synchronicities may shift from affirmation to oppression; the self can erode into delusion. At that threshold, the operative's duty is not to press forward but to withdraw. Silence becomes the higher magic.

The path of return is simple, though rarely easy:
Still the mind. Empty the assumptions. Begin again.

Read the Scriptures—not as cipher or code, but plainly, from Genesis to Revelation, without omission. Allow the text to reframe your narrative faculties. Fast if you are able; limit sensory overload; step away from the public stage. In this state of deliberate reduction, even the most complex magical architecture can be dismantled and the foundation reset.

For this reason, I have collaborated with Joseph Lumpkin and Fifth Estate Publishing to produce *The Universal Bible*—a compendium of all ninety-five books recognized by the seven churches of early Christianity. This work, encompassing far more than the sixty-six books of the King James Version, offers a complete spiritual framework—an anchor for the mystical, the moral, the practical, and the esoteric. It restores to the seeker a fixed point from which to discern and recalibrate, whether their journey began in a cathedral, a conjuration circle, or the pages of an old grimoire.

If the disquiet is urgent—if fear, instability, or confusion dominate—seek help without hesitation: call emergency services, consult a trusted elder in your tradition, or find a guide trained to redirect and balance forces beyond your current grasp.

The *Greater Key of Solomon* is not merely a relic of medieval magic. It is a mirror—reflecting both the creative and destructive capacities of the human spirit. It may inspire a work of art, a rebellion of conscience, or a lifetime of devotion. But its deepest wisdom lies in the paradox it embodies: mastery is not only the ability to go further, but the wisdom to turn back.

Appendix A
Ceremonial Items Checklist

I. Tools & Implements (with locations)

- **Sword** – described for circle consecration and exorcism (pp. 65–66)
- **White-handled knife** – cutting herbs & parchment (p. 71)
- **Black-handled knife** – other ceremonial uses (p. 71)
- **Lance, wand, staff, sickle** – noted among optional implements (p. 73)
- **Parchment/paper, pen, ink** – for pentacles (p. 103)
- **Censer, brazier** – fumigations (p. 104)
- **Mortar & pestle** – grinding incense (p. 105)

II. Vestments & Textiles

- **White linen robe** – worn after ritual bathing (p. 58)
- **Girdle (belt)** – inscribed, worn with robe (p. 58)
- **Silk cloths** – covering tools (p. 73)
- **Head covering** – with divine names (p. 58)

III. Perfumes, Incense, & Aromatics

(All with page refs where they are listed for consecrations and fumigations)

- **Frankincense, Myrrh, Mastic, Benzoin, Storax** (p. 105)
- **Aloeswood, Cinnamon, Cloves, Saffron, Camphor** (p. 105)
- **Rose, Vervain, Coriander seed, Anise, Nutmeg** (p. 105)
- **Costus, Galangal, Nard, Cardamom, Balsam** (p. 105)
- **Juniper berries, Laurel leaves, Thyme, Rue** (p. 105)
- **Violets, Hyssop, Mint, Pennyroyal, Savory, Rosemary, Wormwood** (p. 105)

IV. Herbs for Baths & Sprinklings

- **Vervain, Rue, Hyssop, Bay/Laurel** – ritual baths & sprinkling water (p. 59)

V. Waters, Oils, and Compounds

- **Holy water with exorcised salt** (p. 59)
- **Olive oil (blessed)** – anointing (p. 61)
- **Perfumed oil** – Exodus 30:23–25 style (p. 105)
- **Wine** – libations (p. 62)

VI. Other Offerings

- **Bread, Honey, Milk** – as offerings in specific rites (p. 62)

VII. Protective & Symbolic Items

- **Pentacles** – made of parchment, vellum, or metal (p. 103)
- **Circle** – chalk or charcoal (p. 64)
- **Divine Names** – inscribed on tools, vestments, and pentacles (multiple pages, e.g., p. 58–59, p. 103–104)

Note on "Virgin Parchment" and "Abramelin Oil"

In the early 20th century, publishers like L.W. de Laurence routinely appended procurement notes in grimoires, advising that certain items—*virgin parchment* or "Abramelin oil"—should be ordered directly from their company. This was, in part, a sales tactic: by positioning themselves as the sole "authentic" supplier, they could monetize not just the text but the materials it prescribed.

Historically, *virgin parchment* referred to animal skin (sheep, goat, calf) that had never before been written upon. In medieval and early modern periods, parchment was expensive, so many manuscripts were palimpsests—skins scraped and reused. The term "virgin" was a guarantee of freshness, purity, and exclusivity. Today, genuine animal parchment is more accessible through specialist suppliers, but the symbolic logic remains: the medium should be ritually "unblemished" and dedicated solely to the magical operation.

For modern practice, *virgin parchment* need not be animal in origin—especially if your moral compass points away from using goat or lamb skin. A freshly prepared, uncoated, archival-quality organic fiber paper can fulfill the requirement if it is pure, unused, and ritually consecrated. The operative principle is *dedicated purity*, not the suffering of livestock.

As for *Abramelin oil*—a perfume blend mentioned in the medieval *Book of Abramelin*—its formula is adapted from the holy anointing oil of Exodus 30:23–25. In grimoire revival culture, it was romanticized as a "must-have" for Solomon's operations, though the *Greater Key* does not require it by name. De Laurence's editions often folded it in, along with lists of incense and perfumes, to make their catalogue indispensable.

For the neophyte, this is a good example of why unpacking wording in old grimoires matters: terms like "virgin parchment" are often symbolic shorthand for purity, dedication, and singular use—not a rigid demand for ancient livestock husbandry. Otherwise, taken to extremes, one might as well ask— *why not human babies!?* (We joke, of course... but the point is that discernment is part of magical literacy.)

Appendix B: Understanding Roman Numerals

Roman numerals, the numerical system of ancient Rome, are still in use today in liturgical, ceremonial, and esoteric contexts. In the *Greater Key of Solomon*, they frequently appear in the citation of Psalms, chapters, and ritual sequences. For readers unfamiliar with the system—or those who have not encountered it for many years—a brief refresher is in order.

Roman numerals are based on seven Latin letters, each with a fixed value. By combining these letters in specific ways, a wide range of numbers can be expressed without the use of zero. In the ceremonial tradition, Roman numerals are often rendered in capitals, but lower-case forms are equally valid in modern print.

Core Symbols

Capital	Lowercase	Value
I	i	1
V	v	5
X	x	10
L	l	50
C	c	100
D	d	500
M	m	1,000

Quick Reference Table

Value	Capital	Lowercase
1	I	i
2	II	ii
3	III	iii
4	IV	iv
5	V	v
6	VI	vi
7	VII	vii
8	VIII	viii
9	IX	ix
10	X	x
20	XX	xx
30	XXX	xxx
40	XL	xl
50	L	l
60	LX	lx
70	LXX	lxx
80	LXXX	lxxx
90	XC	xc
100	C	c
200	CC	cc
300	CCC	ccc
400	CD	cd
500	D	d
600	DC	dc
700	DCC	dcc
800	DCCC	dccc
900	CM	cm
1,000	M	m
2,000	MM	mm
3,000	MMM	mmm

Principles of Formation

1. **Addition** — When a smaller numeral follows a larger one, the values are added.
   o Example: VI = 5 + 1 = **6**; XV = 10 + 5 = **15**.
2. **Subtraction** — When a smaller numeral precedes a larger one, the smaller value is subtracted.
   o Example: IV = 5 − 1 = **4**; IX = 10 − 1 = **9**.
3. **Repetition** — A numeral can be repeated up to three times in succession to indicate multiples.
   o Example: XX = 20; XXX = 30.
   o Four in a row is never used; subtraction is preferred (e.g., 40 = XL, not XXXX).
4. **Order Matters** — Roman numerals are read from left to right, applying addition or subtraction according to these rules.

Special Notes for the Ritual Reader

- **Psalm Citations** — In grimoire texts, Psalms are often indicated by Roman numerals alone (e.g., *cxix.* = Psalm 119).
- **No Zero** — Roman numerals lack a zero; each number is constructed from existing symbols.
- **Large Numbers** — While the Romans had ways of writing numbers above 3,999 (such as placing a bar over a numeral to indicate multiplication by 1,000), these are rare in Biblical and ceremonial contexts and are not used in the *Greater Key of Solomon.*

Practical Tip for Neophytes and Returning Readers:
When working with the Psalms in ritual form, it is worth keeping this table at hand. This will save time when cross-referencing the Roman numerals of the grimoire with the standard numbering in a modern Bible. Many practitioners keep a "Psalter index" in the margins of their own *Key of Solomon* for instant recognition.

Appendix C: Benedicite Omnia Opera

Benedicite Omnia Opera—"Bless the Lord, all ye works [of the Lord]"—is the opening line of the *Benedicite*, a hymn also known as the *Song of the Three Holy Children*, the *Canticle of the Three Young Men*, or, in some traditions, the *Song of Creation*. Its origin lies in the Greek additions to the Book of Daniel preserved in the *Septuagint* (Daniel 3:57–88 LXX), where Shadrach, Meshach, and Abednego lift their voices in praise after their miraculous deliverance from Nebuchadnezzar's fiery furnace.

This hymn is absent from the Hebrew/Aramaic Masoretic Text—the basis of most Protestant Old Testaments—and thus from the canonical form of Daniel in modern English Protestant Bibles. In Catholic and Eastern Orthodox Bibles, however, it remains fully integrated into the book, typically inserted between Daniel 3:23 and 3:24. In most Protestant traditions it survives in the Apocrypha, often as part of *The Prayer of Azariah*, which contains both Azariah's supplication (attributed to Abednego) and the subsequent canticle of praise. The 1611 King James Bible preserves it in this form, and it continues to appear in Anglican and Episcopal liturgy, notably in the *Benedicite* canticle used at Morning Prayer.

The preservation of this hymn in the *Septuagint* and *Vulgate* reflects its roots in Hellenistic Jewish manuscript traditions, which included several additions to Daniel that were later excluded from the Masoretic canon during the Reformers' standardization of the Old Testament. When early English translators such as Wycliffe, Coverdale, and the King James committee worked from the Latin *Vulgate*, they retained the passage but set it apart in the Apocrypha rather than alongside the Hebrew-derived chapters of Daniel.

Liturgically, *Benedicite Omnia Opera* occupies a place of honor in the Latin rite, traditionally chanted during Lauds on feast days. It is a sweeping invocation, summoning all of creation—angels, the heavens, waters above, sun, moon, stars, winds, mountains, beasts, and humankind—to bless and praise the Creator.

Within the context of ceremonial magic and the grimoire tradition, its inclusion—particularly in works like the *Greater Key of Solomon*—expands the ritual frame to encompass the entire cosmic order. It functions as both declaration and alignment: a call for every force of creation to witness, sanctify, and affirm the sacred operation being undertaken. Just as the psalms in such texts serve to consecrate the rite and bind it to divine authority, so too does the *Benedicite*, anchoring the work within the praise and dominion of the Creator.

Benedicite, Omnia Opera Domini

(Daniel 3:57–88 LXX - Song of the Three Holy Children)

Greek (Septuagint)

57 εὐλογεῖτε πάντα τὰ ἔργα τοῦ κυρίου τὸν κύριον ὑμνεῖτε καὶ ὑπερυψοῦτε αὐτὸν εἰς τοὺς αἰῶνας

58 εὐλογεῖτε ἄγγελοι κυρίου τὸν κύριον ὑμνεῖτε καὶ ὑπερυψοῦτε αὐτὸν εἰς τοὺς αἰῶνας

59 εὐλογεῖτε οὐρανοί τὸν κύριον ὑμνεῖτε καὶ ὑπερυψοῦτε αὐτὸν εἰς τοὺς αἰῶνας

60 εὐλογεῖτε ὕδατα πάντα τὰ ἐπάνω τοῦ οὐρανοῦ τὸν κύριον ὑμνεῖτε καὶ ὑπερυψοῦτε αὐτὸν εἰς τοὺς αἰῶνας

61 εὐλογεῖτε πᾶσαι αἱ δυνάμεις κυρίου τὸν κύριον ὑμνεῖτε καὶ ὑπερυψοῦτε αὐτὸν εἰς τοὺς αἰῶνας

62 εὐλογεῖτε ἥλιος καὶ σελήνη τὸν κύριον ὑμνεῖτε καὶ ὑπερυψοῦτε αὐτὸν εἰς τοὺς αἰῶνας

63 εὐλογεῖτε ἄστρα τοῦ οὐρανοῦ τὸν κύριον ὑμνεῖτε καὶ ὑπερυψοῦτε αὐτὸν εἰς τοὺς αἰῶνας

64 εὐλογεῖτε πᾶς ὄμβρος καὶ δρόσος τὸν κύριον ὑμνεῖτε καὶ ὑπερυψοῦτε αὐτὸν εἰς τοὺς αἰῶνας

65 εὐλογεῖτε πάντα τὰ πνεύματα τὸν κύριον ὑμνεῖτε καὶ ὑπερυψοῦτε αὐτὸν εἰς τοὺς αἰῶνας

66 εὐλογεῖτε πῦρ καὶ καῦμα τὸν κύριον ὑμνεῖτε καὶ ὑπερυψοῦτε αὐτὸν εἰς τοὺς αἰῶνας

67 εὐλογεῖτε ῥῖγος καὶ ψῦχος τὸν κύριον ὑμνεῖτε καὶ ὑπερυψοῦτε αὐτὸν εἰς τοὺς αἰῶνας

68 εὐλογεῖτε δρόσοι καὶ νιφετοί τὸν κύριον ὑμνεῖτε καὶ ὑπερυψοῦτε αὐτὸν εἰς τοὺς αἰῶνας

69 εὐλογεῖτε πάγοι καὶ ψῦχος τὸν κύριον ὑμνεῖτε καὶ ὑπερυψοῦτε αὐτὸν εἰς τοὺς αἰῶνας

70 εὐλογεῖτε πάχναι καὶ χιόνες τὸν κύριον ὑμνεῖτε καὶ ὑπερυψοῦτε αὐτὸν εἰς τοὺς αἰῶνας

71 εὐλογεῖτε νύκτες καὶ ἡμέραι τὸν κύριον ὑμνεῖτε καὶ ὑπερυψοῦτε αὐτὸν εἰς τοὺς αἰῶνας

72 εὐλογεῖτε φῶς καὶ σκότος τὸν κύριον ὑμνεῖτε καὶ ὑπερυψοῦτε αὐτὸν εἰς τοὺς αἰῶνας

73 εὐλογεῖτε ἀστραπαὶ καὶ νεφέλαι
τὸν κύριον ὑμνεῖτε καὶ ὑπερυψοῦτε
αὐτὸν εἰς τοὺς αἰῶνας

74 εὐλογείτω ἡ γῆ τὸν κύριον ὑμνείτω
καὶ ὑπερυψούτω αὐτὸν εἰς τοὺς
αἰῶνας

75 εὐλογεῖτε ὄρη καὶ βουνοί τὸν κύριον
ὑμνεῖτε καὶ ὑπερυψοῦτε αὐτὸν εἰς
τοὺς αἰῶνας

76 εὐλογεῖτε πάντα τὰ φυόμενα ἐπὶ
τῆς γῆς τὸν κύριον ὑμνεῖτε καὶ
ὑπερυψοῦτε αὐτὸν εἰς τοὺς αἰῶνας

77 εὐλογεῖτε αἱ πηγαί τὸν κύριον
ὑμνεῖτε καὶ ὑπερυψοῦτε αὐτὸν εἰς
τοὺς αἰῶνας

78 εὐλογεῖτε θάλασσαι καὶ ποταμοί
τὸν κύριον ὑμνεῖτε καὶ ὑπερυψοῦτε
αὐτὸν εἰς τοὺς αἰῶνας

79 εὐλογεῖτε κήτη καὶ πάντα τὰ
κινούμενα ἐν τοῖς ὕδασι τὸν κύριον
ὑμνεῖτε καὶ ὑπερυψοῦτε αὐτὸν εἰς
τοὺς αἰῶνας

80 εὐλογεῖτε πάντα τὰ πετεινὰ τοῦ
οὐρανοῦ τὸν κύριον ὑμνεῖτε καὶ
ὑπερυψοῦτε αὐτὸν εἰς τοὺς αἰῶνας

81 εὐλογεῖτε τετράποδα καὶ θηρία τῆς
γῆς τὸν κύριον ὑμνεῖτε καὶ
ὑπερυψοῦτε αὐτὸν εἰς τοὺς αἰῶνας

82 εὐλογεῖτε οἱ υἱοὶ τῶν ἀνθρώπων
τὸν κύριον ὑμνεῖτε καὶ ὑπερυψοῦτε
αὐτὸν εἰς τοὺς αἰῶνας

83 εὐλογεῖτε Ισραηλ τὸν κύριον
ὑμνεῖτε καὶ ὑπερυψοῦτε αὐτὸν εἰς
τοὺς αἰῶνας

84 εὐλογεῖτε ἱερεῖς τὸν κύριον ὑμνεῖτε
καὶ ὑπερυψοῦτε αὐτὸν εἰς τοὺς
αἰῶνας

85 εὐλογεῖτε δοῦλοι τὸν κύριον ὑμνεῖτε
καὶ ὑπερυψοῦτε αὐτὸν εἰς τοὺς
αἰῶνας

86 εὐλογεῖτε πνεύματα καὶ ψυχαὶ
δικαίων τὸν κύριον ὑμνεῖτε καὶ
ὑπερυψοῦτε αὐτὸν εἰς τοὺς αἰῶνας

87 εὐλογεῖτε ὅσιοι καὶ ταπεινοὶ καρδία
τὸν κύριον ὑμνεῖτε καὶ ὑπερυψοῦτε
αὐτὸν εἰς τοὺς αἰῶνας

88 εὐλογεῖτε Ανανια Αζαρια Μισαηλ
τὸν κύριον ὑμνεῖτε καὶ ὑπερυψοῦτε
αὐτὸν εἰς τοὺς αἰῶνας ὅτι ἐξείλετο
ἡμᾶς ἐξ ᾅδου καὶ ἔσωσεν ἡμᾶς ἐκ
χειρὸς θανάτου καὶ ἐρρύσατο ἡμᾶς ἐκ
μέσου καιομένης φλογὸς καὶ ἐκ τοῦ
πυρὸς ἐλυτρώσατο ἡμᾶς

Latin (Vulgate)

57 Benedicite, omnia opera Domini,
Domino:
laudate et superexaltate eum in sæcula.

58 Benedicite, angeli Domini, Domino:
laudate et superexaltate eum in sæcula.

59 Benedicite, cæli, Domino:
laudate et superexaltate eum in sæcula.

60 Benedicite, aquæ omnes, quæ super cælos sunt, Domino:
laudate et superexaltate eum in sæcula.

61 Benedicite, omnes virtutes Domini, Domino:
laudate et superexaltate eum in sæcula.

62 Benedicite, sol et luna, Domino:
laudate et superexaltate eum in sæcula.

63 Benedicite, stellæ cæli, Domino:
laudate et superexaltate eum in sæcula.

64 Benedicite, omnis imber et ros, Domino:
laudate et superexaltate eum in sæcula.

65 Benedicite, omnes spiritus Dei, Domino:
laudate et superexaltate eum in sæcula.

66 Benedicite, ignis et æstus, Domino:
laudate et superexaltate eum in sæcula.

67 Benedicite, frigus et æstus, Domino:
laudate et superexaltate eum in sæcula.

68 Benedicite, rores et pruina, Domino:
laudate et superexaltate eum in sæcula.

69 Benedicite, gelu et frigus, Domino:
laudate et superexaltate eum in sæcula.

70 Benedicite, glacies et nives, Domino:
laudate et superexaltate eum in sæcula.

71 Benedicite, noctes et dies, Domino
laudate et superexaltate eum in sæcula.

72 Benedicite, lux et tenebræ, Domino:
laudate et superexaltate eum in sæcula.

73 Benedicite, fulgura et nubes, Domino:
laudate et superexaltate eum in sæcula.

74 Benedicat terra Dominum:
laudet et superexaltet eum in sæcula.

75 Benedicite, montes et colles, Domino:
laudate et superexaltate eum in sæcula.

76 Benedicite, universa germinantia in terra, Domino:
laudate et superexaltate eum in sæcula.

77 Benedicite, fontes, Domino:
laudate et superexaltate eum in sæcula.

78 Benedicite, maria et flumina, Domino:
laudate et superexaltate eum in sæcula.

79 Benedicite, cete, et omnia quæ moventur in aquis, Domino:
laudate et superexaltate eum in sæcula.

80 Benedicite, omnes volucres cæli, Domino:
laudate et superexaltate eum in sæcula.

81 Benedicite, omnes bestiæ et pecora, Domino:
laudate et superexaltate eum in sæcula.

82 Benedicite, filii hominum, Domino:
laudate et superexaltate eum in sæcula.

83 Benedicat Israël Dominum:
laudet et superexaltet eum in sæcula.

84 Benedicite, sacerdotes Domini,
Domino:
laudate et superexaltate eum in sæcula.

85 Benedicite, servi Domini, Domino:
laudate et superexaltate eum in sæcula.

86 Benedicite, spiritus et animæ
justorum, Domino:
laudate et superexaltate eum in sæcula.

87 Benedicite, sancti et humiles corde,
Domino:
laudate et superexaltate eum in sæcula.

88 Benedicite, Anania, Azaria, Misaël,
Domino:
laudate et superexaltate eum in sæcula:
quia eruit nos de inferno,
et salvos fecit de manu mortis:
et liberavit nos de medio ardentis
flammæ,
et de medio ignis eruit nos.

English Translation

O all ye works of the Lord, bless ye the
Lord: praise and exalt him above all for
ever.
O ye angels of the Lord, bless ye the
Lord: praise and exalt him above all for
ever.
O ye heavens, bless ye the Lord: praise
and exalt him above all for ever.
O ye waters that be above the
firmament, bless ye the Lord: praise and
exalt him above all for ever.
O all ye powers of the Lord, bless ye the
Lord: praise and exalt him above all for
ever.
O ye sun and moon, bless ye the Lord:
praise and exalt him above all for ever.

O ye stars of heaven, bless ye the Lord:
praise and exalt him above all for ever.
O every shower and dew, bless ye the
Lord: praise and exalt him above all for
ever.
O all ye winds of God, bless ye the Lord:
praise and exalt him above all for ever.
O ye fire and heat, bless ye the Lord:
praise and exalt him above all for ever.
O ye winter and summer, bless ye the
Lord: praise and exalt him above all for
ever.
O ye dews and frosts, bless ye the Lord:
praise and exalt him above all for ever.
O ye frost and cold, bless ye the Lord:
praise and exalt him above all for ever.
O ye ice and snow, bless ye the Lord:
praise and exalt him above all for ever.
O ye nights and days, bless ye the Lord:
praise and exalt him above all for ever.
O ye light and darkness, bless ye the
Lord: praise and exalt him above all for
ever.
O ye lightnings and clouds, bless ye the
Lord: praise and exalt him above all for
ever.
O let the earth bless the Lord: praise
and exalt him above all for ever.
O ye mountains and hills, bless ye the
Lord: praise and exalt him above all for
ever.
O all ye things that grow in the earth,
bless ye the Lord: praise and exalt him
above all for ever.
O ye fountains, bless ye the Lord: praise
and exalt him above all for ever.
O ye seas and rivers, bless ye the Lord:
praise and exalt him above all for ever.
O ye whales, and all that move in the
waters, bless ye the Lord: praise and
exalt him above all for ever.
O all ye fowls of the air, bless ye the
Lord: praise and exalt him above all for

ever.

O all ye beasts and cattle, bless ye the Lord: praise and exalt him above all for ever.

O ye children of men, bless ye the Lord: praise and exalt him above all for ever.

O Israel, bless ye the Lord: praise and exalt him above all for ever.

O ye priests of the Lord, bless ye the Lord: praise and exalt him above all for ever.

O ye servants of the Lord, bless ye the Lord: praise and exalt him above all for ever.

O ye spirits and souls of the righteous, bless ye the Lord: praise and exalt him above all for ever.

O ye holy and humble men of heart, bless ye the Lord: praise and exalt him above all for ever.

O Ananias, Azarias, and Misael, bless ye the Lord: praise and exalt him above all for ever, for he hath delivered us from hell, and saved us from the hand of death, and delivered us out of the midst of the furnace of burning flame, even out of the midst of the fire hath he delivered us.

O give thanks unto the Lord, because he is gracious: for his mercy endureth for ever.

O all ye that worship the Lord, bless the God of gods: praise him, and give him thanks; for his mercy endureth for ever.

Prayer of Azariah

1 And they walked in the midst of the fire, praising God, and blessing the Lord.

2 Then Azarias stood up, and prayed on this manner; and opening his mouth in the midst of the fire said,

3 Blessed art thou, O Lord God of our fathers: thy name is worthy to be praised and glorified for evermore:

4 For thou art righteous in all the things that thou hast done to us: yea, true are all thy works, thy ways are right, and all thy judgments truth.

5 In all the things that thou hast brought upon us, and upon the holy city of our fathers, even Jerusalem, thou hast executed true judgment: for according to truth and judgment didst thou bring all these things upon us because of our sins.

6 For we have sinned and committed iniquity, departing from thee.

7 In all things have we trespassed, and not obeyed thy commandments, nor kept them, neither done as thou hast commanded us, that it might go well with us.

8 Wherefore all that thou hast brought upon us, and every thing that thou hast done to us, thou hast done in true judgment.

9 And thou didst deliver us into the hands of lawless enemies, most hateful forsakers of God, and to an unjust king, and the most wicked in all the world.

10 And now we cannot open our mouths, we are become a shame and reproach to thy servants; and to them that worship thee.

11 Yet deliver us not up wholly, for thy name's sake, neither disannul thou thy covenant:

12 And cause not thy mercy to depart from us, for thy beloved Abraham's sake, for thy servant Issac's sake, and for thy holy Israel's sake;

13 To whom thou hast spoken and promised, that thou wouldest multiply their seed as the stars of heaven, and as the sand that lieth upon the seashore.

14 For we, O Lord, are become less than any nation, and be kept under this day in all the world because of our sins.

15 Neither is there at this time prince, or prophet, or leader, or burnt offering, or sacrifice, or oblation, or incense, or place to sacrifice before thee, and to find mercy.

16 Nevertheless in a contrite heart and an humble spirit let us be accepted.

17 Like as in the burnt offerings of rams and bullocks, and like as in ten thousands of fat lambs: so let our sacrifice be in thy sight this day, and grant that we may wholly go after thee: for they shall not be confounded that put their trust in thee.

18 And now we follow thee with all our heart, we fear thee, and seek thy face.

19 Put us not to shame: but deal with us after thy lovingkindness, and according to the multitude of thy mercies.

20 Deliver us also according to thy marvellous works, and give glory to thy name, O Lord: and let all them that do thy servants hurt be ashamed;

21 And let them be confounded in all their power and might, and let their strength be broken;

22 And let them know that thou art God, the only God, and glorious over the whole world.

23 And the king's servants, that put them in, ceased not to make the oven hot with rosin, pitch, tow, and small wood;

24 So that the flame streamed forth above the furnace forty and nine cubits.

25 And it passed through, and burned those Chaldeans it found about the furnace.

26 But the angel of the Lord came down into the oven together with Azarias and his fellows, and smote the flame of the fire out of the oven;

27 And made the midst of the furnace as it had been a moist whistling wind, so that the fire touched them not at all, neither hurt nor troubled them.

28 Then the three, as out of one mouth, praised, glorified, and blessed, God in the furnace, saying,

29 Blessed art thou, O Lord God of our fathers: and to be praised and exalted above all for ever.

30 And blessed is thy glorious and holy name: and to be praised and exalted above all for ever.

31 Blessed art thou in the temple of thine holy glory: and to be praised and glorified above all for ever.

32 Blessed art thou that beholdest the depths, and sittest upon the cherubims: and to be praised and exalted above all for ever.

33 Blessed art thou on the glorious throne of thy kingdom: and to be praised and glorified above all for ever.

34 Blessed art thou in the firmament of heaven: and above ail to be praised and glorified for ever.

35 O all ye works of the Lord, bless ye the Lord : praise and exalt him above all for ever,

36 O ye heavens, bless ye the Lord : praise and exalt him above all for ever.

37 O ye angels of the Lord, bless ye the Lord: praise and exalt him above all for ever.

38 O all ye waters that be above the heaven, bless ye the Lord: praise and exalt him above all for ever.

39 O all ye powers of the Lord, bless ye the Lord: praise and exalt him above all for ever.

40 O ye sun and moon, bless ye the Lord: praise and exalt him above all for ever.

41 O ye stars of heaven, bless ye the Lord: praise and exalt him above all for ever.

42 O every shower and dew, bless ye the Lord: praise and exalt him above all for ever.

43 O all ye winds, bless ye the Lord: praise and exalt him above all for ever,

44 O ye fire and heat, bless ye the Lord: praise and exalt him above all for ever.

45 O ye winter and summer, bless ye the Lord: praise and exalt him above all for ever.

46 o ye dews and storms of snow, bless ye the Lord: praise and exalt him above all for ever.

47 O ye nights and days, bless ye the Lord: bless and exalt him above all for ever.

48 O ye light and darkness, bless ye the Lord: praise and exalt him above all for ever.

49 O ye ice and cold, bless ye the Lord: praise and exalt him above all for ever.

50 O ye frost and snow, bless ye the Lord: praise and exalt him above all for ever.

51 O ye lightnings and clouds, bless ye the Lord: praise and exalt him above all for ever.

52 O let the earth bless the Lord: praise and exalt him above all for ever.

53 O ye mountains and little hills, bless ye the Lord: praise and exalt him above all for ever.

54 O all ye things that grow in the earth, bless ye the Lord: praise and exalt him above all for ever.

55 O ye mountains, bless ye the Lord: Praise and exalt him above all for ever.

56 O ye seas and rivers, bless ye the Lord: praise and exalt him above all for ever.

57 O ye whales, and all that move in the waters, bless ye the Lord: praise and exalt him above all for ever.

58 O all ye fowls of the air, bless ye the Lord: praise and exalt him above all for ever.

59 O all ye beasts and cattle, bless ye the Lord: praise and exalt him above all for ever.

60 O ye children of men, bless ye the Lord: praise and exalt him above all for ever.

61 O Israel, bless ye the Lord: praise and exalt him above all for ever.

62 O ye priests of the Lord, bless ye the Lord: praise and exalt him above all for ever.

63 O ye servants of the Lord, bless ye the Lord: praise and exalt him above all for ever.

64 O ye spirits and souls of the righteous, bless ye the Lord: praise and exalt him above all for ever.

65 O ye holy and humble men of heart, bless ye the Lord: praise and exalt him above all for ever.

66 O Ananias, Azarias, and Misael, bless ye the Lord: praise and exalt him above all for ever: far he hath delivered us from hell, and saved us from the hand of death, and delivered us out of the midst of the furnace and burning flame: even out of the midst of the fire hath he delivered us.

67 O give thanks unto the Lord, because he is gracious: for his mercy endureth for ever.

68 O all ye that worship the Lord, bless the God of gods, praise him, and give him thanks: for his mercy endureth for ever.

Appendix D: The Gallican Psalter and the Greater Key of Solomon

In approaching the *Greater Key of Solomon* with historical accuracy, one must recognize that the psalms it prescribes were never intended to be read from a modern English Bible. The conjurations, blessings, and penitential prayers in the Key were composed during a period when the Latin Vulgate—specifically Jerome's Gallican Psalter—was the universal liturgical standard across Catholic Europe. This was the text heard in monasteries, recited in cathedrals, and committed to memory by clerics, scholars, and those engaged in ceremonial practice.

Why the Gallican Psalter Matters

The Gallican Psalter is Jerome's fourth-century revision of the Greek Septuagint Psalms, completed at a time when Latin was replacing Greek as the language of the Western Church. By the fifteenth century—when the *Greater Key* reached its most complete medieval form—the Gallican Psalter was deeply embedded in the fabric of religious life. Its psalm numbering follows the Septuagint and Vulgate sequence, which differs in places from the Hebrew (Masoretic) system later adopted by Protestant Bibles. This makes it historically and contextually appropriate for aligning our understanding of the Key's instructions with the worldview of its original compilers.

Latin as the Original Soundscape

Latin is more than a language here—it is part of the rite itself. Its cadences, vowel sounds, and rhythm are not incidental. In the *Greater Key*, when the operator is told to recite Psalm LI (*Miserere mei, Deus*), the expectation is that it will be spoken or chanted in Latin, not in translation. The very phonetics of the Latin text, shaped by centuries of repetition in prayer, were themselves considered part of the invocation's force. Including the psalms in Latin preserves this "soundscape," allowing both the scholar and the practitioner to experience the text as it was intended to be heard.

Why Not a Fifth-Century Manuscript?

While the Gallican Psalter's origins trace back to the fourth or fifth century, consulting an actual early medieval codex is impractical. Surviving manuscripts are rare, fragile, often incomplete, and written in scripts (uncials, half-uncials, or early Gothic hands) that require specialist training to read. Moreover, access is restricted to archives and special collections, making it inaccessible to most readers—scholars and practitioners alike.

The Value of the 1911 Bernard Edition

For this reason, we turn to *The Psalter in Latin and English*, edited by J. H. Bernard, D.D., and published in 1911. This edition preserves the Gallican text exactly as it appeared in the liturgy for centuries, paired with a faithful and elegant English translation. The Latin is standardized in modern type, free from scribal abbreviation marks and idiosyncrasies that might obscure meaning for the untrained reader. The side-by-side presentation allows for immediate cross-reference between Latin and English, ensuring that even those unfamiliar with ecclesiastical Latin can follow the meaning without interrupting the flow of study or ritual.

Why Only Seven Psalms Are Included Here

This appendix presents only the seven psalms most often cited in the *Greater Key of Solomon*. Their inclusion in both Latin and English serves two purposes: to preserve the historical form and to ensure modern practitioners can understand their meaning. A separate appendix contains all psalms in English from the King James Version referenced in The Greater Key of Solomon, allowing for full contextual study. Together, these resources bridge the gap between the original medieval working environment and the needs of the modern reader.

Language or Intention?

It is worth asking whether the efficacy of these rites depends on their being performed in Latin, or whether a faithful translation—spoken with clarity and intention—can suffice. The answer may depend on one's perspective: traditionalists may hold that the original tongue carries a unique spiritual and vibrational authority, while others may see intention, focus, and sincerity as the true engines of the work. Either way, by presenting these psalms in their original liturgical form alongside an accurate English rendering, this edition ensures that the choice is an informed one, made with full awareness of the tradition from which the *Greater Key* emerged.

Psalms Most Frequently Used in the Greater Key of Solomon From the Vulgate (Latin) Against English (KJV) Translation

Psalmus XLVI – Omnes gentes, plaudite manibus *(Vulgate)*
Psalm 47 – O clap your hands, all ye people *(KJV)*

Vulgate Latin	KJV English
1. Omnes gentes, plaudite manibus: jubilate Deo in voce exsultationis.	1. O clap your hands, all ye people; shout unto God with the voice of triumph.
2. Quoniam Dominus excelsus, terribilis, rex magnus super omnem terram.	2. For the LORD most high is terrible; he is a great King over all the earth.
3. Subjecit populos nobis, et gentes sub pedibus nostris.	3. He shall subdue the people under us, and the nations under our feet.
4. Elegit nobis hereditatem suam, speciem Jacob quam dilexit.	4. He shall choose our inheritance for us, the excellency of Jacob whom he loved. Selah.
5. Ascendit Deus in jubilo, et Dominus in voce tubæ.	5. God is gone up with a shout, the LORD with the sound of a trumpet.
6. Psallite Deo nostro, psallite: psallite regi nostro, psallite.	6. Sing praises to God, sing praises: sing praises unto our King, sing praises.
7. Quoniam rex omnis terræ Deus: psallite sapienter.	7. For God is the King of all the earth: sing ye praises with understanding.
8. Regnabit Deus super gentes: Deus sedet super sedem sanctam suam.	8. God reigneth over the heathen: God sitteth upon the throne of his holiness.
9. Principes populorum congregati sunt cum Deo Abraham: quoniam dii fortes terræ vehementer elevati sunt.	9. The princes of the people are gathered together, even the people of the God of Abraham: for the shields of the earth belong unto God: he is greatly exalted.

Psalmus L – Miserere mei, Deus *(Vulgate)*
Psalm 51 – Have mercy upon me, O God *(KJV)*

Vulgate Latin

1. Miserere mei, Deus, secundum magnam misericordiam tuam; et secundum multitudinem miserationum tuarum, dele iniquitatem meam.

2. Amplius lava me ab iniquitate mea: et a peccato meo munda me.

3. Quoniam iniquitatem meam ego cognosco: et peccatum meum contra me est semper.

4. Tibi soli peccavi, et malum coram te feci: ut justificeris in sermonibus tuis, et vincas cum judicaris.

5. Ecce enim in iniquitatibus conceptus sum: et in peccatis concepit me mater mea.

6. Ecce enim veritatem dilexisti: incerta et occulta sapientiae tuae manifestasti mihi.

7. Asperges me hyssopo, et mundabor: lavabis me, et super nivem dealbabor.

8. Auditui meo dabis gaudium et laetitiam: et exsultabunt ossa humiliata.

9. Averte faciem tuam a peccatis meis: et omnes iniquitates meas dele.

10. Cor mundum crea in me, Deus: et spiritum rectum innova in visceribus meis.

KJV English

1. Have mercy upon me, O God, according to thy lovingkindness: according unto the multitude of thy tender mercies blot out my transgressions.

2. Wash me throughly from mine iniquity, and cleanse me from my sin.

3. For I acknowledge my transgressions: and my sin is ever before me.

4. Against thee, thee only, have I sinned, and done this evil in thy sight: that thou mightest be justified when thou speakest, and be clear when thou judgest.

5. Behold, I was shapen in iniquity; and in sin did my mother conceive me.

6. Behold, thou desirest truth in the inward parts: and in the hidden part thou shalt make me to know wisdom.

7. Purge me with hyssop, and I shall be clean: wash me, and I shall be whiter than snow.

8. Make me to hear joy and gladness; that the bones which thou hast broken may rejoice.

9. Hide thy face from my sins, and blot out all mine iniquities.

10. Create in me a clean heart, O God; and renew a right spirit within me.

Vulgate Latin	KJV English

11. Ne projicias me a facie tua: et spiritum sanctum tuum ne auferas a me.

11. Cast me not away from thy presence; and take not thy holy spirit from me.

12. Redde mihi laetitiam salutaris tui: et spiritu principali confirma me.

12. Restore unto me the joy of thy salvation; and uphold me with thy free spirit.

13. Docebo iniquos vias tuas: et impii ad te convertentur.

13. Then will I teach transgressors thy ways; and sinners shall be converted unto thee.

14. Libera me de sanguinibus, Deus, Deus salutis meae: et exsultabit lingua mea justitiam tuam.

14. Deliver me from bloodguiltiness, O God, thou God of my salvation: and my tongue shall sing aloud of thy righteousness.

15. Domine, labia mea aperies: et os meum annuntiabit laudem tuam.

15. O Lord, open thou my lips; and my mouth shall shew forth thy praise.

16. Quoniam si voluisses sacrificium, dedissem utique: holocaustis non delectaberis.

16. For thou desirest not sacrifice; else would I give it: thou delightest not in burnt offering.

17. Sacrificium Deo spiritus contribulatus: cor contritum et humiliatum, Deus, non despicies.

17. The sacrifices of God are a broken spirit: a broken and a contrite heart, O God, thou wilt not despise.

18. Benigne fac, Domine, in bona voluntate tua Sion: ut aedificentur muri Jerusalem.

18. Do good in thy good pleasure unto Zion: build thou the walls of Jerusalem.

19. Tunc acceptabis sacrificium justitiae, oblationes et holocausta: tunc imponent super altare tuum vitulos.

19. Then shalt thou be pleased with the sacrifices of righteousness, with burnt offering and whole burnt offering: then shall they offer bullocks upon thine altar.

Psalmus LIII – Deus, in nomine tuo *(Vulgate)*
Psalm 54 – Save me, O God, by thy name *(KJV)*

Vulgate Latin

1. Deus, in nomine tuo salvum me fac: et in virtute tua judica me.

2. Deus, exaudi orationem meam: auribus percipe verba oris mei.

3. Quoniam alieni insurrexerunt adversum me, et fortes quaesierunt animam meam: et non proposuerunt Deum ante conspectum suum.

4. Ecce enim Deus adjuvat me: et Dominus susceptor est animae meae.

5. Averte mala inimicis meis: et in veritate tua disperde illos.

6. Voluntarie sacrificabo tibi, et confitebor nomini tuo, Domine: quoniam bonum est.

7. Quoniam ex omni tribulatione eripuisti me: et super inimicos meos despexit oculus meus.

KJV English

1. Save me, O God, by thy name, and judge me by thy strength.

2. Hear my prayer, O God; give ear to the words of my mouth.

3. For strangers are risen up against me, and oppressors seek after my soul: they have not set God before them. Selah.

4. Behold, God is mine helper: the Lord is with them that uphold my soul.

5. He shall reward evil unto mine enemies: cut them off in thy truth.

6. I will freely sacrifice unto thee: I will praise thy name, O Lord; for it is good.

7. For he hath delivered me out of all trouble: and mine eye hath seen his desire upon mine enemies.

Psalmus LXVI – Deus misereatur nostri *(Vulgate)*
Psalm 67 – God be merciful unto us *(KJV)*

Vulgate Latin

1. Deus misereatur nostri, et benedicat nobis: illuminet vultum suum super nos, et misereatur nostri.

2. Ut cognoscamus in terra viam tuam, in omnibus gentibus salutare tuum.

3. Confiteantur tibi populi, Deus: confiteantur tibi populi omnes.

4. Laetentur et exsultent gentes: quoniam judicas populos in aequitate, et gentes in terra dirigis.

5. Confiteantur tibi populi, Deus: confiteantur tibi populi omnes.

6. Terra dedit fructum suum: benedicat nos Deus, Deus noster!

7. Benedicat nos Deus: et metuant eum omnes fines terrae.

KJV English

1. God be merciful unto us, and bless us; and cause his face to shine upon us; Selah.

2. That thy way may be known upon earth, thy saving health among all nations.

3. Let the people praise thee, O God; let all the people praise thee.

4. O let the nations be glad and sing for joy: for thou shalt judge the people righteously, and govern the nations upon earth. Selah.

5. Let the people praise thee, O God; let all the people praise thee.

6. Then shall the earth yield her increase; and God, even our own God, shall bless us.

7. God shall bless us; and all the ends of the earth shall fear him.

Psalmus LXXI – Deus, judicium tuum *(Vulgate)*
Psalm 72 – Give the king thy judgments *(KJV)*

Vulgate Latin

1. Deus, judicium tuum regi da: et justitiam tuam filio regis;

2. Judicare populum tuum in justitia, et pauperes tuos in judicio.

3. Suscipiant montes pacem populo: et colles justitiam.

4. Judicabit pauperes populi, et salvos faciet filios pauperum: et humiliabit calumniatorem.

5. Et permanebit cum sole, et ante lunam, in generatione et generationem.

6. Descendet sicut pluvia in vellus: et sicut stillicidia stillantia super terram.

7. Orietur in diebus ejus justitia, et abundantia pacis: donec auferatur luna.

8. Et dominabitur a mari usque ad mare: et a flumine usque ad terminos orbis terrarum.

9. Coram illo procident Aethiopes: et inimici ejus terram lingent.

10. Reges Tharsis, et insulae munera offerent: reges Arabum et Saba dona adducent.

11. Et adorabunt eum omnes reges terrae: omnes gentes servient ei;

KJV English

1. Give the king thy judgments, O God, and thy righteousness unto the king's son.

2. He shall judge thy people with righteousness, and thy poor with judgment.

3. The mountains shall bring peace to the people, and the little hills, by righteousness.

4. He shall judge the poor of the people, he shall save the children of the needy, and shall break in pieces the oppressor.

5. They shall fear thee as long as the sun and moon endure, throughout all generations.

6. He shall come down like rain upon the mown grass: as showers that water the earth.

7. In his days shall the righteous flourish; and abundance of peace so long as the moon endureth.

8. He shall have dominion also from sea to sea, and from the river unto the ends of the earth.

9. They that dwell in the wilderness shall bow before him; and his enemies shall lick the dust.

10. The kings of Tarshish and of the isles shall bring presents: the kings of Sheba and Seba shall offer gifts.

11. Yea, all kings shall fall down before him: all nations shall serve him.

Vulgate Latin	KJV English

12. Quia liberabit pauperem a potente: et pauperem, cui non erat adjutor.

12. For he shall deliver the needy when he crieth; the poor also, and him that hath no helper.

13. Parcet pauperi et inopi: et animas pauperum salvas faciet.

13. He shall spare the poor and needy, and shall save the souls of the needy.

14. Ex usuris et iniquitate redimet animas eorum: et honorabile nomen eorum coram illo.

14. He shall redeem their soul from deceit and violence: and precious shall their blood be in his sight.

15. Et vivet, et dabitur ei de auro Arabiae, et adorabunt de ipso semper: tota die benedicent ei.

15. And he shall live, and to him shall be given of the gold of Sheba: prayer also shall be made for him continually; and daily shall he be praised.

16. Et erit firmamentum in terra in summis montium, superextolletur super Libanum fructus ejus: et florebunt de civitate sicut foenum terrae.

16. There shall be an handful of corn in the earth upon the top of the mountains; the fruit thereof shall shake like Lebanon: and they of the city shall flourish like grass of the earth.

17. Sit nomen ejus benedictum in saecula: ante solem permanet nomen ejus; et benedicentur in ipso omnes tribus terrae: omnes gentes magnificabunt eum.

17. His name shall endure for ever: his name shall be continued as long as the sun: and men shall be blessed in him: all nations shall call him blessed.

18. Benedictus Dominus Deus Israel, qui facit mirabilia solus.

18. Blessed be the LORD God, the God of Israel, who only doeth wondrous things.

19. Et benedictum nomen majestatis ejus in aeternum: et replebitur majestate ejus omnis terra: fiat, fiat.

19. And blessed be his glorious name for ever: and let the whole earth be filled with his glory; Amen, and Amen.

20. Defecerunt orationes David filii Jesse.

20. The prayers of David the son of Jesse are ended.

Psalmus CI – Domine, exaudi orationem meam *(Vulgate)*
Psalm 102 – Hear my prayer, O LORD *(KJV)*

Vulgate Latin

1. Domine, exaudi orationem meam: et clamor meus ad te veniat.

2. Non avertas faciem tuam a me: in quacumque die tribulor, inclina ad me aurem tuam. In quacumque die invocavero te, velociter exaudi me.

3. Quia defecerunt sicut fumus dies mei: et ossa mea sicut cremium aruerunt.

4. Percussus sum ut fœnum, et aruit cor meum: quia oblitus sum comedere panem meum.

5. A voce gemitus mei adhaesit os meum carni meae.

6. Similis factus sum pellicano solitudinis: factus sum sicut nycticorax in domicilio.

7. Vigilavi, et factus sum sicut passer solitarius in tecto.

8. Tota die exprobrabant mihi inimici mei: et qui laudabant me, adversum me jurabant.

9. Quia cinerem tamquam panem manducabam, et potum meum cum fletu miscebam.

10. A facie iræ et indignationis tuæ: quia elevans allisisti me.

11. Dies mei sicut umbra declinaverunt: et ego sicut fœnum arui.

KJV English

1. Hear my prayer, O LORD, and let my cry come unto thee.

2. Hide not thy face from me in the day when I am in trouble; incline thine ear unto me: in the day when I call answer me speedily.

3. For my days are consumed like smoke, and my bones are burned as an hearth.

4. My heart is smitten, and withered like grass; so that I forget to eat my bread.

5. By reason of the voice of my groaning my bones cleave to my skin.

6. I am like a pelican of the wilderness: I am like an owl of the desert.

7. I watch, and am as a sparrow alone upon the house top.

8. Mine enemies reproach me all the day; and they that are mad against me are sworn against me.

9. For I have eaten ashes like bread, and mingled my drink with weeping.

10. Because of thine indignation and thy wrath: for thou hast lifted me up, and cast me down.

11. My days are like a shadow that declineth; and I am withered like grass.

Vulgate Latin	KJV English
12. Tu autem, Domine, in æternum permanes: et memoriale tuum in generationem et generationem.	12. But thou, O LORD, shalt endure for ever; and thy remembrance unto all generations.
13. Tu exsurgens misereberis Sion: quia tempus miserendi ejus, quia venit tempus.	13. Thou shalt arise, and have mercy upon Zion: for the time to favour her, yea, the set time, is come.
14. Quoniam placuerunt servis tuis lapides ejus: et terræ ejus miserebuntur.	14. For thy servants take pleasure in her stones, and favour the dust thereof.
15. Et timebunt gentes nomen tuum, Domine: et omnes reges terræ gloriam tuam.	15. So the heathen shall fear the name of the LORD, and all the kings of the earth thy glory.
16. Quia ædificavit Dominus Sion: et videbitur in gloria sua.	16. When the LORD shall build up Zion, he shall appear in his glory.
17. Respexit in orationem humilium: et non sprevit precem eorum.	17. He will regard the prayer of the destitute, and not despise their prayer.
18. Scribantur hæc in generatione altera: et populus qui creabitur, laudabit Dominum.	18. This shall be written for the generation to come: and the people which shall be created shall praise the LORD.
19. Quia prospexit de excelso sancto suo: Dominus de cælo in terram aspexit.	19. For he hath looked down from the height of his sanctuary; from heaven did the LORD behold the earth;
20. Ut audiret gemitus compeditorum: ut solveret filios interemptorum.	20. To hear the groaning of the prisoner; to loose those that are appointed to death;
21. Ut annuntient in Sion nomen Domini: et laudem ejus in Jerusalem.	21. To declare the name of the LORD in Zion, and his praise in Jerusalem;
22. In conveniendo populos in unum, et reges ut serviant Domino.	22. When the people are gathered together, and the kingdoms, to serve the LORD.
23. Respondit ei in via virtutis suæ: Paucitatem dierum meorum nuntia mihi;	23. He weakened my strength in the way; he shortened my days.

Vulgate Latin	KJV English
24. Ne revoces me in dimidio dierum meorum: in generationem et generationem anni tui.	24. I said, O my God, take me not away in the midst of my days: thy years are throughout all generations.
25. Initio tu, Domine, terram fundasti: et opera manuum tuarum sunt cæli.	25. Of old hast thou laid the foundation of the earth: and the heavens are the work of thy hands.
26. Ipsi peribunt, tu autem permanes: et omnes sicut vestimentum veterascent.	26. They shall perish, but thou shalt endure: yea, all of them shall wax old like a garment; as a vesture shalt thou change them, and they shall be changed:
27. Et sicut opertorium mutabis eos, et mutabuntur: tu autem idem ipse es, et anni tui non deficient.	27. But thou art the same, and thy years shall have no end.
28. Filii servorum tuorum habitabunt: et semen eorum in sæculum dirigetur.	28. The children of thy servants shall continue, and their seed shall be established before thee.

Psalmus CXVI – Laudate Dominum omnes gentes *(Vulgate)*
Psalm 117 – O praise the LORD, all ye nations *(KJV)*

Vulgate Latin	KJV English
1. Laudate Dominum, omnes gentes: laudate eum, omnes populi.	1. O praise the LORD, all ye nations: praise him, all ye people.
2. Quoniam confirmata est super nos misericordia ejus: et veritas Domini manet in æternum.	2. For his merciful kindness is great toward us: and the truth of the LORD endureth for ever. Praise ye the LORD.

Appendix E: Full Psalms Referenced in the *Greater Key of Solomon*

Throughout the *Greater Key of Solomon*, the Psalms of David are invoked as part of the ritual framework. Their use varies: in some operations the psalm is to be recited in its entirety—often as a consecration, invocation, or act of purification—while in others a single verse is cited for its precise thematic or symbolic value.

Including the **full text** of every psalm referenced, drawn here from the King James Version, serves two purposes.
First, it preserves the integrity of the original instruction. Even when only a single verse is named, the surrounding verses can deepen understanding of the intended spiritual effect, reveal the psalm's complete thematic arc, and prevent misinterpretation that might arise from reading an isolated line.
Second, it provides immediate accessibility for the operator or student. Rather than interrupting the work to consult an external Bible, the full psalm is present within the same volume, enabling seamless ritual flow and more immersive engagement.

This inclusion also aids scholarly comparison. Cross-referencing the psalms in their entirety allows the adept, academic, or neophyte to examine patterns in their selection—whether for protection, supplication, praise, or dismissal—and to discern the theological logic underpinning the *Greater Key's* liturgical structure.

By keeping the complete text at hand, the reader is better equipped to **extrapolate context**, trace scriptural resonance, and integrate the psalmody into both ceremonial and contemplative practice without risk of omission or partial understanding.

Psalms Referenced in The Greater Key of Solomon

Psalms Chapter 2

1 Why do the heathen rage, and the people imagine a vain thing?

2 The kings of the earth set themselves, and the rulers take counsel together, against the LORD, and against his anointed, saying,

3 Let us break their bands asunder, and cast away their cords from us.

4 He that sitteth in the heavens shall laugh: the LORD shall have them in derision.

5 Then shall he speak unto them in his wrath, and vex them in his sore displeasure.

6 Yet have I set my king upon my holy hill of Zion.

7 I will declare the decree: the LORD hath said unto me, Thou art my Son; this day have I begotten thee.

8 Ask of me, and I shall give thee the heathen for thine inheritance, and the uttermost parts of the earth for thy possession.

9 Thou shalt break them with a rod of iron; thou shalt dash them in pieces like a potter's vessel.

10 Be wise now therefore, O ye kings: be instructed, ye judges of the earth.

11 Serve the LORD with fear, and rejoice with trembling.

12 Kiss the Son, lest he be angry, and ye perish from the way, when his wrath is kindled but a little. Blessed are all they that put their trust in him.

Psalms Chapter 3

1 Lord, how are they increased that trouble me! many are they that rise up against me.

2 Many there be which say of my soul, There is no help for him in God. Selah.

3 But thou, O LORD, art a shield for me; my glory, and the lifter up of mine head.

4 I cried unto the LORD with my voice, and he heard me out of his holy hill. Selah.

5 I laid me down and slept; I awaked; for the LORD sustained me.

6 I will not be afraid of ten thousands of people, that have set themselves against me round about.

7 Arise, O LORD; save me, O my God: for thou hast smitten all mine enemies upon the cheek bone; thou hast broken the teeth of the ungodly.

8 Salvation belongeth unto the LORD: thy blessing is upon thy people. Selah.

Psalms Chapter 4

1 Hear me when I call, O God of
my righteousness: thou hast enlarged
me when I was in distress;
have mercy upon me, and hear
my prayer.

2 O ye sons of men, how long will ye
turn my glory into shame? how long will
ye love vanity, and seek
after leasing? Selah.

3 But know that the LORD hath set
apart him that is godly for himself: the
LORD will hear when I call unto him.

4 Stand in awe, and sin not: commune
with your own heart upon your bed, and
be still. Selah.

5 Offer the sacrifices of righteousness,
and put your trust in the LORD.

6 There be many that say, Who will
shew us any good? LORD, lift thou up
the light of thy countenance upon us.

7 Thou hast put gladness in my heart,
more than in the time that their corn and
their wine increased.

8 I will both lay me down in peace, and
sleep: for thou, LORD, only makest me
dwell in safety.

Psalms Chapter 5

1 Give ear to my words, O LORD,
consider my meditation.

2 Hearken unto the voice of my cry,
my King, and my God: for unto thee will
I pray.

3 My voice shalt thou hear in the
morning, O LORD; in the morning will
I direct my prayer unto thee, and will
look up.

4 For thou art not a God that hath
pleasure in wickedness: neither shall evil
dwell with thee.

5 The foolish shall not stand in thy sight:
thou hatest all workers of iniquity.

6 Thou shalt destroy them that
speak leasing: the LORD will abhor the
bloody and deceitful man.

7 But as for me, I will come into thy
house in the multitude of thy mercy: and
in thy fear will I worship toward thy
holy temple.

8 Lead me, O LORD, in
thy righteousness because of mine
enemies; make thy way straight before
my face.

9 For there is no faithfulness in their
mouth; their inward part is very
wickedness; their throat is an
open sepulchre; they flatter with their
tongue.

10 Destroy thou them, O God; let them
fall by their own counsels; cast them out
in the multitude of their transgressions;
for they have rebelled against thee.

11 But let all those that put their trust in thee rejoice: let them ever shout for joy, because thou defendest them: let them also that love thy name be joyful in thee.

12 For thou, LORD, wilt bless the righteous; with favour wilt thou compass him as with a shield.

Psalms Chapter 6

1 O LORD, rebuke me not in thine anger, neither chasten me in thy hot displeasure.

2 Have mercy upon me, O LORD; for I am weak: O LORD, heal me; for my bones are vexed.

3 My soul is also sore vexed: but thou, O LORD, how long?

4 Return, O LORD, deliver my soul: oh save me for thy mercies' sake.

5 For in death there is no remembrance of thee: in the grave who shall give thee thanks?

6 I am weary with my groaning; all the night make I my bed to swim; I water my couch with my tears.

7 Mine eye is consumed because of grief; it waxeth old because of all mine enemies.

8 Depart from me, all ye workers of iniquity; for the LORD hath heard the voice of my weeping.

9 The LORD hath heard my supplication; the LORD will receive my prayer.

10 Let all mine enemies be ashamed and sore vexed: let them return and be ashamed suddenly.

Psalms Chapter 8

1 O LORD, our Lord, how excellent is thy name in all the earth! who hast set thy glory above the heavens.

2 Out of the mouth of babes and sucklings hast thou ordained strength because of thine enemies, that thou mightest still the enemy and the avenger.

3 When I consider thy heavens, the work of thy fingers, the moon and the stars, which thou hast ordained;

4 What is man, that thou art mindful of him? and the son of man, that thou visitest him?

5 For thou hast made him a little lower than the angels, and hast crowned him with glory and honour.

6 Thou madest him to have dominion over the works of thy hands; thou hast put all things under his feet:

7 All sheep and oxen, yea, and the beasts of the field;

8 The fowl of the air, and the fish of the sea, and whatsoever passeth through the paths of the seas.

9 O LORD our Lord, how excellent is thy name in all the earth!

Psalms Chapter 9

1 I will praise thee, O LORD, with my whole heart; I will shew forth all thy marvellous works.

2 I will be glad and rejoice in thee: I will sing praise to thy name, O thou most High.

3 When mine enemies are turned back, they shall fall and perish at thy presence.

4 For thou hast maintained my right and my cause; thou satest in the throne judging right.

5 Thou hast rebuked the heathen, thou hast destroyed the wicked, thou hast put out their name for ever and ever.

6 O thou enemy, destructions are come to a perpetual end: and thou hast destroyed cities; their memorial is perished with them.

7 But the LORD shall endure for ever: he hath prepared his throne for judgment.

8 And he shall judge the world in righteousness, he shall minister judgment to the people in uprightness.

9 The LORD also will be a refuge for the oppressed, a refuge in times of trouble.

10 And they that know thy name will put their trust in thee: for thou, LORD, hast not forsaken them that seek thee.

11 Sing praises to the LORD, which dwelleth in Zion: declare among the people his doings.

12 When he maketh inquisition for blood, he remembereth them: he forgetteth not the cry of the humble.

13 Have mercy upon me, O LORD; consider my trouble which I suffer of them that hate me, thou that liftest me up from the gates of death:

14 That I may shew forth all thy praise in the gates of the daughter of Zion: I will rejoice in thy salvation.

15 The heathen are sunk down in the pit that they made: in the net which they hid is their own foot taken.

16 The LORD is known by the judgment which he executeth: the wicked is snared in the work of his own hands. Higgaion. Selah.

17 The wicked shall be turned into hell, and all the nations that forget God.

18 For the needy shall not alway be forgotten: the expectation of the poor shall not perish for ever.

19 Arise, O LORD; let not man prevail: let the heathen be judged in thy sight.

20 Put them in fear, O LORD: that the nations may know themselves to be but men. Selah.

Psalms Chapter 13

1 How long wilt thou forget me, O LORD? for ever? how long wilt thou hide thy face from me?

2 How long shall I take counsel in my soul, having sorrow in my heart daily? how long shall mine enemy be exalted over me?

3 Consider and hear me, O LORD my God: lighten mine eyes, lest I sleep the sleep of death;

4 Lest mine enemy say, I have prevailed against him; and those that trouble me rejoice when I am moved.

5 But I have trusted in thy mercy; my heart shall rejoice in thy salvation.

6 I will sing unto the LORD, because he hath dealt bountifully with me.

Psalms Chapter 15

1 Lord, who shall abide in thy tabernacle? who shall dwell in thy holy hill?

2 He that walketh uprightly, and worketh righteousness, and speaketh the truth in his heart.

3 He that backbiteth not with his tongue, nor doeth evil to his neighbour, nor taketh up a reproach against his neighbour.

4 In whose eyes a vile person is contemned; but he honoureth them that fear the LORD. He that sweareth to his own hurt, and changeth not.

5 He that putteth not out his money to usury, nor taketh reward against the innocent. He that doeth these things shall never be moved.

Psalms Chapter 18

1 I will love thee, O LORD, my strength.

2 The LORD is my rock, and my fortress, and my deliverer; my God, my strength, in whom I will trust; my buckler, and the horn of my salvation, and my high tower.

3 I will call upon the LORD, who is worthy to be praised: so shall I be saved from mine enemies.

4 The sorrows of death compassed me, and the floods of ungodly men made me afraid.

5 The sorrows of hell compassed me about: the snares of death prevented me.

6 In my distress I called upon the LORD, and cried unto my God: he heard my voice out of his temple, and my cry came before him, even into his ears.

7 Then the earth shook and trembled; the foundations also of the hills moved and were shaken, because he was wroth.

8 There went up a smoke out of his nostrils, and fire out of his mouth devoured: coals were kindled by it.

9 He bowed the heavens also, and came down: and darkness was under his feet.

10 And he rode upon a cherub, and did fly: yea, he did fly upon the wings of the wind.

11 He made darkness his secret place; his pavilion round about him were dark waters and thick clouds of the skies.

12 At the brightness that was before him his thick clouds passed, hail stones and coals of fire.

13 The LORD also thundered in the heavens, and the Highest gave his voice; hail stones and coals of fire.

14 Yea, he sent out his arrows, and scattered them; and he shot out lightnings, and discomfited them.

15 Then the channels of waters were seen, and the foundations of the world were discovered at thy rebuke, O LORD, at the blast of the breath of thy nostrils.

16 He sent from above, he took me, he drew me out of many waters.

17 He delivered me from my strong enemy, and from them which hated me: for they were too strong for me.

18 They prevented me in the day of my calamity: but the LORD was my stay.

19 He brought me forth also into a large place; he delivered me, because he delighted in me.

20 The LORD rewarded me according to my righteousness; according to the cleanness of my hands hath he recompensed me.

21 For I have kept the ways of the LORD, and have not wickedly departed from my God.

22 For all his judgments were before me, and I did not put away his statutes from me.

23 I was also upright before him, and I kept myself from mine iniquity.

24 Therefore hath the LORD recompensed me according to my righteousness, according to the cleanness of my hands in his eyesight.

25 With the merciful thou wilt shew thyself merciful; with an upright man thou wilt shew thyself upright;

26 With the pure thou wilt shew thyself pure; and with the froward thou wilt shew thyself froward.

27 For thou wilt save the afflicted people; but wilt bring down high looks.

28 For thou wilt light my candle: the LORD my God will enlighten my darkness.

29 For by thee I have run through a troop; and by my God have I leaped over a wall.

30 As for God, his way is perfect: the word of the LORD is tried: he is a buckler to all those that trust in him.

31 For who is God save the LORD? or who is a rock save our God?

32 It is God that girdeth me with strength, and maketh my way perfect.

33 He maketh my feet like hinds' feet, and setteth me upon my high places.

34 He teacheth my hands to war, so that a bow of steel is broken by mine arms.

35 Thou hast also given me the shield of thy salvation: and thy right hand hath holden me up, and thy gentleness hath made me great.

36 Thou hast enlarged my steps under me, that my feet did not slip.

37 I have pursued mine enemies, and overtaken them: neither did I turn again till they were consumed.

38 I have wounded them that they were not able to rise: they are fallen under my feet.

39 For thou hast girded me with strength unto the battle: thou hast subdued under me those that rose up against me.

40 Thou hast also given me the necks of mine enemies; that I might destroy them that hate me.

41 They cried, but there was none to save them: even unto the LORD, but he answered them not.

42 Then did I beat them small as the dust before the wind: I did cast them out as the dirt in the streets.

43 Thou hast delivered me from the strivings of the people; and thou hast made me the head of the heathen: a people whom I have not known shall serve me.

44 As soon as they hear of me, they shall obey me: the strangers shall submit themselves unto me.

45 The strangers shall fade away, and be afraid out of their close places.

46 The LORD liveth; and blessed be my rock; and let the God of my salvation be exalted.

47 It is God that avengeth me, and subdueth the people under me.

48 He delivereth me from mine enemies: yea, thou liftest me up above those that rise up against me: thou hast delivered me from the violent man.

49 Therefore will I give thanks unto thee, O LORD, among the heathen, and sing praises unto thy name.

50 Great deliverance giveth he to his king; and sheweth mercy to his anointed, to David, and to his seed for evermore.

Psalms Chapter 21

1 The king shall joy in thy strength, O LORD; and in thy salvation how greatly shall he rejoice!

2 Thou hast given him his heart's desire, and hast not withholden the request of his lips. Selah.

3 For thou preventest him with the blessings of goodness: thou settest a crown of pure gold on his head.

4 He asked life of thee, and thou gavest it him, even length of days for ever and ever.

5 His glory is great in thy salvation: honour and majesty hast thou laid upon him.

6 For thou hast made him most blessed for ever: thou hast made him exceeding glad with thy countenance.

7 For the king trusteth in the LORD, and through the mercy of the most High he shall not be moved.

8 Thine hand shall find out all thine enemies: thy right hand shall find out those that hate thee.

9 Thou shalt make them as a fiery oven in the time of thine anger: the LORD shall swallow them up in his wrath, and the fire shall devour them.

10 Their fruit shalt thou destroy from the earth, and their seed from among the children of men.

11 For they intended evil against thee: they imagined a mischievous device, which they are not able to perform.

12 Therefore shalt thou make them turn their back, when thou shalt make ready thine arrows upon thy strings against the face of them.

13 Be thou exalted, LORD, in thine own strength: so will we sing and praise thy power.

Psalms Chapter 22

1 My God, my God, why hast thou forsaken me? why art thou so far from helping me, and from the words of my roaring?

2 O my God, I cry in the day time, but thou hearest not; and in the night season, and am not silent.

3 But thou art holy, O thou that inhabitest the praises of Israel.

4 Our fathers trusted in thee: they trusted, and thou didst deliver them.

5 They cried unto thee, and were delivered: they trusted in thee, and were not confounded.

6 But I am a worm, and no man; a reproach of men, and despised of the people.

7 All they that see me laugh me to scorn: they shoot out the lip, they shake the head, saying,

8 He trusted on the LORD that he would deliver him: let him deliver him, seeing he delighted in him.

9 But thou art he that took me out of the womb: thou didst make me hope when I was upon my mother's breasts.

10 I was cast upon thee from the womb: thou art my God from my mother's belly.

11 Be not far from me; for trouble is near; for there is none to help.

12 Many bulls have compassed me: strong bulls of Bashan have beset me round.

13 They gaped upon me with their mouths, as a ravening and a roaring lion.

14 I am poured out like water, and all my bones are out of joint: my heart is like wax; it is melted in the midst of my bowels.

15 My strength is dried up like a potsherd; and my tongue cleaveth to my jaws; and thou hast brought me into the dust of death.

16 For dogs have compassed me: the assembly of the wicked have inclosed me: they pierced my hands and my feet.

17 I may tell all my bones: they look and stare upon me.

18 They part my garments among them, and cast lots upon my vesture.

19 But be not thou far from me, O LORD: O my strength, haste thee to help me.

20 Deliver my soul from the sword; my darling from the power of the dog.

21 Save me from the lion's mouth: for thou hast heard me from the horns of the unicorns.

22 I will declare thy name unto my brethren: in the midst of the congregation will I praise thee.

23 Ye that fear the LORD, praise him; all ye the seed of Jacob, glorify him; and fear him, all ye the seed of Israel.

24 For he hath not despised nor abhorred the affliction of the afflicted; neither hath he hid his face from him; but when he cried unto him, he heard.

25 My praise shall be of thee in the great congregation: I will pay my vows before them that fear him.

26 The meek shall eat and be satisfied: they shall praise the LORD that seek him: your heart shall live for ever.

27 All the ends of the world shall remember and turn unto the LORD: and all the kindreds of the nations shall worshipbefore thee.

28 For the kingdom is the LORD's: and he is the governor among the nations.

29 All they that be fat upon earth shall eat and worship: all they that go down to the dust shall bow before him: and none can keep alive his own soul.

30 A seed shall serve him; it shall be accounted to the Lord for a generation.

31 They shall come, and shall declare his righteousness unto a people that shall be born, that he hath done this.

Psalms Chapter 24

1 The earth is the LORD's, and the fulness thereof; the world, and they that dwell therein.

2 For he hath founded it upon the seas, and established it upon the floods.

3 Who shall ascend into the hill of the LORD? or who shall stand in his holy place?

4 He that hath clean hands, and a pure heart; who hath not lifted up his soul unto vanity, nor sworn deceitfully.

5 He shall receive the blessing from the LORD, and righteousness from the God of his salvation.

6 This is the generation of them that seek him, that seek thy face, O Jacob. Selah.

7 Lift up your heads, O ye gates; and be ye lift up, ye everlasting doors; and the King of glory shall come in.

8 Who is this King of glory? The LORD strong and mighty, the LORD mighty in battle.

9 Lift up your heads, O ye gates; even lift them up, ye everlasting doors; and the King of glory shall come in.

10 Who is this King of glory? The LORD of hosts, he is the King of glory. Selah.

Psalms Chapter 27

1 The LORD is my light and my salvation; whom shall I fear? the LORD is the strength of my life; of whom shall I be afraid?

2 When the wicked, even mine enemies and my foes, came upon me to eat up my flesh, they stumbled and fell.

3 Though an host should encamp against me, my heart shall not fear: though war should rise against me, in this will I be confident.

4 One thing have I desired of the LORD, that will I seek after; that I may dwell in the house of the LORD all the days of my life, to behold the beauty of

the LORD, and to enquire in
his temple.

5 For in the time of trouble he shall hide
me in his pavilion: in the secret of
his tabernacle shall he hide me; he shall
set me up upon a rock.

6 And now shall mine head be lifted up
above mine enemies round about me:
therefore will I offer in
his tabernaclesacrifices of joy; I will sing,
yea, I will sing praises unto the LORD.

7 Hear, O LORD, when I cry with my
voice: have mercy also upon me, and
answer me.

8 When thou saidst, Seek ye my face; my
heart said unto thee, Thy face, LORD,
will I seek.

9 Hide not thy face far from me; put not
thy servant away in anger: thou hast
been my help; leave me not, neither
forsake me, O God of my salvation.

10 When my father and my mother
forsake me, then the LORD will take
me up.

11 Teach me thy way, O LORD, and
lead me in a plain path, because of mine
enemies.

12 Deliver me not over unto the will of
mine enemies: for false witnesses are
risen up against me, and such as breathe
out cruelty.

13 I had fainted, unless I had believed to
see the goodness of the LORD in the
land of the living.

14 Wait on the LORD: be of good
courage, and he shall strengthen thine
heart: wait, I say, on the LORD.

Psalms Chapter 29

1 Give unto the LORD, O ye mighty,
give unto the LORD glory and
strength.

2 Give unto the LORD the glory due
unto his name; worship the LORD in
the beauty of holiness.

3 The voice of the LORD is upon the
waters: the God of glory thundereth: the
LORD is upon many waters.

4 The voice of the LORD is powerful;
the voice of the LORD is full of majesty.

5 The voice of the LORD breaketh the
cedars; yea, the LORD breaketh the
cedars of Lebanon.

6 He maketh them also to skip like
a calf; Lebanon and Sirion like a
young unicorn.

7 The voice of the LORD divideth the
flames of fire.

8 The voice of the LORD shaketh
the wilderness; the LORD shaketh
the wilderness of Kadesh.

9 The voice of the LORD maketh the
hinds to calve, and discovereth the

forests: and in his temple doth every one speak of his glory.

10 The LORD sitteth upon the flood; yea, the LORD sitteth King for ever.

11 The LORD will give strength unto his people; the LORD will bless his people with peace.

Psalms Chapter 30

1 I will extol thee, O LORD; for thou hast lifted me up, and hast not made my foes to rejoice over me.

2 O LORD my God, I cried unto thee, and thou hast healed me.

3 O LORD, thou hast brought up my soul from the grave: thou hast kept me alive, that I should not go down to the pit.

4 Sing unto the LORD, O ye saints of his, and give thanks at the remembrance of his holiness.

5 For his anger endureth but a moment; in his favour is life: weeping may endure for a night, but joy cometh in the morning.

6 And in my prosperity I said, I shall never be moved.

7 LORD, by thy favour thou hast made my mountain to stand strong: thou didst hide thy face, and I was troubled.

8 I cried to thee, O LORD; and unto the LORD I made supplication.

9 What profit is there in my blood, when I go down to the pit? Shall the dust praise thee? shall it declare thy truth?

10 Hear, O LORD, and have mercy upon me: LORD, be thou my helper.

11 Thou hast turned for me my mourning into dancing: thou hast put off my sackcloth, and girded me with gladness;

12 To the end that my glory may sing praise to thee, and not be silent. O LORD my God, I will give thanks unto thee for ever.

Psalms Chapter 31

1 In thee, O LORD, do I put my trust; let me never be ashamed: deliver me in thy righteousness.

2 Bow down thine ear to me; deliver me speedily: be thou my strong rock, for an house of defence to save me.

3 For thou art my rock and my fortress; therefore for thy name's sake lead me, and guide me.

4 Pull me out of the net that they have laid privily for me: for thou art my strength.

5 Into thine hand I commit my spirit: thou hast redeemed me, O LORD God of truth.

6 I have hated them that regard lying vanities: but I trust in the LORD.

7 I will be glad and rejoice in thy mercy: for thou hast considered my trouble; thou hast known my soul in adversities;

8 And hast not shut me up into the hand of the enemy: thou hast set my feet in a large room.

9 Have mercy upon me, O LORD, for I am in trouble: mine eye is consumed with grief, yea, my soul and my belly.

10 For my life is spent with grief, and my years with sighing: my strength faileth because of mine iniquity, and my bones are consumed.

11 I was a reproach among all mine enemies, but especially among my neighbours, and a fear to mine acquaintance: they that did see me without fled from me.

12 I am forgotten as a dead man out of mind: I am like a broken vessel.

13 For I have heard the slander of many: fear was on every side: while they took counsel together against me, they devised to take away my life.

14 But I trusted in thee, O LORD: I said, Thou art my God.

15 My times are in thy hand: deliver me from the hand of mine enemies, and from them that persecute me.

16 Make thy face to shine upon thy servant: save me for thy mercies' sake.

17 Let me not be ashamed, O LORD; for I have called upon thee: let the wicked be ashamed, and let them be silent in the grave.

18 Let the lying lips be put to silence; which speak grievous things proudly and contemptuously against the righteous.

19 Oh how great is thy goodness, which thou hast laid up for them that fear thee; which thou hast wrought for them that trust in thee before the sons of men!

20 Thou shalt hide them in the secret of thy presence from the pride of man: thou shalt keep them secretly in a pavilion from the strife of tongues.

21 Blessed be the LORD: for he hath shewed me his marvellous kindness in a strong city.

22 For I said in my haste, I am cut off from before thine eyes: nevertheless thou heardest the voice of my supplications when I cried unto thee.

23 O love the LORD, all ye his saints: for the LORD preserveth the faithful, and plentifully rewardeth the proud doer.

24 Be of good courage, and he shall strengthen your heart, all ye that hope in the LORD.

Psalms Chapter 32

1 Blessed is he whose transgression is forgiven, whose sin is covered.

2 Blessed is the man unto whom the LORD imputeth not iniquity, and in whose spirit there is no guile.

3 When I kept silence, my bones waxed old through my roaring all the day long.

4 For day and night thy hand was heavy upon me: my moisture is turned into the drought of summer. Selah.

5 I acknowledge my sin unto thee, and mine iniquity have I not hid. I said, I will confess my transgressions unto the LORD; and thou forgavest the iniquity of my sin. Selah.

6 For this shall every one that is godly pray unto thee in a time when thou mayest be found: surely in the floods of great waters they shall not come nigh unto him.

7 Thou art my hiding place; thou shalt preserve me from trouble; thou shalt compass me about with songs of deliverance. Selah.

8 I will instruct thee and teach thee in the way which thou shalt go: I will guide thee with mine eye.

9 Be ye not as the horse, or as the mule, which have no understanding: whose mouth must be held in with bit and bridle, lest they come near unto thee.

10 Many sorrows shall be to the wicked: but he that trusteth in the LORD, mercy shall compass him about.

11 Be glad in the LORD, and rejoice, ye righteous: and shout for joy, all ye that are upright in heart.

Psalms Chapter 37

1 Fret not thyself because of evildoers, neither be thou envious against the workers of iniquity.

2 For they shall soon be cut down like the grass, and wither as the green herb.

3 Trust in the LORD, and do good; so shalt thou dwell in the land, and verily thou shalt be fed.

4 Delight thyself also in the LORD: and he shall give thee the desires of thine heart.

5 Commit thy way unto the LORD; trust also in him; and he shall bring it to pass.

6 And he shall bring forth thy righteousness as the light, and thy judgment as the noonday.

7 Rest in the LORD, and wait patiently for him: fret not thyself because of him who prospereth in his way, because of the man who bringeth wicked devices to pass.

8 Cease from anger, and forsake wrath: fret not thyself in any wise to do evil.

9 For evildoers shall be cut off: but those that wait upon the LORD, they shall inherit the earth.

10 For yet a little while, and the wicked shall not be: yea, thou shalt diligently consider his place, and it shall not be.

11 But the meek shall inherit the earth; and shall delight themselves in the abundance of peace.

12 The wicked plotteth against the just, and gnasheth upon him with his teeth.

13 The LORD shall laugh at him: for he seeth that his day is coming.

14 The wicked have drawn out the sword, and have bent their bow, to cast down the poor and needy, and to slay such as be of upright conversation.

15 Their sword shall enter into their own heart, and their bows shall be broken.

16 A little that a righteous man hath is better than the riches of many wicked.

17 For the arms of the wicked shall be broken: but the LORD upholdeth the righteous.

18 The LORD knoweth the days of the upright: and their inheritance shall be for ever.

19 They shall not be ashamed in the evil time: and in the days of famine they shall be satisfied.

20 But the wicked shall perish, and the enemies of the LORD shall be as the fat of lambs: they shall consume; into smoke shall they consume away.

21 The wicked borroweth, and payeth not again: but the righteous sheweth mercy, and giveth.

22 For such as be blessed of him shall inherit the earth; and they that be cursed of him shall be cut off.

23 The steps of a good man are ordered by the LORD: and he delighteth in his way.

24 Though he fall, he shall not be utterly cast down: for the LORD upholdeth him with his hand.

25 I have been young, and now am old; yet have I not seen the righteous forsaken, nor his seed begging bread.

26 He is ever merciful, and lendeth; and his seed is blessed.

27 Depart from evil, and do good; and dwell for evermore.

28 For the LORD loveth judgment, and forsaketh not his saints; they are preserved for ever: but the seed of the wicked shall be cut off.

29 The righteous shall inherit the land, and dwell therein for ever.

30 The mouth of the righteous speaketh wisdom, and his tongue talketh of judgment.

31 The law of his God is in his heart; none of his steps shall slide.

32 The wicked watcheth the righteous, and seeketh to slay him.

33 The LORD will not leave him in his hand, nor condemn him when he is judged.

34 Wait on the LORD, and keep his way, and he shall exalt thee to inherit the land: when the wicked are cut off, thou shalt see it.

35 I have seen the wicked in great power, and spreading himself like a green bay tree.

36 Yet he passed away, and, lo, he was not: yea, I sought him, but he could not be found.

37 Mark the perfect man, and behold the upright: for the end of that man is peace.

38 But the transgressors shall be destroyed together: the end of the wicked shall be cut off.

39 But the salvation of the righteous is of the LORD: he is their strength in the time of trouble.

40 And the LORD shall help them, and deliver them: he shall deliver them from the wicked, and save them, because they trust in him.

Psalms Chapter 39

1 I said, I will take heed to my ways, that I sin not with my tongue: I will keep my mouth with a bridle, while the wicked is before me.

2 I was dumb with silence, I held my peace, even from good; and my sorrow was stirred.

3 My heart was hot within me, while I was musing the fire burned: then spake I with my tongue,

4 LORD, make me to know mine end, and the measure of my days, what it is: that I may know how frail I am.

5 Behold, thou hast made my days as an handbreadth; and mine age is as nothing before thee: verily every man at his best state is altogether vanity. Selah.

6 Surely every man walketh in a vain shew: surely they are disquieted in vain: he heapeth up riches, and knoweth not who shall gather them.

7 And now, Lord, what wait I for? my hope is in thee.

8 Deliver me from all my transgressions: make me not the reproach of the foolish.

9 I was dumb, I opened not my mouth; because thou didst it.

10 Remove thy stroke away from me: I am consumed by the blow of thine hand.

11 When thou with rebukes dost correct man for iniquity, thou makest his beauty to consume away like a moth: surely every man is vanity. Selah.

12 Hear my prayer, O LORD, and give ear unto my cry; hold not thy peace at my tears: for I am a stranger with thee, and a sojourner, as all my fathers were.

13 O spare me, that I may recover strength, before I go hence, and be no more.

Psalms Chapter 40

1 I waited patiently for the LORD; and he inclined unto me, and heard my cry.

2 He brought me up also out of an horrible pit, out of the miry clay, and set my feet upon a rock, and established my goings.

3 And he hath put a new song in my mouth, even praise unto our God: many shall see it, and fear, and shall trust in the LORD.

4 Blessed is that man that maketh the LORD his trust, and respecteth not the proud, nor such as turn aside to lies.

5 Many, O LORD my God, are thy wonderful works which thou hast done, and thy thoughts which are to us-ward: they cannot be reckoned up in order unto thee: if I would declare and speak of them, they are more than can be numbered.

6 Sacrifice and offering thou didst not desire; mine ears hast thou opened: burnt offering and sin offering hast thou not required.

7 Then said I, Lo, I come: in the volume of the book it is written of me,

8 I delight to do thy will, O my God: yea, thy law is within my heart.

9 I have preached righteousness in the great congregation: lo, I have not refrained my lips, O LORD, thou knowest.

10 I have not hid thy righteousness within my heart; I have declared thy faithfulness and thy salvation: I have not concealed thy lovingkindness and thy truth from the great congregation.

11 Withhold not thou thy tender mercies from me, O LORD: let thy lovingkindness and thy truth continually preserve me.

12 For innumerable evils have compassed me about: mine iniquities have taken hold upon me, so that I am not able to look up; they are more than the hairs of mine head: therefore my heart faileth me.

13 Be pleased, O LORD, to deliver me: O LORD, make haste to help me.

14 Let them be ashamed and confounded together that seek after my soul to destroy it; let them be driven

backward and put to shame that wish me evil.

15 Let them be desolate for a reward of their shame that say unto me, Aha, aha.

16 Let all those that seek thee rejoice and be glad in thee: let such as love thy salvation say continually, The LORD be magnified.

17 But I am poor and needy; yet the Lord thinketh upon me: thou art my help and my deliverer; make no tarrying, O my God.

Psalms Chapter 42

1 As the hart panteth after the water brooks, so panteth my soul after thee, O God.

2 My soul thirsteth for God, for the living God: when shall I come and appear before God?

3 My tears have been my meat day and night, while they continually say unto me, Where is thy God?

4 When I remember these things, I pour out my soul in me: for I had gone with the multitude, I went with them to the house of God, with the voice of joy and praise, with a multitude that kept holyday.

5 Why art thou cast down, O my soul? and why art thou disquieted in me? hope thou in God: for I shall yet praise him for the help of his countenance.

6 O my God, my soul is cast down within me: therefore will I remember thee from the land of Jordan, and of the Hermonites, from the hill Mizar.

7 Deep calleth unto deep at the noise of thy waterspouts: all thy waves and thy billows are gone over me.

8 Yet the LORD will command his lovingkindness in the day time, and in the night his song shall be with me, and my prayer unto the God of my life.

9 I will say unto God my rock, Why hast thou forgotten me? why go I mourning because of the oppression of the enemy?

10 As with a sword in my bones, mine enemies reproach me; while they say daily unto me, Where is thy God?

11 Why art thou cast down, O my soul? and why art thou disquieted within me? hope thou in God: for I shall yet praise him, who is the health of my countenance, and my God.

Psalms Chapter 46

1 God is our refuge and strength, a very present help in trouble.

2 Therefore will not we fear, though the earth be removed, and though the mountains be carried into the midst of the sea;

3 Though the waters thereof roar and be troubled, though the mountains shake with the swelling thereof. Selah.

4 There is a river, the streams whereof shall make glad the city of God, the holy place of the tabernacles of the most High.

5 God is in the midst of her; she shall not be moved: God shall help her, and that right early.

6 The heathen raged, the kingdoms were moved: he uttered his voice, the earth melted.

7 The LORD of hosts is with us; the God of Jacob is our refuge. Selah.

8 Come, behold the works of the LORD, what desolations he hath made in the earth.

9 He maketh wars to cease unto the end of the earth; he breaketh the bow, and cutteth the spear in sunder; he burneth the chariot in the fire.

10 Be still, and know that I am God: I will be exalted among the heathen, I will be exalted in the earth.

11 The LORD of hosts is with us; the God of Jacob is our refuge. Selah.

Psalms Chapter 47

1 O clap your hands, all ye people; shout unto God with the voice of triumph.

2 For the LORD most high is terrible; he is a great King over all the earth.

3 He shall subdue the people under us, and the nations under our feet.

4 He shall choose our inheritance for us, the excellency of Jacob whom he loved. Selah.

5 God is gone up with a shout, the LORD with the sound of a trumpet.

6 Sing praises to God, sing praises: sing praises unto our King, sing praises.

7 For God is the King of all the earth: sing ye praises with understanding.

8 God reigneth over the heathen: God sitteth upon the throne of his holiness.

9 The princes of the people are gathered together, even the people of the God of Abraham: for the shields of the earth belong unto God: he is greatly exalted.

Psalms Chapter 48

1 Great is the LORD, and greatly to be praised in the city of our God, in the mountain of his holiness.

2 Beautiful for situation, the joy of the whole earth, is mount Zion, on the sides of the north, the city of the great King.

3 God is known in her palaces for a refuge.

4 For, lo, the kings were assembled, they passed by together.

5 They saw it, and so they marvelled; they were troubled, and hasted away.

6 Fear took hold upon them there, and pain, as of a woman in travail.

7 Thou breakest
the ships of Tarshish with an east wind.

8 As we have heard, so have we seen in
the city of the LORD of hosts, in the
city of our God: God will establish it for
ever. Selah.

9 We have thought of thy
lovingkindness, O God, in the midst of
thy temple.

10 According to thy name, O God, so is
thy praise unto the ends of the earth: thy
right hand is full of righteousness.

11 Let mount Zion rejoice, let the
daughters of Judah be glad, because of
thy judgments.

12 Walk about Zion, and go round about
her: tell the towers thereof.

13 Mark ye well her bulwarks, consider
her palaces; that ye may tell it to
the generation following.

14 For this God is our God for ever and
ever: he will be our guide even unto
death.

Psalms Chapter 49

1 Hear this, all ye people; give ear, all ye
inhabitants of the world:

2 Both low and high, rich and poor,
together.

3 My mouth shall speak of wisdom; and
the meditation of my heart shall be of
understanding.

4 I will incline mine ear to a parable: I
will open my dark saying upon the harp.

5 Wherefore should I fear in the days of
evil, when the iniquity of my heels shall
compass me about?

6 They that trust in their wealth, and
boast themselves in the multitude of
their riches;

7 None of them can by any means
redeem his brother, nor give to God
a ransom for him:

8 (For the redemption of their soul is
precious, and it ceaseth for ever:)

9 That he should still live for ever, and
not see corruption.

10 For he seeth that wise men die,
likewise the fool and the brutish person
perish, and leave their wealth to others.

11 Their inward thought is, that their
houses shall continue for ever, and their
dwelling places to all generations; they
call their lands after their own names.

12 Nevertheless man being in honour
abideth not: he is like the beasts that
perish.

13 This their way is their folly: yet their
posterity approve their sayings. Selah.

14 Like sheep they are laid in the grave;
death shall feed on them; and the
upright shall have dominion over them
in the morning; and their beauty shall

consume in the grave from their dwelling.

15 But God will redeem my soul from the power of the grave: for he shall receive me. Selah.

16 Be not thou afraid when one is made rich, when the glory of his house is increased;

17 For when he dieth he shall carry nothing away: his glory shall not descend after him.

18 Though while he lived he blessed his soul: and men will praise thee, when thou doest well to thyself.

19 He shall go to the generation of his fathers; they shall never see light.

20 Man that is in honour, and understandeth not, is like the beasts that perish.

Psalms Chapter 51

1 Have mercy upon me, O God, according to thy lovingkindness: according unto the multitude of thy tender mercies blot out my transgressions.

2 Wash me throughly from mine iniquity, and cleanse me from my sin.

3 For I acknowledge my transgressions: and my sin is ever before me.

4 Against thee, thee only, have I sinned, and done this evil in thy sight: that thou mightest be justified when thou speakest, and be clear when thou judgest.

5 Behold, I was shapen in iniquity; and in sin did my mother conceive me.

6 Behold, thou desirest truth in the inward parts: and in the hidden part thou shalt make me to know wisdom.

7 Purge me with hyssop, and I shall be clean: wash me, and I shall be whiter than snow.

8 Make me to hear joy and gladness; that the bones which thou hast broken may rejoice.

9 Hide thy face from my sins, and blot out all mine iniquities.

10 Create in me a clean heart, O God; and renew a right spirit within me.

11 Cast me not away from thy presence; and take not thy holy spirit from me.

12 Restore unto me the joy of thy salvation; and uphold me with thy free spirit.

13 Then will I teach transgressors thy ways; and sinners shall be converted unto thee.

14 Deliver me from bloodguiltiness, O God, thou God of my salvation: and my tongue shall sing aloud of thy righteousness.

15 O Lord, open thou my lips; and my mouth shall shew forth thy praise.

16 For thou desirest not sacrifice; else would I give it: thou delightest not in burnt offering.

17 The sacrifices of God are a broken spirit: a broken and a contrite heart, O God, thou wilt not despise.

18 Do good in thy good pleasure unto Zion: build thou the walls of Jerusalem.

19 Then shalt thou be pleased with the sacrifices of righteousness, with burnt offering and whole burnt offering: then shall they offer bullocks upon thine altar.

Psalms Chapter 53

1 The fool hath said in his heart, There is no God. Corrupt are they, and have done abominable iniquity: there is none that doeth good.

2 God looked down from heaven upon the children of men, to see if there were any that did understand, that did seek God.

3 Every one of them is gone back: they are altogether become filthy; there is none that doeth good, no, not one.

4 Have the workers of iniquity no knowledge? who eat up my people as they eat bread: they have not called upon God.

5 There were they in great fear, where no fear was: for God hath scattered the bones of him that encampeth against thee: thou hast put them to shame, because God hath despised them.

6 Oh that the salvation of Israel were come out of Zion! When God bringeth back the captivity of his people, Jacob shall rejoice, and Israel shall be glad.

Psalms Chapter 54

1 Save me, O God, by thy name, and judge me by thy strength.

2 Hear my prayer, O God; give ear to the words of my mouth.

3 For strangers are risen up against me, and oppressors seek after my soul: they have not set God before them. Selah.

4 Behold, God is mine helper: the Lord is with them that uphold my soul.

5 He shall reward evil unto mine enemies: cut them off in thy truth.

6 I will freely sacrifice unto thee: I will praise thy name, O LORD; for it is good.

7 For he hath delivered me out of all trouble: and mine eye hath seen his desire upon mine enemies.

Psalms Chapter 56

1 Be merciful unto me, O God: for man would swallow me up; he fighting daily oppresseth me.

2 Mine enemies would daily swallow me up: for they be many that fight against me, O thou most High.

3 What time I am afraid, I will trust in thee.

4 In God I will praise his word, in God I have put my trust; I will not fear what flesh can do unto me.

5 Every day they wrest my words: all their thoughts are against me for evil.

6 They gather themselves together, they hide themselves, they mark my steps, when they wait for my soul.

7 Shall they escape by iniquity? in thine anger cast down the people, O God.

8 Thou tellest my wanderings: put thou my tears into thy bottle: are they not in thy book?

9 When I cry unto thee, then shall mine enemies turn back: this I know; for God is for me.

10 In God will I praise his word: in the LORD will I praise his word.

11 In God have I put my trust: I will not be afraid what man can do unto me.

12 Thy vows are upon me, O God: I will render praises unto thee.

13 For thou hast delivered my soul from death: wilt not thou deliver my feet from falling, that I may walk before God in the light of the living?

Psalms Chapter 60

1 O God, thou hast cast us off, thou hast scattered us, thou hast been displeased; O turn thyself to us again.

2 Thou hast made the earth to tremble; thou hast broken it: heal the breaches thereof; for it shaketh.

3 Thou hast shewed thy people hard things: thou hast made us to drink the wine of astonishment.

4 Thou hast given a banner to them that fear thee, that it may be displayed because of the truth. Selah.

5 That thy beloved may be delivered; save with thy right hand, and hear me.

6 God hath spoken in his holiness; I will rejoice, I will divide Shechem, and mete out the valley of Succoth.

7 Gilead is mine, and Manasseh is mine; Ephraim also is the strength of mine head; Judah is my lawgiver;

8 Moab is my washpot; over Edom will I cast out my shoe: Philistia, triumph thou because of me.

9 Who will bring me into the strong city? who will lead me into Edom?

10 Wilt not thou, O God, which hadst cast us off? and thou, O God, which didst not go out with our armies?

11 Give us help from trouble: for vain is the help of man.

12 Through God we shall do valiantly: for he it is that shall tread down our enemies.

Psalms Chapter 64

1 Hear my voice, O God, in my prayer: preserve my life from fear of the enemy.

2 Hide me from the secret counsel of the wicked; from the insurrection of the workers of iniquity:

3 Who whet their tongue like a sword, and bend their bows to shoot their arrows, even bitter words:

4 That they may shoot in secret at the perfect: suddenly do they shoot at him, and fear not.

5 They encourage themselves in an evil matter: they commune of laying snares privily; they say, Who shall see them?

6 They search out iniquities; they accomplish a diligent search: both the inward thought of every one of them, and the heart, is deep.

7 But God shall shoot at them with an arrow; suddenly shall they be wounded.

8 So they shall make their own tongue to fall upon themselves: all that see them shall flee away.

9 And all men shall fear, and shall declare the work of God; for they shall wisely consider of his doing.

10 The righteous shall be glad in the LORD, and shall trust in him; and all the upright in heart shall glory.

Psalms Chapter 67

1 God be merciful unto us, and bless us; and cause his face to shine upon us; Selah.

2 That thy way may be known upon earth, thy saving health among all nations.

3 Let the people praise thee, O God; let all the people praise thee.

4 O let the nations be glad and sing for joy: for thou shalt judge the people righteously, and govern the nations upon earth. Selah.

5 Let the people praise thee, O God; let all the people praise thee.

6 Then shall the earth yield her increase; and God, even our own God, shall bless us.

7 God shall bless us; and all the ends of the earth shall fear him.

Psalms Chapter 68

1 Let God arise, let his enemies be scattered: let them also that hate him flee before him.

2 As smoke is driven away, so drive them away: as wax melteth before the fire, so let the wicked perish at the presence of God.

3 But let the righteous be glad; let them rejoice before God: yea, let them exceedingly rejoice.

4 Sing unto God, sing praises to his name: extol him that rideth upon the heavens by his name JAH, and rejoice before him.

5 A father of the fatherless, and a judge of the widows, is God in his holy habitation.

6 God setteth the solitary in families: he bringeth out those which are bound with chains: but the rebellious dwell in a dry land.

7 O God, when thou wentest forth before thy people, when thou didst march through the wilderness; Selah:

8 The earth shook, the heavens also dropped at the presence of God: even Sinai itself was moved at the presence of God, the God of Israel.

9 Thou, O God, didst send a plentiful rain, whereby thou didst confirm thine inheritance, when it was weary.

10 Thy congregation hath dwelt therein: thou, O God, hast prepared of thy goodness for the poor.

11 The Lord gave the word: great was the company of those that published it.

12 Kings of armies did flee apace: and she that tarried at home divided the spoil.

13 Though ye have lien among the pots, yet shall ye be as the wings of a dove covered with silver, and her feathers with yellow gold.

14 When the Almighty scattered kings in it, it was white as snow in Salmon.

15 The hill of God is as the hill of Bashan; an high hill as the hill of Bashan.

16 Why leap ye, ye high hills? this is the hill which God desireth to dwell in; yea, the LORD will dwell in it for ever.

17 The chariots of God are twenty thousand, even thousands of angels: the Lord is among them, as in Sinai, in the holy place.

18 Thou hast ascended on high, thou hast led captivity captive: thou hast received gifts for men; yea, for the rebellious also, that the LORD God might dwell among them.

19 Blessed be the Lord, who daily loadeth us with benefits, even the God of our salvation. Selah.

20 He that is our God is the God
of salvation; and unto GOD the Lord
belong the issues from death.

21 But God shall wound the head of his
enemies, and the hairy scalp of such an
one as goeth on still in his trespasses.

22 The Lord said, I will bring again
from Bashan, I will bring my people
again from the depths of the sea:

23 That thy foot may be dipped in
the blood of thine enemies, and the
tongue of thy dogs in the same.

24 They have seen thy goings, O God;
even the goings of my God, my King, in
the sanctuary.

25 The singers went before, the players
on instruments followed after; among
them were the damsels playing with
timbrels.

26 Bless ye God in the congregations,
even the Lord, from
the fountain of Israel.

27 There is little Benjamin with their
ruler, the princes of Judah and
their council, the princes of Zebulun,
and the princes of Naphtali.

28 Thy God hath commanded thy
strength: strengthen, O God, that which
thou hast wrought for us.

29 Because of
thy temple at Jerusalem shall kings bring
presents unto thee.

30 Rebuke the company of spearmen,
the multitude of the bulls, with the
calves of the people, till every one submit
himself with pieces of silver: scatter thou
the people that delight in war.

31 Princes shall come out
of Egypt; Ethiopia shall soon stretch out
her hands unto God.

32 Sing unto God, ye kingdoms of the
earth; O sing praises unto the
Lord; Selah:

33 To him that rideth upon the heavens
of heavens, which were of old; lo, he
doth send out his voice, and that a
mighty voice.

34 Ascribe ye strength unto God: his
excellency is over Israel, and his strength
is in the clouds.

35 O God, thou art terrible out of thy
holy places: the God of Israel is he that
giveth strength and power unto his
people. Blessed be God.

Psalms Chapter 72

1 Give the king thy judgments, O God,
and thy righteousness unto the king's
son.

2 He shall judge thy people
with righteousness, and thy poor with
judgment.

3 The mountains shall bring peace to the
people, and the little hills,
by righteousness.

4 He shall judge the poor of the people, he shall save the children of the needy, and shall break in pieces the oppressor.

5 They shall fear thee as long as the sun and moon endure, throughout all generations.

6 He shall come down like rain upon the mown grass: as showers that water the earth.

7 In his days shall the righteous flourish; and abundance of peace so long as the moon endureth.

8 He shall have dominion also from sea to sea, and from the river unto the ends of the earth.

9 They that dwell in the wilderness shall bow before him; and his enemies shall lick the dust.

10 The kings of Tarshish and of the isles shall bring presents: the kings of Sheba and Seba shall offer gifts.

11 Yea, all kings shall fall down before him: all nations shall serve him.

12 For he shall deliver the needy when he crieth; the poor also, and him that hath no helper.

13 He shall spare the poor and needy, and shall save the souls of the needy.

14 He shall redeem their soul from deceit and violence: and precious shall their blood be in his sight.

15 And he shall live, and to him shall be given of the gold of Sheba: prayer also shall be made for him continually; and daily shall he be praised.

16 There shall be an handful of corn in the earth upon the top of the mountains; the fruit thereof shall shake like Lebanon: and they of the city shall flourish like grass of the earth.

17 His name shall endure for ever: his name shall be continued as long as the sun: and men shall be blessed in him: all nations shall call him blessed.

18 Blessed be the LORD God, the God of Israel, who only doeth wondrous things.

19 And blessed be his glorious name for ever: and let the whole earth be filled with his glory; Amen, and Amen.

20 The prayers of David the son of Jesse are ended.

Psalms Chapter 76

1 In Judah is God known: his name is great in Israel.

2 In Salem also is his tabernacle, and his dwelling place in Zion.

3 There brake he the arrows of the bow, the shield, and the sword, and the battle. Selah.

4 Thou art more glorious and excellent than the mountains of prey.

5 The stouthearted are spoiled, they have slept their sleep: and none of the men of might have found their hands.

6 At thy rebuke, O God of Jacob, both the chariot and horse are cast into a dead sleep.

7 Thou, even thou, art to be feared: and who may stand in thy sight when once thou art angry?

8 Thou didst cause judgment to be heard from heaven; the earth feared, and was still,

9 When God arose to judgment, to save all the meek of the earth. Selah.

10 Surely the wrath of man shall praise thee: the remainder of wrath shalt thou restrain.

11 Vow, and pay unto the LORD your God: let all that be round about him bring presents unto him that ought to be feared.

12 He shall cut off the spirit of princes: he is terrible to the kings of the earth.

Psalms Chapter 77

1 I cried unto God with my voice, even unto God with my voice; and he gave ear unto me.

2 In the day of my trouble I sought the Lord: my sore ran in the night, and ceased not: my soul refused to be comforted.

3 I remembered God, and was troubled: I complained, and my spirit was overwhelmed. Selah.

4 Thou holdest mine eyes waking: I am so troubled that I cannot speak.

5 I have considered the days of old, the years of ancient times.

6 I call to remembrance my song in the night: I commune with mine own heart: and my spirit made diligent search.

7 Will the Lord cast off for ever? and will he be favourable no more?

8 Is his mercy clean gone for ever? doth his promise fail for evermore?

9 Hath God forgotten to be gracious? hath he in anger shut up his tender mercies? Selah.

10 And I said, This is my infirmity: but I will remember the years of the right hand of the most High.

11 I will remember the works of the LORD: surely I will remember thy wonders of old.

12 I will meditate also of all thy work, and talk of thy doings.

13 Thy way, O God, is in the sanctuary: who is so great a God as our God?

14 Thou art the God that doest wonders: thou hast declared thy strength among the people.

15 Thou hast with thine arm redeemed thy people, the sons of Jacob and Joseph. Selah.

16 The waters saw thee, O God, the waters saw thee; they were afraid: the depths also were troubled.

17 The clouds poured out water: the skies sent out a sound: thine arrows also went abroad.

18 The voice of thy thunder was in the heaven: the lightnings lightened the world: the earth trembled and shook.

19 Thy way is in the sea, and thy path in the great waters, and thy footsteps are not known.

20 Thou leddest thy people like a flock by the hand of Moses and Aaron.

Psalms Chapter 81

1 Sing aloud unto God our strength: make a joyful noise unto the God of Jacob.

2 Take a psalm, and bring hither the timbrel, the pleasant harp with the psaltery.

3 Blow up the trumpet in the new moon, in the time appointed, on our solemn feast day.

4 For this was a statute for Israel, and a law of the God of Jacob.

5 This he ordained in Joseph for a testimony, when he went out through the land of Egypt: where I heard a language that I understood not.

6 I removed his shoulder from the burden: his hands were delivered from the pots.

7 Thou calledst in trouble, and I delivered thee; I answered thee in the secret place of thunder: I proved thee at the waters of Meribah. Selah.

8 Hear, O my people, and I will testify unto thee: O Israel, if thou wilt hearken unto me;

9 There shall no strange god be in thee; neither shalt thou worship any strange god.

10 I am the LORD thy God, which brought thee out of the land of Egypt: open thy mouth wide, and I will fill it.

11 But my people would not hearken to my voice; and Israel would none of me.

12 So I gave them up unto their own hearts' lust: and they walked in their own counsels.

13 Oh that my people had hearkened unto me, and Israel had walked in my ways!

14 I should soon have subdued their enemies, and turned my hand against their adversaries.

15 The haters of the LORD should have submitted themselves unto him: but their time should have endured for ever.

16 He should have fed them also with
the finest of the wheat: and
with honey out of the rock should I have
satisfied thee.

Psalms Chapter 82

1 God standeth in the congregation of
the mighty; he judgeth among the gods.

2 How long will ye judge unjustly, and
accept the persons of the wicked? Selah.

3 Defend the poor and fatherless:
do justice to the afflicted and needy.

4 Deliver the poor and needy: rid them
out of the hand of the wicked.

5 They know not, neither will they
understand; they walk on in darkness: all
the foundations of the earth are out of
course.

6 I have said, Ye are gods; and all of you
are children of the most High.

7 But ye shall die like men, and fall like
one of the princes.

8 Arise, O God, judge the earth: for
thou shalt inherit all nations.

Psalms Chapter 84

1 How amiable are thy tabernacles, O
LORD of hosts!

2 My soul longeth, yea, even fainteth for
the courts of the LORD: my heart and
my flesh crieth out for the living God.

3 Yea, the sparrow hath found an house,
and the swallow a nest for herself, where
she may lay her young, even thine altars,
O LORD of hosts, my King, and my
God.

4 Blessed are they that dwell in thy
house: they will be still praising
thee. Selah.

5 Blessed is the man whose strength is in
thee; in whose heart are the ways of
them.

6 Who passing through the valley of
Baca make it a well; the rain also filleth
the pools.

7 They go from strength to strength,
every one of them in Zion appeareth
before God.

8 O LORD God of hosts, hear
my prayer: give ear, O God
of Jacob. Selah.

9 Behold, O God our shield, and look
upon the face of thine anointed.

10 For a day in thy courts is better than a
thousand. I had rather be a doorkeeper
in the house of my God, than to dwell in
the tents of wickedness.

11 For the LORD God is
a sun and shield: the LORD will
give grace and glory: no good thing will
he withhold from them that walk
uprightly.

12 O LORD of hosts, blessed is the man
that trusteth in thee.

Psalms Chapter 91

1 He that dwelleth in the secret place of the most High shall abide under the shadow of the Almighty.

2 I will say of the LORD, He is my refuge and my fortress: my God; in him will I trust.

3 Surely he shall deliver thee from the snare of the fowler, and from the noisome pestilence.

4 He shall cover thee with his feathers, and under his wings shalt thou trust: his truth shall be thy shield and buckler.

5 Thou shalt not be afraid for the terror by night; nor for the arrow that flieth by day;

6 Nor for the pestilence that walketh in darkness; nor for the destruction that wasteth at noonday.

7 A thousand shall fall at thy side, and ten thousand at thy right hand; but it shall not come nigh thee.

8 Only with thine eyes shalt thou behold and see the reward of the wicked.

9 Because thou hast made the LORD, which is my refuge, even the most High, thy habitation;

10 There shall no evil befall thee, neither shall any plague come nigh thy dwelling.

11 For he shall give his angels charge over thee, to keep thee in all thy ways.

12 They shall bear thee up in their hands, lest thou dash thy foot against a stone.

13 Thou shalt tread upon the lion and adder: the young lion and the dragon shalt thou trample under feet.

14 Because he hath set his love upon me, therefore will I deliver him: I will set him on high, because he hath known my name.

15 He shall call upon me, and I will answer him: I will be with him in trouble; I will deliver him, and honour him.

16 With long life will I satisfy him, and shew him my salvation.

Psalms Chapter 102

1 Hear my prayer, O LORD, and let my cry come unto thee.

2 Hide not thy face from me in the day when I am in trouble; incline thine ear unto me: in the day when I call answer me speedily.

3 For my days are consumed like smoke, and my bones are burned as an hearth.

4 My heart is smitten, and withered like grass; so that I forget to eat my bread.

5 By reason of the voice of my groaning my bones cleave to my skin.

6 I am like a pelican of the wilderness: I am like an owl of the desert.

7 I watch, and am as a sparrow alone upon the house top.

8 Mine enemies reproach me all the day; and they that are mad against me are sworn against me.

9 For I have eaten ashes like bread, and mingled my drink with weeping.

10 Because of thine indignation and thy wrath: for thou hast lifted me up, and cast me down.

11 My days are like a shadow that declineth; and I am withered like grass.

12 But thou, O LORD, shall endure for ever; and thy remembrance unto all generations.

13 Thou shalt arise, and have mercy upon Zion: for the time to favour her, yea, the set time, is come.

14 For thy servants take pleasure in her stones, and favour the dust thereof.

15 So the heathen shall fear the name of the LORD, and all the kings of the earth thy glory.

16 When the LORD shall build up Zion, he shall appear in his glory.

17 He will regard the prayer of the destitute, and not despise their prayer.

18 This shall be written for the generation to come: and the people which shall be created shall praise the LORD.

19 For he hath looked down from the height of his sanctuary; from heaven did the LORD behold the earth;

20 To hear the groaning of the prisoner; to loose those that are appointed to death;

21 To declare the name of the LORD in Zion, and his praise in Jerusalem;

22 When the people are gathered together, and the kingdoms, to serve the LORD.

23 He weakened my strength in the way; he shortened my days.

24 I said, O my God, take me not away in the midst of my days: thy years are throughout all generations.

25 Of old hast thou laid the foundation of the earth: and the heavens are the work of thy hands.

26 They shall perish, but thou shalt endure: yea, all of them shall wax old like a garment; as a vesture shalt thou change them, and they shall be changed:

27 But thou art the same, and thy years shall have no end.

28 The children of thy servants shall continue, and their seed shall be established before thee.

Psalms Chapter 103

1 Bless the LORD, O my soul: and all that is within me, bless his holy name.

2 Bless the LORD, O my soul, and forget not all his benefits:

3 Who forgiveth all thine iniquities; who healeth all thy diseases;

4 Who redeemeth thy life
from destruction; who crowneth thee with lovingkindness and tender mercies;

5 Who satisfieth thy mouth with good things; so that thy youth is renewed like the eagle's.

6 The LORD
executeth righteousness and judgment for all that are oppressed.

7 He made known his ways unto Moses, his acts unto the children of Israel.

8 The LORD is merciful and gracious, slow to anger, and plenteous in mercy.

9 He will not always chide: neither will he keep his anger for ever.

10 He hath not dealt with us after our sins; nor rewarded us according to our iniquities.

11 For as the heaven is high above the earth, so great is his mercy toward them that fear him.

12 As far as the east is from the west, so far hath he removed our transgressions from us.

13 Like as a father pitieth his children, so the LORD pitieth them that fear him.

14 For he knoweth our frame; he remembereth that we are dust.

15 As for man, his days are as grass: as a flower of the field, so he flourisheth.

16 For the wind passeth over it, and it is gone; and the place thereof shall know it no more.

17 But the mercy of the LORD is
from everlasting to everlasting upon them that fear him, and
his righteousness unto children's children;

18 To such as keep his covenant, and to those that remember his commandments to do them.

19 The LORD hath prepared
his throne in the heavens; and his kingdom ruleth over all.

20 Bless the LORD, ye his angels, that excel in strength, that do his commandments, hearkening unto the voice of his word.

21 Bless ye the LORD, all ye his hosts; ye ministers of his, that do his pleasure.

22 Bless the LORD, all his works in all places of his dominion: bless the LORD, O my soul.

Psalms Chapter 104

1 Bless the LORD, O my soul. O LORD my God, thou art very great; thou art clothed with honour and majesty.

2 Who coverest thyself with light as with a garment: who stretchest out the heavens like a curtain:

3 Who layeth the beams of his chambers in the waters: who maketh the clouds his chariot: who walketh upon the wings of the wind:

4 Who maketh his angels spirits; his ministers a flaming fire:

5 Who laid the foundations of the earth, that it should not be removed for ever.

6 Thou coveredst it with the deep as with a garment: the waters stood above the mountains.

7 At thy rebuke they fled; at the voice of thy thunder they hasted away.

8 They go up by the mountains; they go down by the valleys unto the place which thou hast founded for them.

9 Thou hast set a bound that they may not pass over; that they turn not again to cover the earth.

10 He sendeth the springs into the valleys, which run among the hills.

11 They give drink to every beast of the field: the wild asses quench their thirst.

12 By them shall the fowls of the heaven have their habitation, which sing among the branches.

13 He watereth the hills from his chambers: the earth is satisfied with the fruit of thy works.

14 He causeth the grass to grow for the cattle, and herb for the service of man: that he may bring forth food out of the earth;

15 And wine that maketh glad the heart of man, and oil to make his face to shine, and bread which strengtheneth man's heart.

16 The trees of the LORD are full of sap; the cedars of Lebanon, which he hath planted;

17 Where the birds make their nests: as for the stork, the fir trees are her house.

18 The high hills are a refuge for the wild goats; and the rocks for the conies.

19 He appointed the moon for seasons: the sun knoweth his going down.

20 Thou makest darkness, and it is night: wherein all the beasts of the forest do creep forth.

21 The young lions roar after their prey, and seek their meat from God.

22 The sun ariseth, they gather themselves together, and lay them down in their dens.

23 Man goeth forth unto his work and to his labour until the evening.

24 O LORD, how manifold are thy works! in wisdom hast thou made them all: the earth is full of thy riches.

25 So is this great and wide sea, wherein are things creeping innumerable, both small and great beasts.

26 There go the ships: there is that leviathan, whom thou hast made to play therein.

27 These wait all upon thee; that thou mayest give them their meat in due season.

28 That thou givest them they gather: thou openest thine hand, they are filled with good.

29 Thou hidest thy face, they are troubled: thou takest away their breath, they die, and return to their dust.

30 Thou sendest forth thy spirit, they are created: and thou renewest the face of the earth.

31 The glory of the LORD shall endure for ever: the LORD shall rejoice in his works.

32 He looketh on the earth, and it trembleth: he toucheth the hills, and they smoke.

33 I will sing unto the LORD as long as I live: I will sing praise to my God while I have my being.

34 My meditation of him shall be sweet: I will be glad in the LORD.

35 Let the sinners be consumed out of the earth, and let the wicked be no more. Bless thou the LORD, O my soul. Praise ye the LORD.

Psalms Chapter 105

1 O give thanks unto the LORD; call upon his name: make known his deeds among the people.

2 Sing unto him, sing psalms unto him: talk ye of all his wondrous works.

3 Glory ye in his holy name: let the heart of them rejoice that seek the LORD.

4 Seek the LORD, and his strength: seek his face evermore.

5 Remember his marvellous works that he hath done; his wonders, and the judgments of his mouth;

6 O ye seed of Abraham his servant, ye children of Jacob his chosen.

7 He is the LORD our God: his judgments are in all the earth.

8 He hath remembered his covenant for ever, the word which he commanded to a thousand generations.

9 Which covenant he made with Abraham, and his oath unto Isaac;

10 And confirmed the same
unto Jacob for a law, and to Israel for
an everlasting covenant:

11 Saying, Unto thee will I give the land
of Canaan, the lot of your inheritance:

12 When they were but a few men in
number; yea, very few, and strangers in
it.

13 When they went from one nation to
another, from one kingdom to another
people;

14 He suffered no man to do them
wrong: yea, he reproved kings for their
sakes;

15 Saying, Touch not mine anointed,
and do my prophets no harm.

16 Moreover he called for a famine upon
the land: he brake the whole staff
of bread.

17 He sent a man before them,
even Joseph, who was sold for a servant:

18 Whose feet they hurt with fetters: he
was laid in iron:

19 Until the time that his word came:
the word of the LORD tried him.

20 The king sent and loosed him; even
the ruler of the people, and let him go
free.

21 He made him lord of his house, and
ruler of all his substance:

22 To bind his princes at his pleasure;
and teach his senators wisdom.

23 Israel also came into Egypt;
and Jacob sojourned in the land of Ham.

24 And he increased his people greatly;
and made them stronger than their
enemies.

25 He turned their heart to hate his
people, to deal subtilly with his servants.

26 He sent Moses his servant;
and Aaron whom he had chosen.

27 They shewed his signs among them,
and wonders in the land of Ham.

28 He sent darkness, and made it dark;
and they rebelled not against his word.

29 He turned their waters into blood,
and slew their fish.

30 Their land brought forth frogs in
abundance, in the chambers of their
kings.

31 He spake, and there came divers sorts
of flies, and lice in all their coasts.

32 He gave them hail for rain, and
flaming fire in their land.

33 He smote their vines also and
their fig trees; and brake the trees of
their coasts.

34 He spake, and the locusts came, and
caterpillers, and that without number,

35 And did eat up all the herbs in their land, and devoured the fruit of their ground.

36 He smote also all the firstborn in their land, the chief of all their strength.

37 He brought them forth also with silver and gold: and there was not one feeble person among their tribes.

38 Egypt was glad when they departed: for the fear of them fell upon them.

39 He spread a cloud for a covering; and fire to give light in the night.

40 The people asked, and he brought quails, and satisfied them with the bread of heaven.

41 He opened the rock, and the waters gushed out; they ran in the dry places like a river.

42 For he remembered his holy promise, and Abraham his servant.

43 And he brought forth his people with joy, and his chosen with gladness:

44 And gave them the lands of the heathen: and they inherited the labour of the people;

45 That they might observe his statutes, and keep his laws. Praise ye the LORD.

Psalms Chapter 107

1 O give thanks unto the LORD, for he is good: for his mercy endureth for ever.

2 Let the redeemed of the LORD say so, whom he hath redeemed from the hand of the enemy;

3 And gathered them out of the lands, from the east, and from the west, from the north, and from the south.

4 They wandered in the wilderness in a solitary way; they found no city to dwell in.

5 Hungry and thirsty, their soul fainted in them.

6 Then they cried unto the LORD in their trouble, and he delivered them out of their distresses.

7 And he led them forth by the right way, that they might go to a city of habitation.

8 Oh that men would praise the LORD for his goodness, and for his wonderful works to the children of men!

9 For he satisfieth the longing soul, and filleth the hungry soul with goodness.

10 Such as sit in darkness and in the shadow of death, being bound in affliction and iron;

11 Because they rebelled against the words of God, and contemned the counsel of the most High:

12 Therefore he brought down their heart with labour; they fell down, and there was none to help.

13 Then they cried unto the LORD in their trouble, and he saved them out of their distresses.

14 He brought them out of darkness and the shadow of death, and brake their bands in sunder.

15 Oh that men would praise the LORD for his goodness, and for his wonderful works to the children of men!

16 For he hath broken the gates of brass, and cut the bars of iron in sunder.

17 Fools because of their transgression, and because of their iniquities, are afflicted.

18 Their soul abhorreth all manner of meat; and they draw near unto the gates of death.

19 Then they cry unto the LORD in their trouble, and he saveth them out of their distresses.

20 He sent his word, and healed them, and delivered them from their destructions.

21 Oh that men would praise the LORD for his goodness, and for his wonderful works to the children of men!

22 And let them sacrifice the sacrifices of thanksgiving, and declare his works with rejoicing.

23 They that go down to the sea in ships, that do business in great waters;

24 These see the works of the LORD, and his wonders in the deep.

25 For he commandeth, and raiseth the stormy wind, which lifteth up the waves thereof.

26 They mount up to the heaven, they go down again to the depths: their soul is melted because of trouble.

27 They reel to and fro, and stagger like a drunken man, and are at their wit's end.

28 Then they cry unto the LORD in their trouble, and he bringeth them out of their distresses.

29 He maketh the storm a calm, so that the waves thereof are still.

30 Then are they glad because they be quiet; so he bringeth them unto their desired haven.

31 Oh that men would praise the LORD for his goodness, and for his wonderful works to the children of men!

32 Let them exalt him also in the congregation of the people, and praise him in the assembly of the elders.

33 He turneth rivers into a wilderness, and the watersprings into dry ground;

34 A fruitful land into barrenness, for the wickedness of them that dwell therein.

35 He turneth the wilderness into a standing water, and dry ground into watersprings.

36 And there he maketh the hungry to dwell, that they may prepare a city for habitation;

37 And sow the fields, and plant vineyards, which may yield fruits of increase.

38 He blesseth them also, so that they are multiplied greatly; and suffereth not their cattle to decrease.

39 Again, they are minished and brought low through oppression, affliction, and sorrow.

40 He poureth contempt upon princes, and causeth them to wander in the wilderness, where there is no way.

41 Yet setteth he the poor on high from affliction, and maketh him families like a flock.

42 The righteous shall see it, and rejoice: and all iniquity shall stop her mouth.

43 Whoso is wise, and will observe these things, even they shall understand the lovingkindness of the LORD.

Psalms Chapter 109

1 Hold not thy peace, O God of my praise;

2 For the mouth of the wicked and the mouth of the deceitful are opened against me: they have spoken against me with a lying tongue.

3 They compassed me about also with words of hatred; and fought against me without a cause.

4 For my love they are my adversaries: but I give myself unto prayer.

5 And they have rewarded me evil for good, and hatred for my love.

6 Set thou a wicked man over him: and let Satan stand at his right hand.

7 When he shall be judged, let him be condemned: and let his prayer become sin.

8 Let his days be few; and let another take his office.

9 Let his children be fatherless, and his wife a widow.

10 Let his children be continually vagabonds, and beg: let them seek their bread also out of their desolate places.

11 Let the extortioner catch all that he hath; and let the strangers spoil his labour.

12 Let there be none to extend mercy unto him: neither let there be any to favour his fatherless children.

13 Let his posterity be cut off; and in the generation following let their name be blotted out.

14 Let the iniquity of his fathers be remembered with the LORD; and let not the sin of his mother be blotted out.

15 Let them be before the LORD continually, that he may cut off the memory of them from the earth.

16 Because that he remembered not to shew mercy, but persecuted the poor and needy man, that he might even slay the broken in heart.

17 As he loved cursing, so let it come unto him: as he delighted not in blessing, so let it be far from him.

18 As he clothed himself with cursing like as with his garment, so let it come into his bowels like water, and like oil into his bones.

19 Let it be unto him as the garment which covereth him, and for a girdle wherewith he is girded continually.

20 Let this be the reward of mine adversaries from the LORD, and of them that speak evil against my soul.

21 But do thou for me, O GOD the Lord, for thy name's sake: because thy mercy is good, deliver thou me.

22 For I am poor and needy, and my heart is wounded within me.

23 I am gone like the shadow when it declineth: I am tossed up and down as the locust.

24 My knees are weak through fasting; and my flesh faileth of fatness.

25 I became also a reproach unto them: when they looked upon me they shaked their heads.

26 Help me, O LORD my God: O save me according to thy mercy:

27 That they may know that this is thy hand; that thou, LORD, hast done it.

28 Let them curse, but bless thou: when they arise, let them be ashamed; but let thy servant rejoice.

29 Let mine adversaries be clothed with shame, and let them cover themselves with their own confusion, as with a mantle.

30 I will greatly praise the LORD with my mouth; yea, I will praise him among the multitude.

31 For he shall stand at the right hand of the poor, to save him from those that condemn his soul.

Psalms Chapter 110

1 The LORD said unto my Lord, Sit thou at my right hand, until I make thine enemies thy footstool.

2 The LORD shall send the rod of thy strength out of Zion: rule thou in the midst of thine enemies.

3 Thy people shall be willing in the day of thy power, in the beauties

of holiness from the womb of the morning: thou hast the dew of thy youth.

4 The LORD hath sworn, and will not repent, Thou art a priest for ever after the order of Melchizedek.

5 The Lord at thy right hand shall strike through kings in the day of his wrath.

6 He shall judge among the heathen, he shall fill the places with the dead bodies; he shall wound the heads over many countries.

7 He shall drink of the brook in the way: therefore shall he lift up the head.

Psalms Chapter 111

1 Praise ye the LORD. I will praise the LORD with my whole heart, in the assembly of the upright, and in the congregation.

2 The works of the LORD are great, sought out of all them that have pleasure therein.

3 His work is honourable and glorious: and his righteousness endureth for ever.

4 He hath made his wonderful works to be remembered: the LORD is gracious and full of compassion.

5 He hath given meat unto them that fear him: he will ever be mindful of his covenant.

6 He hath shewed his people the power of his works, that he may give them the heritage of the heathen.

7 The works of his hands are verity and judgment; all his commandments are sure.

8 They stand fast for ever and ever, and are done in truth and uprightness.

9 He sent redemption unto his people: he hath commanded his covenant for ever: holy and reverend is his name.

10 The fear of the LORD is the beginning of wisdom: a good understanding have all they that do his commandments: his praise endureth for ever.

Psalms Chapter 112

1 Praise ye the LORD. Blessed is the man that feareth the LORD, that delighteth greatly in his commandments.

2 His seed shall be mighty upon earth: the generation of the upright shall be blessed.

3 Wealth and riches shall be in his house: and his righteousness endureth for ever.

4 Unto the upright there ariseth light in the darkness: he is gracious, and full of compassion, and righteous.

5 A good man sheweth favour, and lendeth: he will guide his affairs with discretion.

6 Surely he shall not be moved for ever: the righteous shall be in everlasting remembrance.

7 He shall not be afraid of evil tidings: his heart is fixed, trusting in the LORD.

8 His heart is established, he shall not be afraid, until he see his desire upon his enemies.

9 He hath dispersed, he hath given to the poor; his righteousness endureth for ever; his horn shall be exalted with honour.

10 The wicked shall see it, and be grieved; he shall gnash with his teeth, and melt away: the desire of the wicked shall perish.

Psalms Chapter 113

1 Praise ye the LORD. Praise, O ye servants of the LORD, praise the name of the LORD.

2 Blessed be the name of the LORD from this time forth and for evermore.

3 From the rising of the sun unto the going down of the same the LORD's name is to be praised.

4 The LORD is high above all nations, and his glory above the heavens.

5 Who is like unto the LORD our God, who dwelleth on high,

6 Who humbleth himself to behold the things that are in heaven, and in the earth!

7 He raiseth up the poor out of the dust, and lifteth the needy out of the dunghill;

8 That he may set him with princes, even with the princes of his people.

9 He maketh the barren woman to keep house, and to be a joyful mother of children. Praise ye the LORD.

Psalms Chapter 114

1 When Israel went out of Egypt, the house of Jacob from a people of strange language;

2 Judah was his sanctuary, and Israel his dominion.

3 The sea saw it, and fled: Jordan was driven back.

4 The mountains skipped like rams, and the little hills like lambs.

5 What ailed thee, O thou sea, that thou fleddest? thou Jordan, that thou wast driven back?

6 Ye mountains, that ye skipped like rams; and ye little hills, like lambs?

7 Tremble, thou earth, at the presence of the Lord, at the presence of the God of Jacob;

8 Which turned the rock into a standing water, the flint into a fountain of waters.

Psalms Chapter 115

1 Not unto us, O LORD, not unto us, but unto thy name give glory, for thy mercy, and for thy truth's sake.

2 Wherefore should the heathen say, Where is now their God?

3 But our God is in the heavens: he hath done whatsoever he hath pleased.

4 Their idols are silver and gold, the work of men's hands.

5 They have mouths, but they speak not: eyes have they, but they see not:

6 They have ears, but they hear not: noses have they, but they smell not:

7 They have hands, but they handle not: feet have they, but they walk not: neither speak they through their throat.

8 They that make them are like unto them; so is every one that trusteth in them.

9 O Israel, trust thou in the LORD: he is their help and their shield.

10 O house of Aaron, trust in the LORD: he is their help and their shield.

11 Ye that fear the LORD, trust in the LORD: he is their help and their shield.

12 The LORD hath been mindful of us: he will bless us; he will bless the house of Israel; he will bless the house of Aaron.

13 He will bless them that fear the LORD, both small and great.

14 The LORD shall increase you more and more, you and your children.

15 Ye are blessed of the LORD which made heaven and earth.

16 The heaven, even the heavens, are the LORD's: but the earth hath he given to the children of men.

17 The dead praise not the LORD, neither any that go down into silence.

18 But we will bless the LORD from this time forth and for evermore. Praise the LORD.

Psalms Chapter 116

1 I love the LORD, because he hath heard my voice and my supplications.

2 Because he hath inclined his ear unto me, therefore will I call upon him as long as I live.

3 The sorrows of death compassed me, and the pains of hell gat hold upon me: I found trouble and sorrow.

4 Then called I upon the name of the LORD; O LORD, I beseech thee, deliver my soul.

5 Gracious is the LORD, and righteous; yea, our God is merciful.

6 The LORD preserveth the simple: I was brought low, and he helped me.

7 Return unto thy rest, O my soul; for the LORD hath dealt bountifully with thee.

8 For thou hast delivered my soul from death, mine eyes from tears, and my feet from falling.

9 I will walk before the LORD in the land of the living.

10 I believed, therefore have I spoken: I was greatly afflicted:

11 I said in my haste, All men are liars.

12 What shall I render unto the LORD for all his benefits toward me?

13 I will take the cup of salvation, and call upon the name of the LORD.

14 I will pay my vows unto the LORD now in the presence of all his people.

15 Precious in the sight of the LORD is the death of his saints.

16 O LORD, truly I am thy servant; I am thy servant, and the son of thine handmaid: thou hast loosed my bonds.

17 I will offer to thee the sacrifice of thanksgiving, and will call upon the name of the LORD.

18 I will pay my vows unto the LORD now in the presence of all his people.

19 In the courts of the LORD's house, in the midst of thee, O Jerusalem. Praise ye the LORD.

Psalms Chapter 117

1 O praise the LORD, all ye nations: praise him, all ye people.

2 For his merciful kindness is great toward us: and the truth of the LORD endureth for ever. Praise ye the LORD.

Psalms Chapter 119

1 Blessed are the undefiled in the way, who walk in the law of the LORD.

2 Blessed are they that keep his testimonies, and that seek him with the whole heart.

3 They also do no iniquity: they walk in his ways.

4 Thou hast commanded us to keep thy precepts diligently.

5 O that my ways were directed to keep thy statutes!

6 Then shall I not be ashamed, when I have respect unto all thy commandments.

7 I will praise thee with uprightness of heart, when I shall have learned thy righteous judgments.

8 I will keep thy statutes: O forsake me not utterly.

9 Wherewithal shall a young man cleanse his way? by taking heed thereto according to thy word.

10 With my whole heart have I sought thee: O let me not wander from thy commandments.

11 Thy word have I hid in mine heart, that I might not sin against thee.

12 Blessed art thou, O LORD: teach me thy statutes.

13 With my lips have I declared all the judgments of thy mouth.

14 I have rejoiced in the way of thy testimonies, as much as in all riches.

15 I will meditate in thy precepts, and have respect unto thy ways.

16 I will delight myself in thy statutes: I will not forget thy word.

17 Deal bountifully with thy servant, that I may live, and keep thy word.

18 Open thou mine eyes, that I may behold wondrous things out of thy law.

19 I am a stranger in the earth: hide not thy commandments from me.

20 My soul breaketh for the longing that it hath unto thy judgments at all times.

21 Thou hast rebuked the proud that are cursed, which do err from thy commandments.

22 Remove from me reproach and contempt; for I have kept thy testimonies.

23 Princes also did sit and speak against me: but thy servant did meditate in thy statutes.

24 Thy testimonies also are my delight and my counsellors.leth.

25 My soul cleaveth unto the dust: quicken thou me according to thy word.

26 I have declared my ways, and thou heardest me: teach me thy statutes.

27 Make me to understand the way of thy precepts: so shall I talk of thy wondrous works.

28 My soul melteth for heaviness: strengthen thou me according unto thy word.

29 Remove from me the way of lying: and grant me thy law graciously.

30 I have chosen the way of truth: thy judgments have I laid before me.

31 I have stuck unto thy testimonies: O LORD, put me not to shame.

32 I will run the way of thy commandments, when thou shalt enlarge my heart.

33 Teach me, O LORD, the way of thy statutes; and I shall keep it unto the end.

34 Give me understanding, and I shall keep thy law; yea, I shall observe it with my whole heart.

35 Make me to go in the path of thy commandments; for therein do I delight.

36 Incline my heart unto thy testimonies, and not to covetousness.

37 Turn away mine eyes from beholding vanity; and quicken thou me in thy way.

38 Stablish thy word unto thy servant, who is devoted to thy fear.

39 Turn away my reproach which I fear: for thy judgments are good.

40 Behold, I have longed after thy precepts: quicken me in thy righteousness.

41 Let thy mercies come also unto me, O LORD, even thy salvation, according to thy word.

42 So shall I have wherewith to answer him that reproacheth me: for I trust in thy word.

43 And take not the word of truth utterly out of my mouth; for I have hoped in thy judgments.

44 So shall I keep thy law continually for ever and ever.

45 And I will walk at liberty: for I seek thy precepts.

46 I will speak of thy testimonies also before kings, and will not be ashamed.

47 And I will delight myself in thy commandments, which I have loved.

48 My hands also will I lift up unto thy commandments, which I have loved; and I will meditate in thy statutes.

49 Remember the word unto thy servant, upon which thou hast caused me to hope.

50 This is my comfort in my affliction: for thy word hath quickened me.

51 The proud have had me greatly in derision: yet have I not declined from thy law.

52 I remembered thy judgments of old, O LORD; and have comforted myself.

53 Horror hath taken hold upon me because of the wicked that forsake thy law.

54 Thy statutes have been my songs in the house of my pilgrimage.

55 I have remembered thy name, O LORD, in the night, and have kept thy law.

56 This I had, because I kept thy precepts.

57 Thou art my portion, O LORD: I have said that I would keep thy words.

58 I intreated thy favour with my whole heart: be merciful unto me according to thy word.

59 I thought on my ways, and turned my feet unto thy testimonies.

60 I made haste, and delayed not to keep thy commandments.

61 The bands of the wicked have robbed me: but I have not forgotten thy law.

62 At midnight I will rise to give thanks unto thee because of thy righteous judgments.

63 I am a companion of all them that fear thee, and of them that keep thy precepts.

64 The earth, O LORD, is full of thy mercy: teach me thy statutes.

65 Thou hast dealt well with thy servant, O LORD, according unto thy word.

66 Teach me good judgment and knowledge: for I have believed thy commandments.

67 Before I was afflicted I went astray: but now have I kept thy word.

68 Thou art good, and doest good; teach me thy statutes.

69 The proud have forged a lie against me: but I will keep thy precepts with my whole heart.

70 Their heart is as fat as grease; but I delight in thy law.

71 It is good for me that I have been afflicted; that I might learn thy statutes.

72 The law of thy mouth is better unto me than thousands of gold and silver.

73 Thy hands have made me and fashioned me: give me understanding, that I may learn thy commandments.

74 They that fear thee will be glad when they see me; because I have hoped in thy word.

75 I know, O LORD, that thy judgments are right, and that thou in faithfulness hast afflicted me.

76 Let, I pray thee, thy merciful kindness be for my comfort, according to thy word unto thy servant.

77 Let thy tender mercies come unto me, that I may live: for thy law is my delight.

78 Let the proud be ashamed; for they dealt perversely with me without a cause: but I will meditate in thy precepts.

79 Let those that fear thee turn unto me, and those that have known thy testimonies.

80 Let my heart be sound in thy statutes; that I be not ashamed.

81 My soul fainteth for thy salvation: but I hope in thy word.

82 Mine eyes fail for thy word, saying, When wilt thou comfort me?

83 For I am become like a bottle in the smoke; yet do I not forget thy statutes.

84 How many are the days of thy servant? when wilt thou execute judgment on them that persecute me?

85 The proud have digged pits for me, which are not after thy law.

86 All thy commandments are faithful: they persecute me wrongfully; help thou me.

87 They had almost consumed me upon earth; but I forsook not thy precepts.

88 Quicken me after thy lovingkindness; so shall I keep the testimony of thy mouth.

89 For ever, O LORD, thy word is settled in heaven.

90 Thy faithfulness is unto all generations: thou hast established the earth, and it abideth.

91 They continue this day according to thine ordinances: for all are thy servants.

92 Unless thy law had been my delights, I should then have perished in mine affliction.

93 I will never forget thy precepts: for with them thou hast quickened me.

94 I am thine, save me: for I have sought thy precepts.

95 The wicked have waited for me to destroy me: but I will consider thy testimonies.

96 I have seen an end of all perfection: but thy commandment is exceeding broad.

97 O how I love thy law! it is my meditation all the day.

98 Thou through thy commandments hast made me wiser than mine enemies: for they are ever with me.

99 I have more understanding than all my teachers: for thy testimonies are my meditation.

100 I understand more than the ancients, because I keep thy precepts.

101 I have refrained my feet from every evil way, that I might keep thy word.

102 I have not departed from thy judgments: for thou hast taught me.

103 How sweet are thy words unto my taste! yea, sweeter than honey to my mouth!

104 Through thy precepts I get understanding: therefore I hate every false way.

105 Thy word is a lamp unto my feet, and a light unto my path.

106 I have sworn, and I will perform it, that I will keep thy righteous judgments.

107 I am afflicted very much: quicken me, O LORD, according unto thy word.

108 Accept, I beseech thee, the freewill offerings of my mouth, O LORD, and teach me thy judgments.

109 My soul is continually in my hand: yet do I not forget thy law.

110 The wicked have laid a snare for me: yet I erred not from thy precepts.

111 Thy testimonies have I taken as an heritage for ever: for they are the rejoicing of my heart.

112 I have inclined mine heart to perform thy statutes alway, even unto the end.

113 I hate vain thoughts: but thy law do I love.

114 Thou art my hiding place and my shield: I hope in thy word.

115 Depart from me, ye evildoers: for I will keep the commandments of my God.

116 Uphold me according unto thy word, that I may live: and let me not be ashamed of my hope.

117 Hold thou me up, and I shall be safe: and I will have respect unto thy statutes continually.

118 Thou hast trodden down all them that err from thy statutes: for their deceit is falsehood.

119 Thou puttest away all the wicked of the earth like dross: therefore I love thy testimonies.

120 My flesh trembleth for fear of thee; and I am afraid of thy judgments.

121 I have done judgment and justice: leave me not to mine oppressors.

122 Be surety for thy servant for good: let not the proud oppress me.

123 Mine eyes fail for thy salvation, and for the word of thy righteousness.

124 Deal with thy servant according unto thy mercy, and teach me thy statutes.

125 I am thy servant; give me understanding, that I may know thy testimonies.

126 It is time for thee, LORD, to work: for they have made void thy law.

127 Therefore I love thy commandments above gold; yea, above fine gold.

128 Therefore I esteem all thy precepts concerning all things to be right; and I hate every false way.

129 Thy testimonies are wonderful: therefore doth my soul keep them.

130 The entrance of thy words giveth light; it giveth understanding unto the simple.

131 I opened my mouth, and panted: for I longed for thy commandments.

132 Look thou upon me, and be merciful unto me, as thou usest to do unto those that love thy name.

133 Order my steps in thy word: and let not any iniquity have dominion over me.

134 Deliver me from the oppression of man: so will I keep thy precepts.

135 Make thy face to shine upon thy servant; and teach me thy statutes.

136 Rivers of waters run down mine eyes, because they keep not thy law.

137 Righteous art thou, O LORD, and upright are thy judgments.

138 Thy testimonies that thou hast commanded are righteous and very faithful.

139 My zeal hath consumed me, because mine enemies have forgotten thy words.

140 Thy word is very pure: therefore thy servant loveth it.

141 I am small and despised: yet do not I forget thy precepts.

142 Thy righteousness is an everlasting righteousness, and thy law is the truth.

143 Trouble and anguish have taken hold on me: yet thy commandments are my delights.

144 The righteousness of thy testimonies is everlasting: give me understanding, and I shall live.

145 I cried with my whole heart; hear me, O LORD: I will keep thy statutes.

146 I cried unto thee; save me, and I shall keep thy testimonies.

147 I prevented the dawning of the morning, and cried: I hoped in thy word.

148 Mine eyes prevent the night watches, that I might meditate in thy word.

149 Hear my voice according unto thy lovingkindness: O LORD, quicken me according to thy judgment.

150 They draw nigh that follow after mischief: they are far from thy law.

151 Thou art near, O LORD; and all thy commandments are truth.

152 Concerning thy testimonies, I have known of old that thou hast founded them for ever.

153 Consider mine affliction, and deliver me: for I do not forget thy law.

154 Plead my cause, and deliver me: quicken me according to thy word.

155 Salvation is far from the wicked: for they seek not thy statutes.

156 Great are thy tender mercies, O LORD: quicken me according to thy judgments.

157 Many are my persecutors and mine enemies; yet do I not decline from thy testimonies.

158 I beheld the transgressors, and was grieved; because they kept not thy word.

159 Consider how I love thy precepts: quicken me, O LORD, according to thy lovingkindness.

160 Thy word is true from the beginning: and every one of thy righteous judgments endureth for ever.

161 Princes have persecuted me without a cause: but my heart standeth in awe of thy word.

162 I rejoice at thy word, as one that findeth great spoil.

163 I hate and abhor lying: but thy law do I love.

164 Seven times a day do I praise thee because of thy righteous judgments.

165 Great peace have they which love thy law: and nothing shall offend them.

166 LORD, I have hoped for thy salvation, and done thy commandments.

167 My soul hath kept thy testimonies; and I love them exceedingly.

168 I have kept thy precepts and thy testimonies: for all my ways are before thee.

169 Let my cry come near before thee, O LORD: give me understanding according to thy word.

170 Let my supplication come before thee: deliver me according to thy word.

171 My lips shall utter praise, when thou hast taught me thy statutes.

172 My tongue shall speak of thy word: for all thy commandments are righteousness.

173 Let thine hand help me; for I have chosen thy precepts.

174 I have longed for thy salvation, O LORD; and thy law is my delight.

175 Let my soul live, and it shall praise thee; and let thy judgments help me.

176 I have gone astray like a lost sheep; seek thy servant; for I do not forget thy commandments.

Psalms Chapter 122

1 I was glad when they said unto me, Let us go into the house of the LORD.

2 Our feet shall stand within thy gates, O Jerusalem.

3 Jerusalem is builded as a city that is compact together:

4 Whither the tribes go up, the tribes of the LORD, unto the testimony of Israel, to give thanks unto the name of the LORD.

5 For there are set thrones of judgment, the thrones of the house of David.

6 Pray for the peace of Jerusalem: they shall prosper that love thee.

7 Peace be within thy walls, and prosperity within thy palaces.

8 For my brethren and companions' sakes, I will now say, Peace be within thee.

9 Because of the house of the LORD our God I will seek thy good.

Psalms Chapter 124

1 If it had not been the LORD who was on our side, now may Israel say;

2 If it had not been the LORD who was on our side, when men rose up against us:

3 Then they had swallowed us up quick, when their wrath was kindled against us:

4 Then the waters had overwhelmed us, the stream had gone over our soul:

5 Then the proud waters had gone over our soul.

6 Blessed be the LORD, who hath not given us as a prey to their teeth.

7 Our soul is escaped as a bird out of the snare of the fowlers: the snare is broken, and we are escaped.

8 Our help is in the name of the LORD, who made heaven and earth.

Psalms Chapter 125

1 They that trust in the LORD shall be as mount Zion, which cannot be removed, but abideth for ever.

2 As the mountains are round about Jerusalem, so the LORD is round about his people from henceforth even for ever.

3 For the rod of the wicked shall not rest upon the lot of the righteous; lest the righteous put forth their hands unto iniquity.

4 Do good, O LORD, unto those that be good, and to them that are upright in their hearts.

5 As for such as turn aside unto their crooked ways, the LORD shall lead them forth with the workers of iniquity: but peace shall be upon Israel.

Psalms Chapter 126

1 When the LORD turned again the captivity of Zion, we were like them that dream.

2 Then was our mouth filled with laughter, and our tongue with singing:

then said they among the heathen, The LORD hath done great things for them.

3 The LORD hath done great things for us; whereof we are glad.

4 Turn again our captivity, O LORD, as the streams in the south.

5 They that sow in tears shall reap in joy.

6 He that goeth forth and weepeth, bearing precious seed, shall doubtless come again with rejoicing, bringing his sheaves with him.

Psalms Chapter 127

1 Except the LORD build the house, they labour in vain that build it: except the LORD keep the city, the watchman waketh but in vain.

2 It is vain for you to rise up early, to sit up late, to eat the bread of sorrows: for so he giveth his beloved sleep.

3 Lo, children are an heritage of the LORD: and the fruit of the womb is his reward.

4 As arrows are in the hand of a mighty man; so are children of the youth.

5 Happy is the man that hath his quiver full of them: they shall not be ashamed, but they shall speak with the enemies in the gate.

Psalms Chapter 130

1 Out of the depths have I cried unto thee, O LORD.

2 Lord, hear my voice: let thine ears be attentive to the voice of my supplications.

3 If thou, LORD, shouldest mark iniquities, O Lord, who shall stand?

4 But there is forgiveness with thee, that thou mayest be feared.

5 I wait for the LORD, my soul doth wait, and in his word do I hope.

6 My soul waiteth for the Lord more than they that watch for the morning: I say, more than they that watch for the morning.

7 Let Israel hope in the LORD: for with the LORD there is mercy, and with him is plenteous redemption.

8 And he shall redeem Israel from all his iniquities.

Psalms Chapter 131

1 Lord, my heart is not haughty, nor mine eyes lofty: neither do I exercise myself in great matters, or in things too high for me.

2 Surely I have behaved and quieted myself, as a child that is weaned of his mother: my soul is even as a weaned child.

3 Let Israel hope in the LORD from henceforth and for ever.

Psalms Chapter 133

1 Behold, how good and how pleasant it is for brethren to dwell together in unity!

2 It is like the precious ointment upon the head, that ran down upon the beard, even Aaron's beard: that went down to the skirts of his garments;

3 As the dew of Hermon, and as the dew that descended upon the mountains of Zion: for there the LORD commanded the blessing, even life for evermore.

Psalms Chapter 134

1 Behold, bless ye the LORD, all ye servants of the LORD, which by night stand in the house of the LORD.

2 Lift up your hands in the sanctuary, and bless the LORD.

3 The LORD that made heaven and earth bless thee out of Zion.

Psalms Chapter 137

1 By the rivers of Babylon, there we sat down, yea, we wept, when we remembered Zion.

2 We hanged our harps upon the willows in the midst thereof.

3 For there they that carried us away captive required of us a song; and they that wasted us required of us mirth, saying, Sing us one of the songs of Zion.

4 How shall we sing the LORD's song in a strange land?

5 If I forget thee, O Jerusalem, let my right hand forget her cunning.

6 If I do not remember thee, let my tongue cleave to the roof of my mouth; if I prefer not Jerusalem above my chief joy.

7 Remember, O LORD, the children of Edom in the day of Jerusalem; who said, Rase it, rase it, even to the foundation thereof.

8 O daughter of Babylon, who art to be destroyed; happy shall he be, that rewardeth thee as thou hast served us.

9 Happy shall he be, that taketh and dasheth thy little ones against the stones.

Psalms Chapter 139

1 O lord, thou hast searched me, and known me.

2 Thou knowest my downsitting and mine uprising, thou understandest my thought afar off.

3 Thou compassest my path and my lying down, and art acquainted with all my ways.

4 For there is not a word in my tongue, but, lo, O LORD, thou knowest it altogether.

5 Thou hast beset me behind and before, and laid thine hand upon me.

6 Such knowledge is too wonderful for me; it is high, I cannot attain unto it.

7 Whither shall I go from thy spirit? or whither shall I flee from thy presence?

8 If I ascend up into heaven, thou art there: if I make my bed in hell, behold, thou art there.

9 If I take the wings of the morning, and dwell in the uttermost parts of the sea;

10 Even there shall thy hand lead me, and thy right hand shall hold me.

11 If I say, Surely the darkness shall cover me; even the night shall be light about me.

12 Yea, the darkness hideth not from thee; but the night shineth as the day: the darkness and the light are both alike to thee.

13 For thou hast possessed my reins: thou hast covered me in my mother's womb.

14 I will praise thee; for I am fearfully and wonderfully made: marvellous are thy works; and that my soul knoweth right well.

15 My substance was not hid from thee, when I was made in secret, and curiously wrought in the lowest parts of the earth.

16 Thine eyes did see my substance, yet being unperfect; and in thy book all my members were written, which in continuance were fashioned, when as yet there was none of them.

17 How precious also are thy thoughts unto me, O God! how great is the sum of them!

18 If I should count them, they are more in number than the sand: when I awake, I am still with thee.

19 Surely thou wilt slay the wicked, O God: depart from me therefore, ye bloody men.

20 For they speak against thee wickedly, and thine enemies take thy name in vain.

21 Do not I hate them, O LORD, that hate thee? and am not I grieved with those that rise up against thee?

22 I hate them with perfect hatred: I count them mine enemies.

23 Search me, O God, and know my heart: try me, and know my thoughts:

24 And see if there be any wicked way in me, and lead me in the way everlasting.

Appendix F:

Scriptural Continuity in the Solomonic Tradition

The Septuagint and the Library of Alexandria:
History and Legend

The *Benedicite omnia opera* and other psalm citations in the *Greater Key of Solomon* ultimately derive from the Greek Septuagint, the earliest major translation of the Hebrew Scriptures. According to the *Letter of Aristeas* (2nd–1st century BCE), this translation was commissioned by Ptolemy II Philadelphus of Egypt, who sought to add the Jewish Law to the holdings of the Library of Alexandria. Seventy-two elders—six from each tribe of Israel—were brought from Jerusalem, each producing an identical translation in seventy-two days, a miracle taken as proof of divine inspiration. Philo of Alexandria, Josephus, and later Christian writers repeated and embellished this account, affirming that the finished work was deposited in the Library.

Whether or not a copy was truly stored in the Library, Alexandria was the most plausible setting for the translation. It was a cosmopolitan hub where Jewish, Greek, and Egyptian cultures intersected, and where the Ptolemaic dynasty sponsored vast translation projects. For early Christians, the Septuagint became their Old Testament, quoted by the apostles and preserved in Greek-speaking churches. The Library connection thus became more than a detail of history—it was a symbolic statement of the Septuagint's intellectual and spiritual authority.

In medieval and Renaissance Europe, the Septuagint reached ritual magic and liturgical tradition chiefly through Jerome's Latin Vulgate, particularly the Gallican Psalter. By the time the *Greater Key of Solomon* was compiled in its most complete form, these psalms—rooted in the Septuagint tradition—were the standard liturgical text. Understanding the Septuagint's association with Alexandria helps explain why the psalms in the *Greater Key* follow a numbering and wording unfamiliar to those reading from modern English Protestant Bibles.

While the legend of the seventy-two translators may be embellished, it shaped centuries of perception. For the ceremonial practitioner or scholar, it is a reminder that the "original" text of a Solomonic rite is not always the Hebrew Bible of today, but the psalter as it was received, recited, and sanctified in the Latin tradition—an inheritance whose roots trace back, at least in legend, to the greatest library of the ancient world.

Condensed Text of the Letter of Aristeas
(A Summary)

The author, Aristeas, writes to his brother Philocrates, explaining his embassy to Eleazar, the Jewish high priest of Jerusalem, at the behest of Ptolemy II Philadelphus of Egypt. The king, urged by Demetrius, librarian of Alexandria, decides to enrich his royal collection with a Greek translation of the Jewish Law, and instructs Aristeas to secure both the text and qualified translators.

In response, Eleazar selects seventy-two respected Jewish scholars—six from each of the twelve tribes—and sends them to Alexandria. Lavish gifts are also bestowed upon the Temple, including gold and silver vessels, richly decorated, and a table adorned with gemstones, designed according to detailed specifications.

Upon the scholars' arrival, Ptolemy holds a lavish seven-day banquet, posing philosophical questions to test their wisdom. Impressed, he rewards them and oversees their departure to the island of Pharos, where they complete the translation in precisely seventy-two days. The translated Law is then read to the Jews of Alexandria, who bless it, request copies, and pronounce a curse on anyone who might alter the text. Upon their return to Jerusalem, each translator is richly rewarded for his work.

This summary is based on the established narrative found in multiple scholarly resources—most notably:
Wikipedia, "Letter of Aristeas", which outlines how "seventy-two interpreters" produced the Septuagint at the request of Ptolemy II Philadelphus .
British–Oxford Classical Dictionary and **Reading Acts** websites, which both characterize the work as a **pseudepigraphal, Hellenistic composition** from mid-2nd century BCE intended to legitimize the Greek translation of the Pentateuch .

Aside: The Fragile Chain of Transmission

The *Greater Key of Solomon* does not exist in a vacuum. It stands at the far end of a chain of preservation that has carried sacred texts across millennia—through conquest, exile, translation, and the slow attrition of time. To understand why the Key is so deeply anchored in Scripture, one must see it against the backdrop of biblical and historical events that shaped the survival of those texts.

c. 10th century BCE - The Ark of the Covenant
and the Menelik Tradition

Ethiopian Orthodox tradition, preserved in the *Kebra Nagast*, claims that Menelik I, son of King Solomon and the Queen of Sheba, took the Ark of the Covenant from Jerusalem to Ethiopia during Solomon's lifetime. If true, the Ark—together with the tablets of the Law—would have been removed centuries before the destruction of the First Temple. Whether literal or symbolic, this tradition is one of the earliest examples of Solomonic legend transcending geographic and cultural boundaries.

586 BCE - The Babylonian Destruction of the First Temple

Under King Nebuchadnezzar II, Babylon's armies sacked Jerusalem, destroyed Solomon's Temple, and carried the people of Judah into exile. The original Torah scrolls and other sacred writings were likely burned or seized. This was a catastrophic rupture: the central symbols of Israel's covenant, the Temple and its archives, were gone.

c. 5th century BCE - Ezra's Restoration of the Torah

After the Persians conquered Babylon, the exiled Jews were allowed to return. Ezra the scribe, according to Jewish tradition, rewrote or recompiled the Torah from memory and surviving fragments, reestablishing it as the cornerstone of Jewish worship and law. This act was more than clerical—it was an early exercise in the sacred preservation of the written word, ensuring that what had been lost in fire could live again in ink and parchment.

3rd-2nd century BCE - The Septuagint and the Library of Alexandria

Under Ptolemy II Philadelphus of Egypt, 72 Jewish scholars were said to have translated the Hebrew Scriptures into Greek—the Septuagint. According to the *Letter of Aristeas*, this translation was made for inclusion in the Library of Alexandria, the great repository of Hellenistic learning. Whether the Torah and other books of the Septuagint actually sat on its shelves remains debated, but the symbolism is unmistakable: sacred Hebrew tradition was now rendered into the lingua franca of the eastern Mediterranean, widening its reach far beyond Judea.

285–246 BCE to 5th century CE – The Rise and Fall of the Library of Alexandria

The Library, founded under the Ptolemies, suffered multiple blows: Julius Caesar's siege of Alexandria in 48 BCE, the city's sacking under Emperor Aurelian in the 270s CE, the destruction of the Serapeum in 391 CE under Patriarch Theophilus, and later accounts of losses during the Arab conquest in 642 CE. By the early 5th century, whatever remained of its original collections was gone. If copies of the Septuagint were once stored there, their preservation would have depended on having already spread beyond its walls.

4th century CE – The Gallican Psalter and Jerome's Vulgate

As Christianity became the dominant faith of the Roman Empire, Latin began to replace Greek in the liturgy of the Western Church. Jerome's translation of the Psalms from the Greek Septuagint into Latin—known as the Gallican Psalter— became the standard for centuries. These are the Psalms that medieval and Renaissance Europe knew, recited, and chanted.

15th–17th centuries CE – The Compilation of the Greater and Lesser Keys

By the time the *Greater Key of Solomon* reached its mature form in late medieval manuscripts, the Gallican Psalter was inseparable from Catholic ceremonial life. The psalms were not read in English, nor in Hebrew, but in the liturgical Latin that had been chanted for generations. The *Lesser Key* would follow a similar path, drawing on biblical and liturgical material rooted in this same transmission.

Why This Matters for the Greater Key

The *Greater Key* presumes a world in which sacred authority is embedded in a chain of unbroken transmission—from Solomon's court, through exile, through the work of scribes like Ezra, through the translation of the Septuagint, through the Latin of Jerome, into the ceremonial handbooks of the late Middle Ages. Its psalms are not there as literary ornament—they are remnants of the same texts preserved against fire, sword, and time.

To perform a rite from the *Greater Key* without understanding this history is to step into a river without knowing its source. Even more, it challenges modern practitioners: the psalms that powered these rituals were meant to be spoken in the language of their time, with the cadence, rhythm, and soundscape that centuries of repetition had made sacred. Whether one believes intention alone can replace this, or whether the ancient tongue carries an irreplaceable charge, is a question every would-be Solomonic operator must answer honestly

The Greater and Lesser Keys as Witness to the Enduring Word

The preceding appendices presented seven of the most frequently cited psalms from the *Greater Key of Solomon* in both Latin and English—drawn from the Gallican Psalter, the very form in which they would have been heard, memorized, and recited by the grimoire's medieval compilers. This was not an aesthetic choice, but an act of historical fidelity: the Latin text preserves the original soundscape of the rite, while the English translation ensures comprehension.

It is worth remembering that these psalms were not incidental to the Key's operations—they were the very breath and backbone of the work. The operator's voice, shaped by the cadence of the Gallican text, stood in direct continuity with centuries of cathedral choirs, monastic offices, and liturgical recitation. To speak them in Latin was to join an unbroken chain of transmission reaching back to Jerome's fourth-century revision, and further still to the seventy-two translators of the Septuagint.

That number—seventy-two—resonates curiously with the seventy-two spirits catalogued in the *Lesser Key of Solomon*. Whether deliberate or coincidental, the symmetry reflects a worldview in which divine order permeates both scripture and the spiritual hierarchies invoked by the Keys. In this sense, the Solomonic tradition affirms not merely the symbolic value of the Bible, but its authority as a historical and spiritual foundation.

It is here that modern skepticism falters. A "Solomonic mage" who dismisses the Bible, or reduces Jesus to a peripheral figure, cuts away the very root from which the Keys draw their power. The conjurations and blessings of the *Greater Key* stand on the covenantal authority of the God of Israel; without that foundation, the work becomes a hollow performance, shorn of its engine.

When placed under the microscope, the *Greater Key of Solomon* does not diminish the Bible's legitimacy—it amplifies it. Pontius Pilate lived. Solomon lived. The psalms attributed to David, Solomon's father, as preserved in the medieval Latin, from the Greek Septuagint, from the Hebrew Torah, were the very ones recited in the operations of the Key. The grimoire's survival into our own century is not simply a testament to medieval magic, but to the unwavering transmission of the written word of God.

To work with the Keys, then, is not merely to rehearse a set of ceremonial forms, but to enter an inheritance: a lineage of scripture, language, and ritual that spans empires, translations, and centuries. Its magic does not lurk between the lines—it is in the lines themselves, in the enduring words preserved, proclaimed, and enacted as the living bridge between divine will and human action.

www.ingramcontent.com/pod-product-compliance
Lightning Source LLC
LaVergne TN
LVHW061304060426
835513LV00013B/1241